MASKIM HUL

Babylonian Magick

Ecstasy and Storm After Creation by Marchozelos

MASKIM HUL
Babylonian Magick

by

MICHAEL W. FORD

The complete gateway to the Union of Anu and Ki, to Irkalla and the fiery spheres of the Seven.

SUCCUBUS PRODUCTIONS

MASKIM HUL
Babylonian Magick
By Michael W. Ford
Illustrated by Marchozelos
ISBN-13:
978-1456492052

ISBN-10:
1456492055

Copyright © 2010 by Michael W. Ford

All rights reserved. No part of this book, in part or in whole, may be reproduced, transmitted, or utilized, in any form or by any means electronic or mechanical, including photocopying, recording, or by any information storage and retrieval system, without written permission in writing from the publisher, except for brief quotations in critical articles, books and reviews. All images without explicit copyright citations are in public domain. Art collage by Michael W. Ford unless otherwise indicated.

First edition 2010 Succubus Productions

Information:
Succubus Productions
PO Box 926344
Houston, TX 77292
US
Website: http://www.luciferianwitchcraft.com
Email: succubusproductions@yahoo.com

TO THE ILU LIMNU

This grimoire is dedicated to the seven malevolent Phantoms of the flames, the Seven Maskim who are Ilu Limnu, Gods who embody rebellion and chaos. May the words within stir them continually from their abode in the heavens and dark earth, by the sea and the realm of the dead. Arise Seven Spirits of the Deep Earth, whose voices resound in the heights. Thou who disturb order, begetting chaos find rule again. Thou malevolent gods, phantoms of the vast heavens, come thou forth to ignite our souls, our minds with the Black Flame.

Acknowledgements

I would like to thank Hope Marie who has put up with my endless workings, obsessive research and most of all, the dissertations and commentary on all questions Babylonian when a simple question is asked of me. Marchozelos, and The Order of Phosphorus for my extended solitude and understanding why. Luciferians and those who seek to extend beyond the defined theology of the day and especially all those who support the works. Thanks to Josh Abbott for Hubris and Serpentis, who have fit in perfectly with the other snakes, P. Watson for the support and advice. In addition, to Christos Beest who so long ago in the 1990's encouraged the continual struggle of the darkness, when Algol was first illuminated before me. Stephen Sennitt, for his paitence in Vampyri and all those I have contact with. I would like to thank all of Enenuru forum who provided ideas for cuneiform, especially to all the students of Mesopotamian archeology and religion.

CONTENTS

CHAPTER ONE
MESOPOTAMIAN ORIGINS AND BACKGROUND OF RELIGIOUS CULTURE..........pg. 23

CHAPTER TWO
THE MESOPOTAMIAN MAGICKIAL WORLD AND CREATION..........pg. 55

CHAPTER THREE
THE ROARING OCEANS OF CHAOS: *A Shadow Ritual & Hymn* ....pg 77

CHAPTER FOUR
THE GODS AND DEMONS OF MESOPOTAMIA….. pg. 101

CHAPTER FIVE
THE DARK GODS AND EVIL SPIRITS….pg. 219

CHAPTER SIX
THE RITES OF THE KASSAPU…..Pg. 287

Part Two of Chapter Six: Necromancy and the rites of Ereshkigal..pg 419

CHAPTER SEVEN
Etemennaki and Ascension..........Pg. 449

Bibliography

Maskim Hul: Babylonian Magick is published on 12.21.2010 and available for order that day. This is in accordance with the Total Lunar Eclipse on the Solstice, the first Total Lunar Eclipse since 1638. "The Ritual of the Eclipse and Devouring of the Moon", a significant ritual in this grimoire is to be performed again by the author at 1.41 AM Central Standard Time near Houston, Texas when the Total Eclipse begins. The rite is more significant than the other times performed as it is completely in line with the forces of darkness and chaos. Additionally, in the Month of Tebetu in an old Babylonian astrological tablet, Tiamat and Kingu join and do battle against Marduk. The Solstice is also sacred in Luciferianism to Lilith, the modern deific mask of the older goddess Lamashtu, Ardat Lili, Lili, Lilu, Ishtar, Ereshkigal and more.

May this book be a gateway and so the gates shall open 12.21.2010.

Michael W. Ford

PREFACE
BABYLONIAN MAGICK
The Will of the Individual

Maskim Hul is a foundation for my Luciferian work and process of initiation. As my previous initiatory work through the years, I gained insight in adapting ancient traditions with modern techniques, with the exception of the Yatuk Dinoih workings, the development of Luciferian cultic material was broad in the association from which it derived.

The Babylonian Magick presented in this grimoire was a great challenge regarding the integrity of an ancient culture and the magical practices. Keeping consistent with those practices, adapting them to a modern world was not as difficult in practice. However, there was much research and "digging" to be done ensuring the depths were explored. This grimoire took a new life from how it was planned; it tested every aspect of my psyche. I am honored to present the sinister to you, the primordial chaos which coils around us like the serpent. I am a *changed* individual and if you apply the works herein, you will be as well. Success is always upon a path of pain, struggle and well-earned rewards along the way.

This living or 'dead' grimoire, Maskim Hul is a gate to not only the Ilu Limnu or 'Evil Gods', yet also the all of the Gods of the Babylonian-Assyrian Pantheon if you apply the structure within. It may be utilized in a way to harmonize with your daily life and without adopting cultural practices which will make little sense to your friends, family and ultimately you! I can attest the Gods and Demons do adapt just as you, for consider that each individual is a temple and gateway to life for them, so there is a "give and take" involved. All worthwhile relationships are "give and take" although many have such with more on one side than the other.

Such is the practice of magick. As a Luciferian I can attest you will find a different perspective on the concept of "light" than you will before you practice the workings herein. If you consistently apply the workings and maintain this you will become an adept.

This, of course is easier read than done and most arm-chair magickians will not be able to apply consistency and discipline long enough to achieve it.

Please do not let my words be of any shock at any rate, this is simply the way of the world. Look around you and see it is over-ripe consumer-quantity daily! It is neither remarkable nor rare; rather such sheep-like behavior is as common as grass in a middle-class neighborhood.

Success, how can I achieve it with this type of magick? What often places the individual into 'elite' status is the ability to maintain consistency in the chosen task. It is that simple. The rest is up to the genetics, intellect and ability of that thing which is you.

I have written this in honor of the Seven Maskim Hul, known as the Sebitti or "Seven Evil Gods". I offer this to the Mother Tiamat and Kingu. I offer this to the Great Gods who emerged within the circle of the crooked serpent. May this provide a gate to your vessel in this world again, may the dead come forth to the living!

A NOTE ON LUCIFERIANISM

My approach was clear: Luciferian. The reader may cringe at the idea; "Lucifer has no place in the Mesopotamian pantheons" is to be thought. This is the moment I must press some clairity in the definition.

Satanism is the rational focus on the self in relation to life here and now. This philosophy is based on carnal fulfillment with consideration for the preservation of self. Magic is practiced as a type of ideological empowerment and psychodrama.

Firstly, Luciferianism is a modern term for the ideological, philosophical and Magickial attainment of applicable knowledge and inner power. The type of knowledge sought is through study, initiation and the continual struggle for self-improvement through spiritual rebellion against the social concept of "God" and "Religion". Luciferianism is different from medieval magic and witchcraft as the Luciferian approaches the art as a psychological, subconscious and conscious foundation. The theory of ritual magick is that the Luciferian understands the "gods", "spirits" and "demons" are the archetypical creation of humanity; that our subconscious feeds the type of energy in which these beings exist through. Luciferians thus seek experience and the darkness within to gain knowledge, wisdom and power.

Luciferianism is thus the ultimate spirituality as it focuses on the growth and expansion of the individual in a rational sense here and now, with the broad range of spiritual exploration as well.

The magick within this book is concerned with the refinement of consciousness, self-empowerment and power attained through knowledge. The self is viewed as the temple which the gods and demons dwell within. The magick of this grimoire is spiritual rebellion- in the model of the Seven Maskim/Sebitti/Evil Gods and Lamashtu.

November 23rd, 2010 6:30 AM.

Michael W. Ford

INTRODUCTION
MY OWN PRIVATE BABYLON

Marchozelos

The power of magick is seen in truth through those who are within its thralls. Those who seek to go beyond the limitations of the imbalances that are apparently inherent in us are those who reach beyond into the fears of primitive man and delve into the mysteries of change and gnosis. I suggested to Magus Akhtya that I write of my own experiences with the power of ancient magick and how it affected my own day-to-day life. As an initiate I have always sought (whether or not with effectiveness that remains to be seen) to push my consciousness to it's limits and mold my perceptions of life towards a non dogmatic concept open to all thought patterns in a disciplined way. Nothing could have prepared me however, for the strenuous and challenging spiritual work that I have done as the artist behind this new book.

For all that has been written on the nature of occult literature and esoteric philosophies none in my estimation have been as important (in recent times) as the workings to be found in the Order of Phosphorus. This is a rather bold statement but one that I find to be true due to my own experiences. We are at the forefront of what is to be seen as the 'edge of the precipice' so to speak, in that we lack dogmatic foundation and consume the essence of the relevant in our surroundings. Action and reaction, pleasure and suffering are alchemically devoured and reconstructed into a new paradigm only to be experienced by the individual in question. The only truth is balance and will. It is not the acquisition of power and notoriety alone that we wish to extract from history and philosophy, but the essence itself marked in the lives of those who have existed since and before time immemorial.

Varying experiences and challenges that I have always sought to overcome has marked my own life. Many years before joining the Order, I like many in our modern society grew up enmeshed in Judeo-Christian dogma, and it was something that marked my life in a deep and profound way. Growing up nominally Roman Catholic, in my early teens I sought out the works of the early church fathers and writings of the scripture as well as history to guide my way towards what (at the time) I believed to be the truth. This lead me to traditionalist non-ecumenical Eastern Orthodox Christianity and it held me in its thralls quite honestly. I became so enmeshed in this belief that I forsook for a time my own family and joined as a novitiate a monastery in the mountains of Colorado, so as to find the knowledge and wisdom that I sought. After much study and personal grief due to my questioning and existential nature, I found in my solitude that which I was lacking. It was not an external source that guided my hunger and thirst for the truth; it was the Light within me all along. That which was so elusive now became in my hour of darkness so real, so tangable I sought it out with all the strength that was within me.

For a time I ignored that silent voice that was within me, yet I knew that it was speaking to me and gathering all my collective experiences to guide my Will towards a new yet ancient path. I did some soul searching so to speak, and I recollected on my earliest memories of being in an old gothic church as a small child, experiencing the rites and passages that were to be found within the old stalwart monolith of the Christian faith. The old sorrowful statues, the priests in their garments flowing of gold and silver, and the chalices filled with wine glistening upon the altars decorated with perfumed frankincense and myrrh. It was not the belief that attracted me so much as it was the emotional and artistic aestheticism of it all. It was the silence and meditation, the desire and strength of the flowing of tears of the nature of motherhood rather than the icon of the Theotokos (Mother of God). The suffering of Christ in the Victorian ochre stained wood became a symbol of transfiguration into that which is ecstasy through suffering and deprivation, rather than guilt and consummation of flesh into spiritual slavery.

With these recollections, I knew that I had the desire and the imagination to reach towards a deeper path, a more ancient path that would be more relevant to my daily experiences of strife and challenges. I did not have the word for what I knew was the concept of 'timelessness' yet it was what would drive me to push forward towards the path of the Black Light of Luciferianism. It was the asceticism of the monastery and the discipline I learned from reading those ancient books that caused me to further my studies towards a more conclusive end. I sought a path that had no end and could not provide answers as 'universal'. I knew inside myself that the so-called 'traditional' conception of Satanism was too limited for my own imagination and thirst for the unquenchable; therefore I continued upon my path and sought the Promethean image of Lucifer in my own path. I found myself seeking that which was beyond the medieval image of the Devil being that who is of darkness only, and I sought the path of the Black Light, which is of struggle, falling into the abyss and coming out triumphant and powerful.

Aestheticism and beauty had always driven my path in life, and I found myself (as I do often today) struggling through depression, anxiety and the thirst for balance between both light and dark, conceptually and philosophically. When reading John Milton's "Paradise Lost" I found myself wondering if there were more ancient origins of the ideas and stories that I had read and studied in western lore. What was the path of the Left Hand in its most undiluted essence, and where could I find that which had eluded me for so many years? Upon my entrance to the Order of Phosphorus I was already well versed in the Pseudomonarchia Demonum of Johann Weyer as well as the Black Pullet grimoires. I had involved myself in a form of self-styled Chaos Magick through intuition and visionary experience, never following the path of strict ritual adherence to the sources available to me. After all, the writers of these books must have either received tradition by word of mouth or experienced their revelations that were specifically inspired by their own particular role in history and innovation and spontaneity must be the key to the spark of light that this new path had to offer me.

I knew that power came neither from culture nor the traditions that had ingrained myself in me, yet the emotional desires and strength I gathered from the visual and sensual input of the rites I had performed had far deeper meaning to me than the substance of them, which I had incorporated from the Christian faith. The old grimoires taught me discipline, strength of character and spiritual empowerment to a certain extent yet I knew that deep inside the source of my devotion must have had a more profound meaning than had been understood by contemporary society. I studied the texts of the Avesta and realized that a lot of the spirits and deific masks expounded upon in later writings shared the majority of the epistemological theorem expounded upon throughout the folklore of civilizations most people are familiar with (i.e. the Roman Empire) yet carried a certain essence which was diluted and compartmentalized throughout centuries of monotheistic social engineering and terrorism.

Upon my embarking on the path of the Seven Maskim/Sebitti and Labartu, rather than the image of Samael and Lilith, I had experienced more profound and visionary experiences than before. I had often worked with the conceptual focus points written of by Austin Osman Spare, particularly in the sigilization of desire and the emanation of the Self through destruction of ego/duality and found myself seeing a startling parallel between what could be interpreted as a very traditional path yet expressed in a manner that is wholly fresh and in tune with modern life. Here was an example that could be interpreted without prejudice or presupposed dogmatic revelation, and at the same time be seen as a gateway towards the empowerment of the individual in an antinomian sense, rather than a collectivist mindset of self-dissolving god worship.

It is true that there is a connection to history in these writings you are about to explore; yet there is a sense of timelessness in that there is no sense of time in the formulaic point of view. One needs to separate oneself from the outer ripples of the limitations of age and circumstance and enfold the mind in a new paradigm of freedom and strength through self-accountability. There is only one mind in the Age beyond all Ages; that have Desire and accumulation of power through self-reliance! Gods and goddesses only hold the truth through an alchemical balance of the attributes of both and this is seen well enough through experience and far-sightedness.

It is often said in Judeo-Christian mythology that narrow is the way of salvation, and wide the way to the gates of hell (sheol) yet I would beg to differ. The human experience is wrought with strife and battles either internal or external, and the only constant knowledge of the 'real' and 'unreal' is through experience and example. One man's truth is another's falsehood. There is no knowledge or spiritual energy attributed to weakness or to ideology alone. All these concepts fall to the wayside and there is only the mirror to gaze upon when truth is razed in the crucible of fate. I have looked upon this mirror and though my horror at the imperfections I perceive through my limited vision, my thirst for life is what shall ultimately be the judge of my actions and breadth of liberation.

The key to one door shall open another. It is through my own journey that I shall gaze upon the precipice and see myself for what I truly am and shall become. Gods and Goddesses are but masks to place on my own face, and as I have done so through a channeling of this ancient energy I shall be one with the vision written of in this tome. The only truth is this: That flesh and blood is to be desired only as far as it's ultimate meaning allows us to transcend limitations and belief and that the Self is beyond restriction; imbibing both lust and carnal knowledge shall be but one key towards the illimitable expansion of our minds. These are not merely words that I speak yet they are the speech of the sylphs, pebbles thrown into the wasteland of modern excess and sobriety, and as I am no prophet, I am also not a fool. There is wisdom in my estimation in listening to the voice that lay within the mind of each and every one of us, for this is the voice that shall be with us to the point of death and beyond. The ancient Sumerians, Akkadians and Assyrians who were devoted and made offerings in their temples knew this, and I am confident that their knowledge shall be passed to you, as it was to myself and shall be a continual process of desire and revelation. If you take from this book one thing, it is this; that with knowledge there is a price, and to become as one with Ardat Lili, Marduk, Sin-Nanna, Ishtar, Ninurta, Ningishzidda, Tiamat and others, you must not part with your Self in the process, yet accumulate these essences into your own knowledge so that you yourself shall become as a god, and not assimilate into the grid of over 2000 years of silence and ignorance. What makes the inscriptions and unearthed icons of the ancients so powerful is not the evocative nature of their art but the sense that through their silence, there will be the few throughout time itself that will break the bonds of literalism and shed all consciousness towards the illumination of self-gnosis and antinomian power.

> *"You were the intruder,*
> *Before Shamash,*
> *May the King of Gods be great!"*

- **Priest Marchozelos III °, TOPH.**

CHAPTER ONE

MESOPOTAMIAN ORIGINS AND BACKGROUND OF RELIGIOUS CULTURE

Assyrians flaying war-captives, heads carried away. Skins were hung on the walls of the temple of not only the war-god but also in the palace in early Assyrian records.

OF THE GODS OF OLD

The Gods and Goddesses of ancient times are fed in this world by humanity. Once the God has been established with function, purpose and representation, then it is fed with the sacrifice of energy of some sort. For many it is the Gods being visualized continually and then offerings of blood or food. This over a period of time and through numerous generations creates what Carl Jung referred to as "Archetypes", prototypes of ideas which exist in the collective unconscious of humanity.

Alexander the Great once wrote to his mother *that "even the higher gods, Jupiter, Juno and Saturn and the others gods, were men, and that the secret was told him by Leo, the high priest of Egyptian sacred things"*[1] and even insisting in his letter that she burn it upon reading it. Obviously, she did not heed his instructions. Upon the physical death of Seleukos I Nikator (King: 305 – 281 BC), founder of the Seleucid Empire, was deified by his successor and son Antiochos I Soter (King 281- 261 BC), who set up temples and altars to his father. In Babylon the Seleucid Empire did not impose Hellenistic views; rather we find that they assimilated for the Hellenistic settlers there the Babylonian Gods with Hellenistic ones, as well as a Temple and offerings made to Seleukos I Nikator ("Victor") and his family.

Understand that the Adversary is a part of each God and Goddess, beginning with Tiamat all through to Marduk. One distinct difference in this grimoire from a Luciferian perspective is that Marduk is not something we as "Children of Tiamat" fight against; rather we invoke the serpent of darkness along with Kingu (who ultimately are the creators of life) through Marduk. The later Greco-Egyptian concepts called "Theurgy" are found in the earliest records of Babylonian and Assyrian Magick, which are laid as foundation methods here.

---

[1] The Worship of the Dead by J. Garnier

The Gods of this grimoire are what can be called "Dead" Gods; they sleep in the abyss of our subconscious minds. When we feed them and communicate with them through invocation, they stir slowly from the depths. Over a period of time they rise up from our subconscious to take new life in our Minds and Bodies. Each god and goddess holds a key to our potential as becoming deified in our own life and beyond.

Luciferians believe in the potential of an informed mind; a strong will and the focus to become a god ensorcelled in darkness beholding light.

Nearly every Babylonian (I refer to this to include the Elam, Assyrian and Chaldean variants) gods are like humans and contain both aspects of darkness as well as light. They destroy and create, they can be vengeful yet also compassionate to those they choose to care about. There is no universal or mindless bliss of "love" as the Judeo-Christians would try to make you believe, nor it there "One God".

A useful method for the Kassapu/Priest/Adept is to for a period of time hold devotional workings towards a specific deific mask/god/goddess. This would be merely invocations, hymns and offerings to one god or goddess to discover their association within you. Remember, as you will see by applying practice here that all the gods and demons manifest through your personally, without us they do not exist to ourselves. Contemplate my deeper meaning of this from a Luciferian perspective.

Tiamat is the source and sacred Mother of creation. Much like any God or Goddess, she is both destructive and life bringing. Invoke her well and listen to your instincts, for she is the most powerful of all. Immortality of the Spirit is possible for the Black Adept, once the Gods have found their awakening in him. His mind, remaining independent like they, shall gather much energy and upon death your spirit shall exist as a Dark God within their current of being.

Understand that ancient religion is not that of today; times, culture and circumstance has us at an advantage to those who lived in ancient Mesopotamia three thousand years ago. We must understand that in your practice of this ancient sorcery you are approaching the experience of nature; the body and the mind to bring close a communion of the ancient with the present time. Stirring the primal sea of the atavistic stream of the ancient serpent is a reality.

This grimoire is dedicated to the Seven Maskim, Tiamat and the Ilu Limnu. I have listened to her primordial voice for many years; my path has led me here as I am now. This grimoire will provide a suitable avenue for initiation, if you dare!

We shall seek to use the drums of the deep to stir her once again, to move upward through us in this world! You will find workings and mediations for many Gods of Light as well, for we are not bound by Judeo-Christian absolutes. Luciferians understand balance and the application of knowledge. Do not dismiss a god if it is at first appearance "of light" or "of darkness". Luciferians as the Kassapu (sorcerer, warlock) will always find a structure of balance between the two. *We do not think in dualistic terms.*

The Akkadians believed that every phenomenon in nature and upon the earth had a spirit or god associated with it, depending on how it affected and how perceived, defined it as malefic or beneficent to life. Some cruel acts could later bring a beneficial result.

HISTORICAL FOUNDATIONS

While this is a grimoire of Magickial practice, it bears some of my responsibility to present some *basic* terms for words used herein; to provide a burgeoning clarity of the texts and their applications therein. While this is not an exhaustive or complete study, it may offer some useful foundation points for further understanding.

AKKADIANS

Akkad also called Agade is an ancient city founded by Sargon I, the King and founder of what is known as the Akkadian dynasty which existed from an estimated 2340 to 2284 B.C. The area was north of Sumer and became the first established unity of an empire for its time. Naram-Sin was the grandson of Sargon of Akkad and is shown of the famous victory stele wearing the horned-cap of divinity, having slain his enemies. Naram-Sin was the first to use the title of **"King of the Four Quarters"**. The four quarters have been used ever since for the traditions of Assyrian and Babylonian Kings, including the Seleucid Empire while it maintained control of Babylon. Interestingly enough, the "four quarters" in Mesopotamian Geography are encircled by the winds, which in turn are circular in movement.

ASSYRIANS

Assyria is an ancient land which lies in present day Iraq and Syria. The center of the region was a major trade route from Anatolia and the Iranian plateau through the Zagros Mountains and south through Babylonia. Assyria was in the northern area above Babylonia and Sumer. The Old Assyrian period is dated 1900 – 1400 B.C., the Middle Assyrian Period is 1400 – 1050 B.C. and the most important was the Neo-Assyrian Empire of 934 – 610 B.C.

The grimoire presented here manifests the wide range of deific interpretations from known Assyrian and Babylonian records.

Shalmaneser II, Priest of Ashur who offers Blood, Spirit and Energy to the Gods. The Pile of Skulls of Assyrian Conquest by Marchozelos

HITTITES

The Hittites were a people composed of Indo-European tribes who settled in Anatolia in the 18th Century B.C. and founded a kingdom. The Hittite Kingdom is dated (both old and new) was from 1650 – 1200 B.C. The Hittites were a major military power which fought against Egypt and the Assyrians frequently. The Hittites had a fairly rich theological pantheon which more or less was compatible with the Assyrian, Chaldean and even the Canaanite deities as well.

There was a god of plague called **Alauwaimis**, a demon who could avert plague with offerings of goat. **Tarpatassis** is a Hittite demon who could grant people a long life by keeping sickness away.

The Gods of the Hittites were interchanged in many ways, with slight exceptions with regard to the Babylonian-Chaldean mythology.

We have **Alalus** who was the king of heaven from which **Anu** was his cupbearer for a number of years until he rebelled and cast him under the earth. **Anu** then took **Kumarbi** or **Kismaras** who is known later as the "Father of the Gods" as his cupbearer. Kumarbi rebelled after some years and became the god who is equated with Enlil and the Syrian Dagan.

Kismaras seems to have later manifested as **Kimaris**, known as the 66th Goetic demon that also has name variants of **Cimejes** and Cimeies. He is described as a Marquis, great and strong who appears as a warrior upon a black horse. Kismaras instructs on grammer, logic, rhetoric and to recover lost treasure or wisdom.

Teshub is the storm god; the calf of Teshub is a bull with a human head called the Sharruma. The Moon god **Kashku** is known to bestow dark omens yet may be satisfied with offerings of sheep. **Shaushka** is the Hurrian/Hittite Ishtar; she is loved by a serpent named **Hedammu**.

BABYLONIANS, CHALDEANS & SUMERIANS

The Sumerians were the people of southern Mesopotamia in 3rd millennium B.C., the center of which was the city UR which was the source of many cuneiform tablets.

The Babylonians are a people established by the king Hammurabi in the 18th Century B.C. from which the city of Babylon was established. The Chaldeans were tribal peoples from southern Mesopotamia. Being composed of numerous tribes, being Bit Amukani, Bit-Yakin and Bit Dakkuri as the most significant they were involved in Maritime trade and were also highly skilled in astrology and magic.

The Chaldeans form a Dynasty in Babylonia and ruled it from 625 to 539 B.C. At this point Chaldean was used to describe "Babylonians" and Babylonia from that point on. In consideration of the grimoire here, Chaldean and Babylonian are interchangeable.

ELAMITES

Elam was a land located in Iran directly from the north-east of Babylon and south-west of Ur. Being a mountainous region, Elam was populated with a fierce yet highly developed people; of which fought with Babylon and the Assyrians at different periods. Their language was not connected with others and they did write in cuneiform. Elam at times was conquered by Akkad and Assyria as well as becoming a powerful sovereign with Kings such as Kiden-Hutran and Untash-Napirisha. The gods and demons of the Elamites were mostly interchanged with both Assyria and Babylonia, although they do have distinct gods. In a Babylonia calendar text dating from around the first millennium

B.C. Elam is associated with Tiamat; Assyria is equated with Kingu and Marduk with Babylonia[2].

LULUBI

The Lulubi were a mountainous, warrior-people who lived in the mountains of what is now Armenia and Persia. They were raiders, much like the later Median and Scythian tribes and fought against the Akkadians numerous times. Naram-Sin describes them as "warriors with bodies of "cave birds[3]", a race with ravens' faces....Tiamat suckled them.." and lived in the "Shining Mountains". Venus or Ishtar declared to Naram-Sin "not to destroy the sons of perdition" as Enlil would summon them for evil, or destruction (plundering, raiding, etc).

The Luluabi are represented in a rock carving near Sar-i-pul in the Zagros mountain area, they are bearded and the Chief of the tribe wears a turban-cap with a sheepskin kil. His weapon is a Gamlu or Axe and his warriors have their scalps shaved above the temples, which is a style shown in the carvings showing the Gutian tribes as well.

GUTIANS

The Gutians were a warlike tribe of people thought to populate the Zagros Mountain range North-East of the Assyrian territories. They came into power as a type of dynasty around 2190 B.C. and were a fierce mountain-people who were highly skilled in hit and run guerilla raids into Assyrian and Sumerian territories. These people were said to have been sent by the

---

[2] F. Reynolds, Stellar Representations of Tiamat and Qingu in a learned calendar text.

[3] Could this be a reference to bats?

Babylonian God Marduk, for the King of Akkad Naram-Sin who destroyed the famed city. The Guti swept down and not only conquered Akkad, but also destroyed it.

The Gutians are described as devastating raiders and after a time conquerors. They, like the Barbarian hordes of Roman-Europe were desecrators and "blasphemers" of the temples and culture of the Akkadians and Sumerians.

Due to their lack of understanding in the customs, religion and general culture of the Akkadians, the Gutians did not keep hold of their conquests for long. Eventually these people were defeated and split off into other cultures of mountainous areas.

The Gutians are known from the "Lament for Ur" as "the snake of the mountains" and were associated with Azag who battled Ninurta.

OF RELIGION AND WAR

"Ninib, the hero, who crushes the wicked and the enemy and lets me attain my heart's desire" – Tiglath-Pileser I

Understanding the balance between gods and their ability to be creative, kind, equally brutal and warlike is found in the culture itself. The Assyrians, Babylonians and Elamites were cultures who were constantly at war with some tribe, neighboring country, each other or busy with revolts within. The entire foundation is centered on warfare, conquering and overmastering the enemy. Through this, is a temporary peace obtained.

While their kingdoms were so long ago, their cultural manifestation of the Gods are the beginnings of Luciferianism as it is now. The ideal of strength, wisdom, beauty, conquering your enemy (being person, fears or challenges) and destroying without mercy are Luciferian ideals found in the mind.

Luciferianism is not based in Judeo-Christian "demons", rather it is found in origin in ancient Babylonia, Persia, Greece and Egypt. The Judeo-Christian influence no doubt has empowering aspects and fuels the Adversarial Spirit, it remains that Luciferianism is far older than its' name or current cultural identity.

Satanic and demonic magick and ritual now is a "mask" for the ancient initiatory practices which involve a balance of both darkness and light; where the individual places no god – imagined or otherwise before the self and that the "Daemon" or spirit of the individual is made strong through working with "deific masks".

The Gutians Warlords (2190-2115 B.C.) are referred to by the Sumerians as "demons" and no doubt assuming the "image" of the Chaldean demons who in a similar fashion come down from the Northern-Mountain lands.

"The Gutians, the fanged serpent of the mountain, who acted with violence against the gods, who carried off the kingship of the land of Sumer to the mountain land, who filled the land of Sumer with wickedness, who away the wife from the one who had a wife, who took away from the who had a child, who put wickedness and evil in the land of Sumer." – R2: 284 of Warfare in the Ancient Near East William J. Hamblin

We find an association between the Mountain Warlords such as the Gutian and the legend of Ninurta. Azag, the demonic enemy of Ninurta is described as coming from the mountainous abode of the Zagros Mountains, similar to the Gutians.

Azag thought to take away the kingship of Ninurta in the Sumerian lands.

In understanding the role of mythology, magick, religion and initiation one must contemplate the world you live in and all the aspects of your life which bear meaning for you. Look to the symbolism of this grimoire to empower your being in both darkness and light. This is why it is significant towards being successful in this type of magick that you understand the culture and all aspects: geographic region, challenges and the mindset of the day based on the records available. Once this is accomplished you may look at the manifestations of the gods and demons and how they apply to your own life *as it is now*. Adaptation to resurrect such ancient archetypes is essential towards a living and breathing current arising from the sleep of ages.

Torture of captives by Assyrian soldiers by Marchozelos

The great Assyrian King, Asurnasirpal II (883-859 B.C.), was renowned for his cruelty and bloodthirsty nature.

"At that time ASSUR the lord, the proclaimer of my name, the enlarger of my kingdom, entrusted his weapon that spares not to the hands of my lordship, (even to me) Assur-natsir-pal the exalted prince, the adorer of the great gods, the mighty monster, the conqueror of cities and mountains to their furthest bounds, the king of lords, the consumer of the violent, who is crowned with terror, who fears not opposition, the

valiant one, the supreme judge who spares not, who overthrows resistance, the king of all princes..."-Annals of Asurnasirpal II

The King would proclaim offerings to each god depending on his campaigns or needs. We see the illuminated nature of the King as a type of "God-Manifest", that being that this deific power(s) have manifest in his nature and rule. It is also significant to understand that the Assyrians were great creators as well, they lived in a world where you had to be cruel to deter others from attacking you.

"The king who has marched with justice in reliance on ASSUR and SAMAS, the gods his helpers, and powerful countries and princes his foemen he has cast down like a reed (and) has subjugated all their lands under his feet, the supplier of the freewill offerings for the great gods, the established prince, who is provident to direct the laws of the temples of his country, the work of whose hands and the gift of whose sacrifices the great gods of heaven and earth desire and have established his high-priesthood in the temples for ever; their strong weapons have they given for the spoil of my lordship; the terror of his weapon, the glory of his lordship, over the kings of the four regions (of the world) have they made strong for him; the enemies of ASSUR to their furthest bounds above and below he has combated, and tribute and gifts he has laid upon them; (he), the conqueror of the foes of ASSUR, the powerful king, the king of ASSYRIA, the son of Tiglath-Uras, the high priest of ASSUR, who upon all his foemen has laid the yoke, has set up the bodies of his adversaries upon stakes" – Annals of Asurnasirpal II

Asurnasirpal was a great leader and conqueror who modernized the Assyrian army and forcefully expanded it.

"The son of the chief of the city of NISTUN, I flayed in the city of ARBELA (and) clothed the wall of the fortress with his skin."-Annals of Asurnasirpal II

Skinning enemies and using their skins to decorate the palace and especially that of the War-Gods was a great sight to the Assyrian kings, a literal terror to their enemies abroad who heard of such practice.

"I erected a pyramid of skulls at the approach to its chief gate. The nobles, as many as had revolted, I flayed; with their skins I covered the pyramid. Some (of these) I immured in the midst of the pyramid; others above the pyramid I impaled on stakes; others round about the pyramid I planted on stakes; many at the exit from my own country I flayed; with their skins I clad the fortress-walls. The limbs of the chief officers who (were) the chief officers of the kings who had rebelled I cut off. I brought Akhi-yababa to NINEVAH (and) flayed him; with his skin I clad the fortress-wall of NINEVAH."-Asurnasirpal II

Assyrian and Babylonian Kings created boundary stones, which were inscribed with symbols and names of the gods along with a curse for any who remove it. Ashurbanipal inscribed a curse on a tablet in his records:

"Psammetichus, King of Egypt, who had thrown off the yoke of my lordship. I heard of it and prayed to Ashur and Ishtar, as follows: 'May be corpse be cast before his enemies, and may they carry away his bones'. - The Rassam Cylinder

Ashurbanipal as well as his father Esarhaddon consulted the Oracle of Ishtar who affirmed the kingship and authority of Ashurbanipal's father after the murder of Sennacherib.

"I conquered that region, laid it waste for a distance of fifteen days' march, and poured disaster upon it. As for Ahsheri, who did not fear my lordship – in accordance with the word of Ishtar who dwells in Arbela, who had said from the beginning, 'I will bring about the death of Ahsheri, King of the Mannai, according to as I have said'. She delivered him into the hands of his servants, and the people of his land made a revolt against him. On the street of his city they cast his corpse" – The Rassam Cylinder

Specific months and seasons were meant for campaigns and war. Ashurbanipal on his fifth campaign marched to Elam. He inscribed that by the "command of Ashur, Sin, Shamash, Ramman, Bel, Nabu, Ishtar of Nineveh, Queen of Kidmuri, Ishtar of Arbela, Ninib, Nergal and Nuski, in the Month Elul, the month of the mission of the Goddesses, the month of Ashur, the king of the gods, the father of the gods, great in his lordship"- The Rassam Cylinder

Tiglath-Pilesar Impaling Enemies by Marchozelos

Ashurbanipal understood as did his predecessors and visers; the significance of showing kindness and favor to those who supported the Assyrian Kingdom and complete cruelty and annihilation to those who opposed it. For if it was not the Assyrians who conquered, they would be vassals of another as we have seen throughout history.

Ishtar of Arbela, the great oracle goddess, the warrior goddess and mistress who bathed in the blood of her enemies along with Ashur played a pivotal role as the inspiration of the Assyrians to go forth and conquer. Ishtar is a perfect example of the Goddess within a state of consistent balance with the God, she is both cruel and kind and she bows to no other god!

The Gods are written about in Assyrian records as having been pacified by the offerings of blood and victims during war. The Gods and Goddesses, even the most "light" oriented enjoyed slaughter of enemies:

"I cut out the tongues of those soldiers in whose mouths were insolence because they had spoken against Ashur, my lord and had plotted evil against me, and I murdered them. As for the rest of the men who were alive, by the bull-colossi, where my grandfather, Sennacherib, had made a slaughter, there I at that time slew those men as a lamentation for him. I let dogs, swine, vultures, eagles, birds of the heavens, and fish of the ocean eat their flesh, which was cut off. After I had done these thingsd and had pacified the hearts of the great gods...threw into heaps the bones of the bodies of the men whom Gira had destroyed, those who had died of hunger and feminine.."-Ramman Cylinder

Ashurbanipal then cleaned the streets and cities, purified the temples and made continual offerings of incense and libation with dirges and penitential prayers. In the Luciferian tradition as I have defined it, this is balance as he destroyed and created with equal measure.

ANCIENT ASSYRIA

"Tiglath-Pileser, the fiery, fierce flame, the mighty battle-storm"
–Inscription of Tiglath-Pileser I, 1100 B.C.

The Sigil of Assur, the Conquering God

The foundation of religion is the needs of its people. Ancient Assyria provides an interesting perspective on a people who adored beauty, loved warfare and fed the gods the blood of their victims. The early high priest of Assyria was the king, who served as the figurehead of the kingdom. Keeping extensive libraries, Ashurbanipal (685-627 BC) is responsible for collecting the largest library of tablets of his day which brought us so much knowledge of the Assyrian religion, culture and ritual working.

While the Assyrians and Babylonians were highly developed culturally, the geographic region and opposing cultures from all areas found both regions in consistent struggle for dominion. Assyria became the primary lordship of the region, with a philosophy and a theological foundation of balance; they were bloodthirsty and cruel in war, yet made consistent offerings to all of the gods and held their banner in the sign of Ashur, the winged god who holds the bow and arrow towards their enemy.

The inscriptions of the kings of Assyria and Babylonia offer some clear insight into the determination and balance of these viable cultures.

"Ashur, great lord, ruler of the divine host..who bestows scepter and crown..Bel, lord and king of all the spirits of the deep...Ishtar, princess among the gods, mistress of destructions, who unchains the terrors of war: Ye great gods, guardians of heaven and earth, whose onset brings fight and battle..." –Inscription of Tiglath-Pileser I, King of Assyria (1100 B.C.)

We see here the invocation of the gods at the beginning of the inscription, Bel being a semi-generic term for "Marduk" of Babylonia, without calling to the god of another city. We do see a separation of Bel and Marduk at times, especially in ancient Assyrian king records however it is considered commonly that Bel and Marduk may be interchanged to avoid confusion. Ashur in many ways takes on a composite god of Marduk and Ninurta to be a god of the Assyrian people. Tiglath-Pileser I was a great king he conquered to a great extent in all directions, including Babylon.

"Like the Thunderer (Adad) I crushed the corpses of their warriors in the battle that caused their overthrow. I made their blood to flow over all the ravines and high places of mountains. I cut off their heads and piled them up at the walls of their cities like heaps of grain." –Tiglath-Pileser I

We see a good example of the God Adad, symbolized as the "Thunderer" representing storms envisioned and manifested in the armies of Tiglath-Pileser. It seems logical that he saw the might of his power as given by the gods and manifest directly through him.

"I made their blood flow into the Tigris and over the heights of the mountains...I headed the bodies of their warriors in great numbers on

the mountain peaks, and let the rive carry off the corpses of their soldiers into the Tigris" –Tiglath-Pileser

Lion Hunt of Ashurbanipal by Marchozelos

The tradition of conquering throughout the near east was a see-saw effect; Assyria went through a period of decline under different kings and saw great periods of resurgence. We do see consistency in the inscriptions of each king, their tradition of documenting their victories and challenges highlighted their great empires.

Shalmaneser II 1031 BC to 1019 BC was a strong king who went on a series of conquests as well. His inscription begins with an invocation to the gods;

"Assur, the great Lord, the King of all, the great gods; Anu, King of the spirits of heaven and the spirits of earth, the god, Lord of the world; Bel the Supreme, Father of the gods, the Creator; Hea, King of the deep, determiner of destinies, the King of crowns, drinking in brilliance" – Inscription of Shalmaneser II

We see Shalmaneser making reference to the gods including Anu, called the king of the spirits of the heavens and earth as well as being lord of the earth. Hea is Ea the King of the Deep, the lord of magick and the spirits or knowledge.

"Merodach, Prince of the gods, Lord of battles; Adar, the terrible, Lord of the spirits of heaven and the spirits of earth, the exceeding strong god; Nergal, the powerful god, King of the battle; Nebo, the bearer of

the high sceptre, the god, the Father above; Beltis, the wife of Bel, mother of the great gods" – Inscription of Shalmanaser II

Merodach, essentially Marduk called the Lord of battles. Adar, Nergal and Nebo are invoked, specifically as dark gods of war.

"The noble offspring of Tiglath-Adar who has laid his yoke upon all lands hostile to him, and has swept them like a whirlwind." – Inscription of Shalmanaser II

The reference of "whirlwind" is associated with the powers wielded by the Seven Sebitti/Maskim, Labartu/Lamashtu and other demons who work in accordance with Ea on occasion. This is another example of association with the forces of nature, the gods and similar deific powers made manifest via the King and the army.

The Neo-Assyrians held titles as described in their tablets and records during their reign which provides insight into the political and religious ideas of the time. Some when having conquered Babylon, who brought forth many strong and wise Babylonian-Chaldean kings who opposed Assyrian rule at different periods, held titles such as "sar Babili" or "King of Babylon".

"Governor of the god Assur"- **Shalmaneser III, Assurnapsirpal II**

"Governor of the gods Bel and Marduk" – **Sargon II**

"Governor of the gods Nabu and Marduk" – **Sargon II**

"Governor of the gods" – **Adad-nirari II, Shalmaneserr I, Tukilti-Ninurta I**

"Governor of Enlil" – **Naram-Sin of Akkad**

Esarhaddon calls himself the exalted autocrat (self-directed ruler) of Ashur, Nabu and Marduk, King of Kings, the unsparing, who burns the stubborn, who is clothed with brilliancy and who does not fear battle; the splendid warrior, the all-powerful, who controls the scepter of kings.

Ashurbanipal (668-626 B.C.) was one of the last great Assyrian kings – even more brutal than some of his predecessors. What makes this king unique is that he learned the "wisdom of Nabu (Nebo)" and that of the royal scribes, which is he learned how to read and write. Ashurbanipal learned also how to shoot with the bow, riding and how to control a chariot. This placed Ashurbanipal at an advantage over some previous kings, as being skilled and knowledgeable; he could allow very few advisors to have their own agendas or to be guided in the wrong direction. He calls himself "a warlike man, the favorite of Ashur and Ishtar.." and is equally an individual who sought to enhance and enlighten his people and subjects accordingly.

Ashurbanipal had the difficult task of maintaining the accomplishments of his father Esarhaddon and Grandfather Sennacherib. One interesting section of his records presents the authority he maintained through cruelty to his enemies:

"The inhabitants of Sais also, and Medes, and Tanis, and the rest of the cities, as many as had sided with them and plotted evil, they the generals destroyed with weapons, both small and great, and left not a man in them. They hung their corpses on gibbets, stripped off their skins, and therewith covered the wall of the city."-The Rassam Cylinder

Ashurbanipal showed kindness as well, the Governor of Sais he had brought in iron chains and then showed mercy to Necho, whom he made a strict new covenant with and had him clothed in rich robes, a gold chain with the insignia of his sovereignty and a golden Assyrian dagger with Ashurbanipal inscribed upon it.

Ashurbanipal did not claim his own divinity directly, however as one may discern from the Assyrian records, the Kings' were vessels of the Gods and their nature moving through the King as the High Priest. Ashurbanipal wrote after confronting Elam that

"After I had made the weapons of Ashur and Ishtar rage over Elam, and had manifested might and power, I turned my face on my return against Dunanu of Gambulu, who had trusted in Elam....I conquered Samgunu, the fortress of Gambulu, I entered into that town; I slaughtered its inhabitants like wild animals.". As may be seen, the Gods were fed for thousands of years on the blood of the enemy in every culture from ancient Persia to Egypt.

"Like the onset of the mighty storm I covered the land of Elam..I cut off the head of Teumman, their king, the rebel who had devised evil. I slew his warriors without number. I filled the plain around Susa with their bodies like as thorns and thistles...I made their blood flow down the river Eulaus, and dyed its water like wool."-The Rassam Cylinder

Assyrian Head-Hunters by Marchozelos

We see on inscriptions and art the impaled bodies and flayed victims who had opposed the will of Assyria, they were proud to display their might and destroy any concept of weakness in their image.

During a famine in Akkad, the people who sided with "Shamash-shum-ukin" a leader who rebelled against Ashurbanipal wrote that they were so hungry that they *"ate the flesh of their sons and daughters in order to satisfy their hunger, and they cut open their stomachs...Ashur, Sin, Shamash, Ramman, Bel, Nabu, Ishtar of Nineveh, Queen of Kidmuri, Ishtar of Arbela, Ninib, Nergal and Nusku, who went before me and subdued my foes, threw Shamash-shum-ukin, the hostile brother who had attacked me, into an abyss of burning fire and destroyed his life."* –Ramman Cylinder

Ashurbanipal was as cruel as he was kind, *"I beheaded them and cut off their lips and took them to Assyria as a spectacle for the people of my land"*, and such treatment of prisoners and especially leaders of rebel cities was a consistent practice.

"Their numerous captives I burned with fire. I captured many of the soldiers alive with the hand. I cut off the hands and feet of some; I cut off the noses, the ears (and) the fingers of others; the eyes of the numerous soldiers I put out. I built up a pyramid of the living (and) a pyramid of heads. In the middle (of them) I suspended their heads on vine-stems in the neighborhood of their city.
I erected a pyramid at the approach to its chief gate. The nobles, as many as had revolted, I flayed; with their skins I covered the pyramid. Some (of these) I immured in the midst of the pyramid; others above the pyramid I impaled on stakes; others round about the pyramid I planted on stakes; many at the exit from my own country I flayed; with their skins I clad the fortress-walls. The limbs of the chief officers who (were) the chief officers of the kings who had rebelled I cut off. I brought Akhi-yababa to NINEVAH and flayed him; with his skin I clad the fortress-wall of NINEVAH. Power and might I laid upon the land of LAQE. While I was staying in the city of SURI the tribute of the kings of the land of LAQE every one of them, with the strength of my army (and with) violent battle I attacked the city. I captured (it) Six hundred of

their fighting men I slew with the sword. Three thousand of their captives I burned with fire. I left not one alive among them to become a hostage. Khula the lord of their city I captured alive with (my) hand. I built their bodies into pyramids. Their young men (and) their maidens I burned to ashes. Khula the lord of their city I flayed. With his skin I clad the fortress-wall of the city of DAMDAMU'SA." –Ashurnasirpal II Inscription

We see here the manifestation of Adversary as a force of balance and the careful consideration of establishing order through controlled chaos. This is the law of both the ancient and modern world.

*"The warlike Pest-god overthrew Uaite, together with his troops, who had not kept my treaty had escaped from before the weapons of Ashur, my lord, and fled before them. Famine arose among them, and for their hunger they ate the flesh of their children. The curses, as many as were inscribed upon their treaty, Ashur, Sin, Shammash, Ramman, Bel, Nabu, Ishtar of Nineveh, Queen of Kidmuri, Ishtar of Arbela, Ninib, Nergal and Nisku suddenly brought upon them...Beltis, the beloved of Bel, the strong one, honored of the goddesses who sits enthroned with Anu and Bel, gored my enemies with her might horns. Ishtar, clothed in flames and arrayed in brilliancy, rained down fire upon Arabia. The warlike pest-god girded on war and overthrew my enemies. Ninib, the lance, the great warrior, the son of Bel, with his sharp arrows cut off my enemies."*Ashurbanipal

Darkness and Light were made manifest in the actions of the Assyrian and other people, they directed in their region the movement of the Gods' just as the Gods manifest through them.

HELLENIC BABYLONIA
Babylonian Customs during the Seleucid Period

Chaldean and Babylonian religion has influenced numerous surrounding cultures throughout time; we must consider the Hellenic influence as well to this grimoire. Hellenic practices were brought to Babylon with Megas Alexandros, "Alexander the Great" of Macedon. Adopting and respecting the customs of Babylon and the Chaldean system, the Hellenic gods were assimilated for the Greeks attempting to understand this new place.

This practice continued with Seleukos I Nikator, the founder of the Seleucid Empire. Consider that many of the tablets which are the sources for many "demon" incantations written in the Seleucid period, from 305 BC to 165 BC. What is most admirable is the Seleucid policy to keep local religious beliefs intact with as little distraction to it as possible. While the ancient Assyrians held a title for their appointed leaders in Babylon, called **Sakkanak Babili**, *"Governor of Babylon"* the Seleucids utilized the Achaemenid title of "Satrap" as the term for the governor of this great ancient city.

The Priesthood in Seleucid Babylonia

The Priesthood of the Gods in Babylonia kept to their sacred practices. As described in "Priest and Temple in Hellenistic Babylonia" by Gilbert J.P. McEwan there were devout and intense daily hymns and offerings to the gods. The Priest was called *erib biti* which means "Temple Enterer". The temples also had cult performers who recited incantations and others. The sesgallu was a temple officer who had a specific role of reading the hymn of Enuma Elish during the Babylonian New Year's

Ritual. This same officer also participated in a ritual called the kinunu festival which was on the 18th of Arahsamna located in the Ekasbarkalama temple in the main Esagila temple.

The famed translator of Hellenic Babylonia Berossus, known for his alternate version of "Enuma Elish" was a priest in the Temple of Marduk in Babylon during the lifetime of Antiochus I Soter would have been a strong part of the ritual structure of Babylonia at this time.

The ritual performer of the hymns was a **kalu**. This cultic performer was deemed the most significant from a text called **'nepes sa qat kali'** in which the King decreed offerings for both the kalu and the satammu priest. In earlier times the Babylonians had the tupsarru or "scribe" and in Hellenistic times a sangu priest, for which each temple had.

The names of the Priesthood even if Hellenic in ethnic origin or influence held often their names with the added God name depending on the Temple which they presided. For instance we know some kalu priesthood names from Uruk as Anu-belsunu, Anu-uballit, Sin-leqe-unnini and many others which combined the names of the gods with the Priest. We see this tradition today in modern magick as the importance of word and association; *in the name there is power*.

Rites and Ceremonies of the Temples

The ceremonies of Seleucid Babylonia are recorded in several tablets dated from the period. There is a rite called **Akitu** which are performed during two festivals of the months **Tasrit** and **Nisan**nu. The **Bajatu** is a ceremony conducted during the night and is conducted directly after the secondary evening meal. The beginning was when the gates of the temple were locked and then ended when the gates were opened at dawn. There was a torchlight ceremony and procession with various statues of deities.

There was a ritual called "**dik biti**" (awakening of the temple) which was held before dawn before the gates of the temple were opened. From what is known the rites were invocations of each god were recited. The Kalu and Naru sang the hymns during the ritual.

The **Naptanu** rite was a ritual meal offered at different gods in the temple during different times throughout the day in accordance with custom. In addition during special occasions the meals were offered as well including the **Akitu** festival in Babylon. *It is during this festival that the Enuma Elish was recited as ritual itself.*

The **'Pit Babi'** or **"Opening of the Gate"** ceremony was conducted at dawn in the temples throughout the region. During Hellenistic times the Zodiac was heavily focused on with associations to the Gods themselves. Modern practitioners will not find it plausible or realistic to conduct strenuous ceremonies daily in addition to daily life, however such a rite may be conducted on special occasions. Consistency in Magick is as significant as any working conducted, without driving towards your goal you may waste much time waiting for it in which it may never come to pass. When importance and consistency is applied nothing is impossible within reason.

The **Kispu** offerings were to the shades of the dead as ancestors however during the Seleucid period is only recorded once during a period of lunar eclipse. During this lunar eclipse, the rite is given as a metaphor for the streams which no longer held water for the Great Gods called the Anunnaki.

There were intense and detailed rituals conducted with the statues of the temple, for which the gods' and their associated powers' were understood to embody the idols as they were consecrated. Clothes, washings and offering food to the statues were common throughout all Babylonian periods.

A Clarification on Statues and Deific Masks

The modern practitioner and more distinctly the Luciferian/Kassapu does not need to dress the statue nor offer food to it other than empowering it as described later in this grimoire. Some practitioners do offer to their statues and altars in the process of projecting the desire to a visible image in willfully compelling the manifestation of it's' power in this world. You do not put any god before yourself and you should be willing to focus on the gods though your own Magickial work. *Taking care of the mind and body of the Kassapu is partially offering to the god within*; for it supports the maintenance of your life on earth. Thus the statue represents a power willfully empowered by the owner and the gods are but mirrors reflected within.

The Hellenic Ruler Cult in Babylon

During the Seleucid period there was a semi-active Cult of the King in which they were worshipped as the benefactors of the kingdom and people, saviors, protectors and conquerors. One temple ceremony of ancient Babylon was called "**dullu sa saluki u maresu**", translated: "**Ritual of Seleucus and his Offspring**" which was based in the Esagila Temple and had consistent status with Bel and Beltia.

In Uruk the Hellenistic Ruler Cult was present to some extent as well. Offerings were made to statues of the kings and its title was "**passuru sa saim sarrani**". After the Seleucid period there was a sharp decline in records of Babylonia, while there is still records through the Parthian period, the Sassanian period no doubt placed a hand over the Chaldean and Babylonian magical traditions, blending it in with the Zoroastrian pantheon. We see evidence of this in the magical lore, spells and Zurvanite records which spread through the Levantine and Asia Minor. Further, the early Christian traditions despite the various so-called "heretical" branches of Christians incorporated in their spells records of various demons of both Mesopotamia and Zoroastrian lore.

CHAPTER TWO

THE MESOPOTAMIAN MAGICKIAL WORLD AND CREATION

THE GEOGRAPHY OF THE MAGICKIAL WORLD ACCORDING TO THE BABYLONIANS

The universe was shaped after the battle from Tiamat and humanity from Kingu's blood by the skill of the Magickian-God, Ea. Marduk was given Kingship for his great victory and created order in the universe. The Babylonian world is composed of the following in a general compilation from two tablets (KAR 307 and AO8196):

UPPER HEAVENS (EMPYREAN) – The Highest Aspect of Spirit, the Throne of Anu, the King of All Spirits, known as **"Samtu sa anim: Samu Anim"** – *The Heaven of Anu.* The term heaven is represented as the element air associated with spirit, this includes violent winds as well. Do not confuse this "original" heaven with a place of "good only" post-death "bliss" kingdom of the Christians. The Seven Maskim/Sebitti/Evil Gods including Lamashtu may transverse here, although Lamashtu was cast down for rebelling against her father, Anu. The colors associated with the Heaven of Anu are red, white and black.

MIDDLE HEAVENS – The abode of the Igigi/Anunnaki of the Heavens (Great Gods) of which there are 300 placed here. They are spirits of the air and Anu is the King of the Anunnaki. Bel (interchangeable with Marduk) is placed here as well at times. Enlil is also associated with the middle and lower heavens at times.

LOWER HEAVENS – The abode of stars and risen gods. The constellations were placed here.

UPPER EARTH – The abode of humanity and all physical life forms. The clay of man was mixed with the blood of Kingu here by Ea, the Lord of Magick and the Depths.

UNDERWORLD (Chthonic/Infernal) – The 600 Anunnaki were "closed in" in the darkness from which Ereshkigal and Nergal reign. These underworld gods often transverse the underworld all the way upward to the heavens. The Irkalla is reachable by the mountains of mashu from which is watched over by two Girtablullu (Scorpion-man and woman). There river of the underworld is guided by a boatman who leads down into the depths. The underworld has Seven Gates and Levels.

THE ABSU (Abyssic Waters) – The freshwater and abyssic abode surrounding the earth, the depths, which Ea holds his kingdom. This was the original kingdom of Tiamat and her first husband and namesake – Absu.

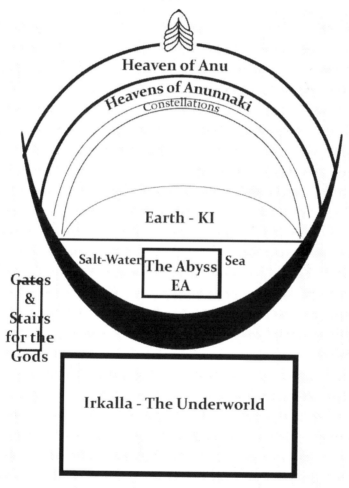

Basic map of Babylonian World

KIPPAT SARE
The Circle of the Winds

The Circle of the Winds or 'kippat sare[4]' is a concept of ancient Mesopotamian cosmography. The four winds are consistently viewed as a square, for which the earth and regions are separated into four parts. As we can see this uniformed association, the elements play a significant role in our Magickial approach and how we commune and ascend/descend as living deities. The winds are visualized as moving within a circular motion. This concept is little different from earlier magickial foundations in our modern age. As all energy moves within a spiral or 'serpent' coil, the winds themselves move in a circular motion. As you grow adept in this concept of using a circle there will come a time when you may summon or invoke a demon, god or spirit within using no physical circle! This is accomplished alone by the will of the Kassapu, nothing more.

THE UNIVERSE AND MAGICK

Magick is the art of compelling change in the universe, within reference to Kassapu, or the sorcerer, change within the subjective and often the objective world. This simply means that change occurs within first; that is subjective, then if possibility exists then in the objective or world around us. The subjective is in early stages of magick a process of inner change and transformation, such as the building of a foundation. From which the will of the Kassapu grows strong through determination and self-belief, then the inner alchemical process creates a slow process of 'ascension' and transformation.

---

[4] Mesopotamian Cosmic Geography by Wayne Horowitz

Ascension means simply to become a God or Goddess in the process of Magick. Adversarial Magick is a balanced approach wherein the Kassapu becomes the 'axis' point for which energy flows, thus the only god which is!

Ascension in Adversarial Magick is to become a being more intelligent, wise through the application of knowledge and strong spiritually and physically (according to your desire). Ascension is not mixed in some whitewashed dualistic concept; rather the Kassapu knows both the desires of darkness and the strength in light.

In Babylonian and Chaldean traditions the planets play a significant role. Decisions were made from the positions of the planets, stars and even wars were committed based on these observations. Having the knowledge we have now concerning science, the Kassapu or Luciferian would not necessarily base his or her life around the position of the planets (while many often do this via astrology) rather we look to the symbolism of the planets and stars.

Within each symbol there is meaning; this relates to our subconscious and conscious selves. The whole aim of this grimoire is to provide the 'hidden' or 'forbidden' knowledge (the unverified experience yet providing a valid process) to gain wisdom (knowledge experienced) to become the self-directed vessel of your earthly experience. In short, becoming a god incarnate is the goal of the work within.

Becoming a God Incarnate in Luciferianism no matter which Adversarial Tradition[5] you work through defines that you are accountable for your destiny. I understand that magick works through a process of expanding beyond your 'comfort zone' and often through pain and struggle, yet is also dependant upon your perception of the subjective world.

---

[5] By tradition in reference to traditional Luciferianism via Persian Yatukih, Medieval Satanic archetypes, Qlippothic, Greek-Hellenic, Babylonian, Egyptian or Ugarit branches of Luciferianism.

In moments of extreme exertion, physical pain through pushing the body and mind to the limits do we then cross the abyss; our subconscious and conscious mind are linked for mere moments. In that period of chemical release in the brain our gate to the gods is open, and then we can better build our inner temple.

Try to perform a hymn or invocation to a god, remembering a few important lines and then exercising or pushing the self to the limits for a period of time via exercise, focusing on the god and their image to you. This gateway you forge will no doubt bring you some interesting results.

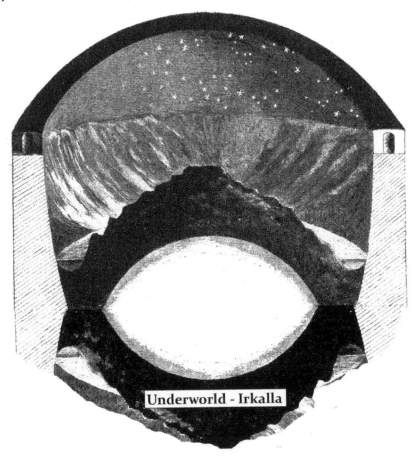

Babylonian World

AKKADIAN & BABYLONIAN MONTHS

The Babylonian Months are somewhat different from the traditional calendar used today, from which the base form still exists. The Kassapu who wishes to utilize the Babylonian months may do so with little ease, for offerings or workings based on the specific deific mask or god the Adept will work with. The bold names on the left are Akkadian spellings and the capitalized Sumerian spellings are to the right of the Akkadian.

Nisannu (ITI.BARA) – March/April

Ajaru (GU) – April/May

Simanu (SIG) – May/June

Du'uzu (SU) – June/July

Abu (NE) – July/August

Ululu (KIN) – August/September

Tasritu (DU) September/October

Arahsamna (APIN) – October/November

Kislimu (GAN) – November/December

Tebetu (AB) – December/January

Sabatu (ZIZ) – January/February

Addaru (SE) – February/March

The first month of the year for the ancient Babylonians was Nisannu being March/April. The most important festival of the year for the Babylonians was Akitu – the New Year rites. The first month of the year is to honor Marduk and Prince Nebo, the scribe and god of divination. Traditionally, Akitu was a celebration of the sowing of barley and was opened in the first of the month. Traditionally, the Babylonian King would make a ritualistic journey to the different temples during this period.

CHALDEAN ASTROLOGY AND GOD ASSOCIATIONS
A Basic Introduction

The Chaldeans, famous for their development of astrology and association with sorcery were a tribal people who lived southeast of Babylon towards UR. Over periods of time various Chaldean sorcerers became interconnected with Babylon and their own Magickial development.

The methodology and depth of Chaldean astrology is highly innovative and insightful of their time. The gods are found among the stars, their associations and movements as planets and constellations play a significant role in their innate power as archetypes in Babylonian theology.

The majority of the gods, goddesses and monsters are represented in the stars and constellations. For a further study, see the Bibliography.

ZODIAC SIGNS

Aries (HUN, LU) – Hired Man

Taurus (MUL.MUL) - Bull of Heaven

Gemini (MAS.MAS) – Twins

Cancer (ALLA) – Crab

Leo (A) – Lion

Virgo (ABSIN) – Furrow

Libra (RIN) – Scales

Scorpio (GIR.TAB) – Scorpion

Sagittarius (PA) – Pabilsag

Capricorn (MAS) – Goat Fish

Aquarius (GU) – Great One

Pisces (ZIB.ME) Tails

PLANETS

Moon – Sin (EN.ZU)

Sun – Shamas (UTU)

Jupiter – Marduk (SAG.ME.GAR)

Venus – Ishtar (MUL.DILBAT / *Istar belit matati*[6])

Mercury – Nebo/Ningishzida/ Ninurta (SIHTU)

Saturn – Ninurta (UDU.IDIM.SAG.US/GENNA)

Mars – Nergal (Salbatanu)

TIAMAT AND KINGU AS CONSTELLATIONS

A lesser-known record surviving of the depiction of Tiamat and Kingu in the night sky occurs within a Babylonian calendar text from first millennium B.C. The published fragments (for which there are three versions[7]) are in King's translations from 1902. This omen-record indictates that Tiamat (Elam) and Kingu (Assyria) in the month of Tebetu are to attack Marduk (Babylon).

The text describes a great astro-mythological battle in which the powers assemble in the region of Tebetu (December-January, yet representing here an area in the night sky). Tiamat and Kingu are the same as Tebetu which means the Sea (Tiamat). In the

---

[6] "Ishtar, Lady of the Lands".

[7] Languages and Cultures in Contact: At the Crossroads of Civilizations in Syrio-Mesopotamian Ream. F. Reynolds, Birmingham. 1993

region of the Goat-Fish constellation, Tiamat gathered to bring battle upon Marduk.

Tiamat and Kingu join as one; the Dark Mother takes the general post and makes all decisions. In this manifestation, she is the She-Goat Constellation. Traditionally, Asakku is equated with Kingu in Astrology. Asakku, a great demon who, like the Seven Sebitti/Maskim was born of the union of Anu and Ki and was a great warrior and disease-bringing demon-god.

As Tiamat and Kingu join as one, they become the She-Goat constellation, associated with the Sorceress Constellation. The Gizzanitu, the Angry Goat or **ki-iz za-ni-tu** and **Pussanitu**, being the Angry Mouth or pu-u-za-ni-tu are the She-Goat Constellation and Corpse Constellation within the Goat-Fish Constellation. The union of the Mouth Constellation and Star is equivalent to the Corpse Constellation, the associated Goddess being Tiamat. Tiamat is named as "Female-Twin" which is **tu-u-am-tu** as she has two faces, one female and one male (Kingu). This would easily explain why some depictions of Tiamat show her with a serpent-penis. This would be explainable by Kingu and Tiamat joined as one, fighting Mardulk.

Interestingly enough, the month name of TEBETU is scribed as tap-pat-tu or tappattu, "Female Friend" which is applied in this calendar text as Kingu. Tiamat is thus one of the original manifestations of the Adversary, a balanced union of two aspects. The records of the Babylonian Priest Berosus supports this dual concept:

"There was a time in which there existed nothing but darkness and an abyss of waters, wherein resided most hideous beings, which were produced on a two-fold principle. There appeared men, some of whom were furnished with two wings, others with four, and with two faces. They had one body but two heads; the one that of a man, the other of a woman; and likewise in their several organs both male and female. Other human figures were to be seen with the legs and horns of goats; some had horses' feet; while others united the hind-quarters of a horse with the body of a man, resembling in shape the hippo-centaurs. Bulls

likewise were bred there with the heads of men, and dogs with four told bodies, terminated in their extremities with the tails of fishes; horses also with the heads of dogs; men too and other animals, with the heads and bodies of horses and the tails of fishes." - The Legend of the Creation According to Berosus and Damascius

We see here the waters of chaos from which the primordial beings emerge, the goddess of these chaos-forms *"The person, who presided over them, was a woman named OMUROCA; which in the Chaldean language is THALATTH; in Greek THALASSA, the sea; but which might equally be interpreted the Moon."*[8]. Tiamat, joined with Kingu represents the Goat-Fish Constellation collectively, while as Tiamat she is the She-Goat and Kingu is the Scorpion constellation and also the Corpse Constellation. The adversary of Tiamat is Marduk, being **sag.me.gar** and the Arrow Star and Bow Constellations are his weapons against the forces of chaos.

Tiamat is the great power which shape-shifts according to her need and desire. We can see this by her form as Ishtar, Kingu in the demon-god Asakku and *partly* Marduk. As Kingu joined with Tiamat (for they in union beget the monsters), becoming one great beast, one head male and the other female gives a clue to the name she bears, **tu-am-tu**, *"The Female Twin"*.

As Ishtar of Nineveh is associated with the Upper Parts of Tiamat in one Assyrian record, Marduk and Ninlil were associated with her lower parts. This presents foundation as why Ishtar was as powerful as both Marduk and Ninlil together and that Tiamat possesses an Adversarial, or dual nature.

---

[8] Berosus

THE SEVEN STARS or MUL.MUL

The Seven Star cluster called by the Greeks as Pleiades is one of the most adversarial (note balanced) of the symbols representing the gods. The Seven Stars together can mean a negative or positive effect on events depending on the astrologers. MUL.MUL is represented by the Seven Evil Gods called Maskim are referred to as *"seven malevolent phantoms of the flames"*. The Seven are not bound to these stars, yet utilize them when they are visable.

As the Seven Stars have always been associated with the Moon, such as on a "standard" year the Seven Stars and the Moon are conjoined on the first day. This no doubt presents a possible origin of the myth of the Seven Evil Gods encircling and attacking Sin. The Seven Stars are known as those who herald the power of Mars being Nergal-Erra, lusting for war and destruction when it suits them.

THE CHAOS-MONSTERS OF TIAMAT AS CONSTELLATIONS

MUSMAHHU– Hydra/Serpent

BASMU – Hydra/Serpent

UGALLU – Leo

URIDIMMU – Wolf

GIRTABLULLU – Scorpio

KULULLU- Aquarius

KUSARIKKU – Taurus

SUHURMAS - Capricorn

GODS AND DEMONS

LAMASHTU –Wolf – Mul.Ur.Barra
ANU – Wolf & Crab
ADAD – Raven
ISHARA – Scorpion
ERESHKIGAL – Serpent
NINGISHZIDA – Serpent
NERGAL – Panther, Star of She-Goats Throne

LEGEND OF CREATION
THE TABLET OF CUTHA

In the Chaldean Account of Genesis by George Smith, there is an alternate tablet of creation described. The significance of this tablet is that Tiamat created many beings with the heads of Ravens, the bodies of birds of the deserts mixed with human beings. These descriptions are obviously influential in the lore of demons later on into the middle ages, which can easily be viewed in grimoire texts such as the Goetia or Lesser Key of Solomon.

This record as re-adapted as a ritual text was found in form on a tablet in Cutha, of which Nergal is the Patron God of. This tradition of Cutha portrays that Tiamat existed with a brood of demon-offspring who ruled the great chaos underground. In addition, Cutha has an association with the underworld due to the temple of Nergal.

The following is an *adapted* ritual text from the translation of George Smith and A.H. Sayce.

CUTHEAN LEGEND OF CREATION
AN ADAPTED EXAMPLE

His word is the command of the gods, fire embraced. His glancing-white instrument is the burning-white instrument of the gods.

The lord of that which is above and that which is below, the lord of the spirits of earth... who drinks turbid waters and drinks not clear waters...
In whose field that warrior's weapon all that rests there... captured and destroyed.
On a tablet he wrote not, he opened not (the mouth), and bodies and produce.
He caused nothing to come forth in the land, and I approached him not.

Warriors with the body of a bird of the desert, men with the faces of ravens[9], did the great old gods create. The old gods of great power, wisdom and brilliance hidden in darkness.

In the ground, the darkness within the earth the gods created his city.
TIAMAT, DRAGON-MOTHER gave them suck; she gave them the blood of life. Their progeny, Sasur, the mistress of the gods created deep within the earth.
In the midst of the mountains, the dark barbarous lands they grew up and became heroes, increasing in number.

---

[9] Refer to the Seven Maskim / Sebitti

Seven kings, brethren, appeared as begetters;

Six thousand (in number were) their armies.

The god BANINI their father king; their mother the queen was MELILI;

The eldest brother who went before them, ME-MANGAB Mu-Ni, "Voice of Thunder" was his name;
The second brother, ME-DU "The Voice above and below" was his name.
The third brother, ME-MAN PAKH was his name;
The fourth brother, ME-DA was his name;
The fifth brother, ME-MAN TAKH was his name;
The sixth brother, ME-RU "The Voice which creates" was his name;
The seventh brother, ME-RA was his name."

"whom Bel shall call, and who shall rule the kingdom, who shall rebuild this house, this tablet I write to thee, in the city of Cutha, in the temple of Sitlam, in the sanctuary of Nergal, I leave for thee;" – From the Creation Tablet of Cutha.

The children of Tiamat, of which she is the mother of life according to the Babylonians, had the first gods as having animal composite parts including the faces of ravens. Ravens are birds associated with the underworld and the shadow. Considering that birds, eagles, hawks, ravens and vultures among others are associated with gods and spirits, one may look to the element of air or the spirit with the association in spiritual matters.

The Priest of Bel-Marduk Berossus in Babylon who compiled Babylonian texts under the Seleucid King Antiochus I Soter provided a great bridge for the ancient writings to continue on. While many of his works do not exist today, some were extensively quoted by other historians after who had access to his works. Damascius, a Pagan philosopher of the 6th century A.D. who was banished to Persia in 529 A.D. by Christian Roman Emperor Justinian wrote of the Babylonian Creation.

Berossus gives and interesting account which identifies the chaos-spirit origins of humanity;

"There was a time in which there existed nothing but darkness and an abyss of waters, wherein resided most hideous beings, which were produced of a two-fold principle. There appeared men, some of whom were furnished with two wings, others with four, and with two faces. They had one body but two heads: the one that of a man, the other of a woman: and likewise in their several organs both male and female. Other human figures were to be seen with the legs and horns of goats: some had horses' feet: while others united the hind quarters of a horse with the body of a man, resembling in shape the hippocentaurs. Bulls likewise were bred there with the heads of men; and dogs with fourfold body, terminated in their extremities with the tails of fishes: horses also with the heads of dogs: men too and other animals, with the heads and bodies of horses and the tails of fishes. In short, there were creatures in which were combined the limbs of every species of animals. In addition to these, fishes, reptiles, serpents, with other monstrous animals, which assumed each other's shape and countenance. Of all which were preserved delineations in the temple of Belus at Babylon" – **Fragments Of Chaldæan History, Berossus: From Alexander Polyhistor from Ancient Fragments by Corey.**

Like the Cutha Tablet, we see that there were beings which were composites of animals and the aspects of chaos. Tiamat is mentioned here as Omoroca who is associated with Water and the moon.

"The person, who presided over them, was a woman named Omoroca; which in the Chaldean language is Thalatth…Belus came, and cut the woman asunder: and of one half of her he formed the earth, and of the other half the heavens; and at the same time destroyed the animals within her (in the abyss). For, the whole universe consisting of moisture, and animals being continually generated therein, the deity above-mentioned took off his own head: upon which the other gods mixed the blood, as it gushed out, with the earth; and from thence were formed men. On this account it is that they are rational, and partake of divine knowledge. This Belus, by whom they signify Jupiter, divided the darkness, and separated the Heavens from the Earth, and reduced universe to order. But the animals, not being able to bear the prevalence of light, died. Belus upon this, seeing a vast space unoccupied, though by nature fruitful, commanded one of the gods to take off his head, and to mix the blood with the earth; and from thence to form other men and animals, which should be capable of bearing the air" –Fragments by Corey

Tiamat is now viewed as the Goddess who brought forth life, although Belus directed the evolution into humans. The figure of Oannes, described by Berossus is a early "Watcher" type God who arises from the depths of sea to instruct humans on the same aspects in which the Watchers do in the later Hebraic texts.

"At Babylon there was (in these times) a great resort of people of various nations, who inhabited Chaldæa, and lived in a lawless manner like the beasts of the field. In the first year there appeared, from that part of the Erythræan sea which borders upon Babylonia, an animal destitute of reason, by name Oannes, whose whole body (according to the account of Apollodorus) was that of a fish; that under the fish's head he had another head, with feet also below, similar to those of a man, subjoined to the fish's tail. His voice too, and language, was articulate and human; and a representation of him is preserved even to this day.

This Being was accustomed to pass the day among men; but took no food at that season; and he gave them an insight into letters and sciences, and arts of every kind. He taught them to construct cities, to found temples, to compile laws, and explained to them the principles of geometrical knowledge. He made them distinguish the seeds of the earth, and showed them how to collect the fruits; in short, he instructed them in everything which could tend to soften manners and humanize their lives. From that time, nothing material has been added by way of improvement to his instructions. And when the sun had set, this Being Oannes, retired again into the sea, and passed the night in the deep; for he was amphibious. After this there appeared other animals like Oannes, of which Berossus proposes to give an account when he comes to the history of the kings. Moreover Oannes wrote concerning the generation of mankind; and of their civil polity; and the following is the purport of what he said:" –Fragments by Corey

From these origins, it seems clear that the Babylonians were instructed by the Gods from the Sea. Oannes is known also as Adapa, the son of Ea who is the first of the Seven Sages who were Apkallu. These Seven Sages were divine beings who resided in the Absu or Depths ruled by Ea. Their rising from the sea prior to the Babylonian flood was to instruct humanity and raise them up in knowledge and practice. At dusk Oannes would then return to the ocean depths for he was in amphibious form.

These same Seven Sages could not only take fish form, yet could also take bird-human form as well, a symbol of the underworld. The Apkallu were thus associated with the subconscious itself; for the knowledge in which they brought emerges from the Depths of the Absu, the very region of Ea the Lord of the Depths.

THE ENUMA ELISH AND THE ROARING OCEANS OF CHAOS AND THE ELEMENTS

The Enuma Elish (meaning "when on high") is a translated series from numerous creation tablets which had its origins in Babylon; however versions of the tablets were translated in not only Babylon but also Assyria. The creation text was meant to be a sacred document, recited during the **Babylonian New Year's Ritual** by the **sesgallu** or **Temple Brother**. It has been noted that these texts were sang as hymns which further demonstrates the power found in vibrations of sound.

The **Enuma Elish as published here** in part has been *ritualistically* scribed during meditations (after a series of solitary invocations) of Tiamat, Kingu and Nebo (the god of divination) to empower and create a suitable Luciferian manifestation denoting the aim of the work itself. The following text is not the exact historical translation.

In the early stages of ritual practice and exploring the essence of Babylonian Magick, *it is advisable for the Kassapu to read, re-read and meditate in a private setting* "The Roaring Oceans of Chaos" to not only awaken the primal atavism and the gateway to the gods.

The rituals of exorcism are based in the elements and the gods invoked are always deeply associated with the phenomena they invoke against the demon or witch. For instance, Nusku is called as "Fire" to "burn" the witch or demon. The elements and nature plays a foundational-role in the gods, spirits and demons in the spiritual world.

The Kassapu works with nature as well. The need for connecting with nature is significant as this plays a deep perspective for understanding your individual instinct and desire. When invoking, always focus on the elements or animal/reptile the god or demon is associated with.

The element of fire is important as it is that which brings us wisdom; i.e. the black flame in luciferianism[10] for instance suggests that through evolution as we gained awareness of the "I" we were able to utilize reason and logic. As the myths tell us, the gods were fearful of this at first or it was our subconscious

---

[10] Adversarial Light – Magick of the Nephilim by Michael W. Ford, Succubus Productions

guilt of creating without the guidance of something above us. Remember, rebellion is in our veins just as darkness is our origin.

In the works of exorcism just as in daily life, fire and water are essentials for physical survival. Fire and water were for the ancient Babylonians the foremost means of removing evil spirits and demons from those they attach themselves to.

The theory of this is that spiritual beings, gods, demons, vampires, ghosts and all other forms are existent in the shadow world; i.e. the astral plane and ghost-world. They commune with us via the dream, thus they work in the darkness of night.

Spirits, Gods, Demons and all the other phantasms of the spirit-world are associated and find their vehicle of manifestation via the element which invigorates them. The underworld itself is associated with water, the Absu which is below where Tiamat slept and where the palace of Ea is. Based on the cycle of the Sun and Moon, the Babylonians[11] made offerings to the Eastern rising of the Sun from out of the depths of the Absu or realm of Ea, to then enter the mountains of darkness in the west. In this alone the Babylonians are superior to the "advanced" Judeo-Christian and later monotheistic faiths as they embrace not only balance yet also have deep associations in nature itself. Later religions especially monotheistic ones bring a separation of balance, making opposites and absolutes, all the while taking one gods and making "him" "all encompassing" without association with the world he created. All of the gods in this grimoire emerged originally in some form from Tiamat and Absu, the very essence of chaos and watery darkness. We see the gods of light such as Ishtar, gaining power by initiation in the underworld. She draws close to her "sister" or "darkside" known as Ereshkigal and gains further power when she returns. Ishtar is a goddess of love and war, balanced yet extreme in passion.

---

[11] I use this term in generic fashion, making a reference to all associated within the gods therein. It includes Assyrians, Elamites and Chaldeans of Ur.

Ea is the lord of magick and sorcery who exists in the watery Absu. His power was gained from usurping the throne of Tiamat's husband Absu from which his great palace was made. Ea takes many forms, some primordial and chaotic as well as more humanlike. Ea is a friend of humanity, sending the Seven Sages to instruct man on the art of magick and the ways of creation in this physical world.

The main cult of Ea was located in the ancient city called Eridu, which was near the mouth of the Euphrates and the Tigris. Interestingly enough, this leads into the ocean wherein is said to be the entrance to the abyss and the kingdom of dark waters.

In exorcisms, Ea instructs Marduk to take water from the two streams or rather the Euphrates and the Tigris and sprinkle water upon a sick man. It seems that all things emerge and are invigorated in the element of water. Exorcists and Magicians would call water "of Eridu" and thus was empowered by both Ea and Marduk.

From the *"me tabuti"*, "good waters" of Ea and the *"me limnuti"*, "evil waters" of Tiamat were the powers of both good and evil gods. Ea we must remember was a usurping god, just as Marduk yet both are found in the ancestral linage of Tiamat and Absu, just as humans are found from Tiamat and Kingu. The word HUL which denoted two words, *limnu*, "evil" and *marru*, "bitter[12]".

The bitter waters were forbidden to man as they were from the undefiled darkness of Tiamat and the Evil Gods and Demons, while the sweet waters were consecrated by Ea and the beneficial gods of man. The Kassapu trespasses the law of the symbol of "sweet" water, to initiate the self in the darkness of Tiamat just as Ea and Marduk did previous. This principle is that of self-directing the Will to emerge stronger from the waters of primordial chaos and become equally as gods on earth.

---

[12] The Doctrine of Sin in the Babylonian Religion, Julian Morgenstern 1905

CHAPTER THREE

THE ROARING OCEANS OF CHAOS
A Shadow Ritual & Hymn

Mushussu dragon-serpent, a chaos-monster of Tiamat which became a powerful force supporting the Gods of Babylon, Assyrian and Ur.

THE ENUMA ELISH
THE ROARING OCEANS OF CHAOS
A Left Hand Path perspective of the Gods

The following text may be either read or recited by the practicing Kassapu during a Temple dedication to Tiamat or the Gods; near the Babylonian New Year or anytime when it inspires. Burn incense and meditate upon by candlelight, connect in your mind the process of the coiling and crooked serpent, all that transpires is the Will of Tiamat. The full circle is made complete in the ascension of Marduk for which the dark gods ascend again.

TIAMAT AND ABSU

In the time before humanity rose from the primal slime of chaos, the darkness stirred and slept within the abyssic void of Tiamat and Absu.

When chaos reigned and darkness was abound when the earth was not named nor embodied Absu, the begetter and Tiamat who bore all life mixed their waters together. It was a time which was not counted, when the dreaming abyss of restful slumber encircled Tiamat and Absu.

Between them two gods Lahmu and Lahamu emerged from their union, their names pronounced and given. Soon after Anshar and Kishar were born from this royal line, wherein years passed until they fully matured.

Anu emerged as powerful as Anshar his father, who gave his power to him. Anu created Nudimmud in his likeness that was also powerful in wisdom and very strong in his might.

These powerful Gods and Goddesses soon stirred in the belly of Tiamat, disturbing the primal chaos of dreams and sleep. Absu sought to quiet the Gods who were loud and chaotic, while Tiamat indulged their behavior although it stirred her.

Tiamat spoke unto Absu, "How can we destroy what we have created? While they are troublesome in our desire to slumber in darkness, they should be allowed to remain." The Viser of Chaos called Mummu counseled Absu; "O great father, end their troublesome ways which keep thee and our Mother from rest by day and sleep by night."

Absu was pleased with this and their plans were laid forth. It was soon after that Ea came to understand these plans that the primal darkness had in store for them. Soon after this, Ea created a spell of sleep which would cause Absu to fall under.

Ea calmed the ancient abyssic waters and recited this spell, for which Absu soon fell under. Viser Mummu was also made to sleep as well. He was chained from the nose to be kept until slaughter. Ea took from Absu his Crown, his belt and the Mantle of Radiance and took it for himself. Ea, like his forebears, was of darkness and could also beget light.

Absu slept and the sweet waters were still. The hunger Ea held for power was not unlike his parents, Absu was held down and slain, and his life as it was consumed by Ea and with it his power. Absu was now as a Great Spirit or shade of darkness, falling again into the abyss.

Ea cried out into the darkness, for he would reside among the Gods now. He had a palace in the abyss created, which he called Absu in honor of his Father. He built a great residence with several chapels or offering points for the Gods.

Ea joined with Damkina and they dwelt among great splendor, dwelling in the Chamber of Destinies. They gave life to Bel, who was very clever and became the Sage of the Gods.

Within Absu, Marduk was created and granted the gifts of the Gods. He was poured the radiance of his parents, Ea who fathered him and Damkina who bore him.

Made perfect, Ea understood that Marduk was while bearing light also a God from the Darkness of the Great Mother Tiamat. Marduk while appearing as a Solar God of victory, still held the passions of darkness within his heart.

Proud was the form of Marduk, his stare was piercing as he grew in power. His knowledge too was great. Looking upon the lore of the Abyssic Dragon-Mother Tiamat, he grew in respect to her even as a future Adversary.

Marduk was raised higher than the other Gods for his radiance was so bright. One form of Marduk was that he had several eyes and from his mouth fire blazed forth. Marduk was to be called one of the greatest of them all.

The God Anu, great God of the Sky as both light and darkness cried out, "Marduk, Son and Majesty of the Gods!"
Marduk was crowned in the radiant mantle of ten gods, terrible and powerful in his countenance. Five fearsome rays from the primal sorceries of the ancient abyss surrounded Marduk.
Anu begot the Four Winds and gave them birth.
Anu placed the Four Winds in the hand of Marduk, "For you shall have this power".
Anu fashioned the dust and the whirlwind which would carry his commands.

TIAMAT AWAKENS

Tiamat, our ancient mother, goddess of darkness,
Serpent-Queen of the primal abyss,
Stirred upward from nightmarish sleep;
The old gods, the primal gods were angered,
Went forth to Tiamat and spoke unto her;
Those who slew your lover Absu sending him into the complete unconsciousness;
They have created the four winds to stir you,
We too cannot sleep in nightmarish sleep;
Mummu has been captured before thee,
Let us destroy the restless ones;
Fill the skies with a battle cry so we may conquer,
Our enemy and devour their spirits.

Tiamat listened well; it pleased her to hear this.
Let us gather and rise up now, for the children have risen

Against my timeless being, fools who would seek to
Destroy what cannot be destroyed!

Tiamat opened forth a vein and with blood aroused the
children of darkness, her mighty powers of chaos.
These demons were fierce, scheming for battle day and
night.
Prowling like Lions they raged about.
They created their weapons and prepared for war

Mother Hubar, Great Imperial Darkness, who fashions all things, could choose the forms she wished to raise from primordial chaos. Her fleshly shadow which took forms which other gods may understand created and bore life in the abyss. Tiamat created the shadow-flesh of Mother Hubar to manifest her Will, this shadow was servitor and of her blood, her consciousness entered Hubar.

She bore giant serpents: Sharp of tooth and unsparing in
fang,
Whose hunger would devour the Sun if she wished it;
Filling their bodies with venom instead of blood,
She cloaked ferocious dragons with fearsome rays;
These fierce dragons were clothed in terror, for they are the
embodiment of night and that which haunts above and
below the earth;
And placed upon them mantles of radiance, for they
became Godlike.

Tiamat chanted her words of power:

"Whoever looks upon you shall collapse in utter terror!

Their bodies shall rear up continually and never turn away!"

From the primal darkness, from the blackened light of the abyss did Tiamat bring forth:

The Horned Serpent, the Mushussu-dragon, the Lahmu-hero…
The Ugallu-demon, a rapid-wolf and a Scorpion-man.
Fearsome and aggressive Umu-demons…
A fish-demon and a bull-man…
For these primal powers shall be forever within my coils.
Their powers unending and forever a wellspring of chthonic wisdom.

Tiamat spoke and her orders would not be disobeyed, for she was Chaos yet also the Order from which Chaos is stilled.

Tiamat created then Eleven Gods, Monsters of Tiamat; Bearers of Great Illuminated Radiance, those who are of the Black Flame bore merciless weapons, for they were fearless in battle.

For the Kassapu who invokes the long dead gods, the life-force which infuses them shall make thus the sorcerer a great force of darkness, hidden in the flesh of a man or woman.

KINGU RECEIVES THE ANU POWER

Kingu, a great Demon-God among them was ascended now as the Husband and champion of Tiamat. She chose him as he would be her general, who would guide and strike at the new Gods.

'For you, Kingu shall bear my power, for you alone shall be the greatest'

Tiamat conferred upon him the leadership of her army, the command of troops and her vast powers.
She places him upon a Throne.

"I cast a spell for you, that you Kingu are the Greatest of the Gods! Your power will rule over all other Gods, for you are my only lover!'

Tiamat then gave the Tablet of Destinies to Kingu and made him clasp it tightly to his breast.

"Kingu, your utterance shall never be altered, your Word shall be Law!" and this power was conferred.

Kingu received the Anu power, for he was illuminated in blackened fire. He ascends as a God of both Darkness and Light.

Kingu, primal adversary, who shall make war against the younger ones, stood in his terrible brilliance.

Wearing the horned tiara, broad shouldered and having clasped the Tablet of Destiny upon his breast, Kingu would lead chaos into the midst of the younger gods.

Decreeing destinies for his sons, Kingu spoke unto them;

"What issues forth from your mouths shall quench fire and your venom shall paralyze and sicken the powerful!"

Kingu alone commanded the powers of the 11 Demons of Tiamat, his forms could be many and his power was great. In a chariot of blackened fire and fearsome weapons he would lead forth an army against the new Gods who would tear their created Order away.

For Kingu was most powerful of the Gods, next to his Queen Tiamat, mother of all terrors and dragons. His mantle was radiance, for he bore the horns of power. His weapons were many, he held the Mace, a sword forged of blackened fire, lightning was his power and the sorcerous spells taught him by Tiamat.

Kingu thirsted for the blood of the new gods, for he would have their spirit-power and dwell next to his queen in the darkness.

MARDUK ARISES

For now Ea had heard of this news and was filled with dread. He went forth to Anshar, the father of Anu and Ki, to tell him of his knowledge. All were filled with dread as the ancient ones who they had first attacked were preparing to illuminate them.

Ea went forth again to learn of Tiamat's strategy and yet he could not find it. Going before Anshar, Ea spoke solemnly; "My spells are not equal to Tiamat's; I could not uncover her plans. She is too strong, mighty and terrible in her power. Her horde is powerful, chaotic and violent. She commands them all. She roared into the darkness and it stirred great fear in me, for she calls for her blood to be reclaimed and returned!"

Ea and the others gods feared who she called a woman, that they considered themselves stronger as they were men. Yet in this, they feared her more than anything.

Marduk felt his ancestral power and primordial instinct within, though his driven goal was power and a new order. The essence of Marduk is to conquer, to overmaster his challenges and ascend as a God or descend again into the darkness of his grandparents.

Marduk told the Gods he would banish Tiamat to the darkness, for his knowledge of Magick was also great. The Gods listened and soon gathered a council to decree the fate. The new Gods were terrified that the ancient mother who bore them now sought to devour them all.

Marduk was given great power by this council, for they sought to make him the most powerful of all the Gods. He was given a bow, designated it as his weapon along with a great arrow. He carried a mace in his right hand, slung the bow at his side.

The body of Marduk was filled with an ever-blazing Black Flame, for this was the gift of Tiamat to all her offspring. They would use this assumed power against her, for they too had the blood of the serpent within them. He then held the power of lightning, the winds and great storms which guided his powerful chariot.

Making a net, Marduk would capture Tiamat within it. He utilized his power to marshal the four winds to his command. Marduk as being an offspring of Tiamat held much power from his blood. For Marduk knew both darkness and inner light just as his primordial mother of dragons.

The four winds served him, the seven winds and the tornado. Marduk, champion of Babylon mounted his mighty storm-chariot and held four horses called "Slayer", "Racer", "Flyer" and "Pitiless" to guide it. These horses would not tire but would destroy all.

Marduk clothed himself in a cloak of awesome armor, his head crowned in the blazing and burning radiance of his ascension.

THE WAR OF CHAOS

Going forth to face Tiamat and her legions of chaos, Marduk was unafraid for he understood fear was weakness.

Marduk looked upon the battle lines, looked for the strategy of Kingu and Tiamat. He could not find it and was confused, his mind grew weak. His Will soon crumbled before Tiamat, who was Mother Darkness and most powerful among all.

The armies of Marduk grew fearful at uncovering the broken Will of their leader.

Tiamat casted her spells, she did not even turn her neck. Her lips spoke of lies, serpents and shape-changing forms confused her enemies.

"How powerful your attacking force is, O Lord of Gods" Tiamat sent goodwill to Marduk and he replied knowing she may be lying;

"Why do you seem so friendly, yet your forces seek to destroy us because the Sons were noisy? Why would you not have compassion for us? You appointed Kingu as your lover and King, you gave him the rites of the Anu-Power, and then you sought to destroy Anshar the Great one of the Gods!"

Before him, Tiamat created a war-body of shadow-flesh; the Great Dragon of Chaos was manifest. Tiamat the Goddess of Chaos embodied her shadow with flesh and much power, for if she stirred as she was nothingness would cast them all into timeless sleep and death.

Omoroca was of the watery abyss, from a time when there was but darkness eternal. When she dwelt in the subconscious of all things as life itself emerges from her, the Terrible Mother of Draconian-Chaos!

For as her Shadow took flesh she formed a black mirror of her true form in the Abyss, a great and powerful dragon bearing the claws of a lion, a serpent-tale which bore venom, the head of a tiger and dragon in one flesh, a griffin like body with scales of a serpent. Her eyes burned with unnatural light and she held great fires within her mouth. Her serpent tongue whispered spells of her desire, which at this moment were of causing the death of their spirit-souls and seeking the blood of the new Gods.

Marduk then challenged her to single combat, for which she lost her control and raged with fury against him.

Her lower parts shook from the depths of the abyss. She recited her incantations and let loose her spells of darkness. Her utterances were terrifying, blood-haunting and creating images of the abyss. Her spell of death would have all the new gods offering their Spirit-Souls to Her and her horde of Chaos-beasts.

"Who would fathom the great mysteries of primal darkness? I will drink your veins dry O frightened children."

Marduk and Tiamat faced each other; he let loose the four winds of terror. Tiamat unleashed her 11 chaos-monsters seeking to devour the gods who stood against Omoroca For Marduk had inherited the blood of Tiamat, so it was sweet and harsh within them. Marduk feared his end, for Tiamat was primordial Chaos embodied. Her shadow great, still not her form which he alone could not fathom.

Marduk, fearful of Her, that great power called upon the four winds to shock and still the 11 chaos-demons who were filled with blood, and to then with a net Marduk created cast upon Tiamat's battle-flesh and capture her, binding her in a desperate moment before he perished before his glaring fangs.

For now Marduk called the Winds which assaulted Tiamat, the great dragon opened forth her mouth to consume these winds. Marduk commands the Imhullu-wind to fill her open mouth that she may not close it.
Marduk sent forth his arrow through her mouth and split this shadow, bleeding now while she curse and cackled before him.

"Darkness is my eternal form, for I coil in the abyss. You cannot destroy that which is immortal, only stilling this body in which I have created. Your blood is mine, for I exist within it already. I shall manifest in ways through you Marduk, and the other Gods. I shall command when you do not see it and your will is nothing but my own. For this shadow flesh shall enter darkness, my spirit will haunt among you all. I shall be the unseen when I command you; you shall think it your own design."

Marduk cut her further with spear and she fell again into darkness. The monsters of chaos now were uncontrolled and Kingu raged against Marduk. The lightning bolt filled Kingu first and he soon fell. Marduk took the Tablets of Destinies from him and he too entered darkness.

Marduk spared the demons of chaos, knowing he was still weak. They would walk among them, uniting for one cause. The spirit of Tiamat commanded this, that she would fulfill her desires unknown to Marduk.

Still shadows bore her blood from her veins and the four winds took it away from the profane. The Priests of Tiamat and the Anu-Power would raise her from ancient slumber again.

From the deceased Kingu whose s pirit went forth sleeping in death still resounded with Tiamat. The blood of Kingu was used to infuse man with higher intellect or that very possibility. Kingu, whose spirit of war was captured within the orb of the Moon, calls out from the abyss.

The Blood of Tiamat infused Kingu with immortality, thus his form would change and re-emerge as Azag or Asakku, a great demon-god of the Zagros Mountains. In the spirit Kingu may seek all of us, for our blood is his and is thus a direct link to our ancestor. As Kingu was granted the Anu-power he thus decreed his destiny as immortal and to always rise from the darkness. For it was arrogance which thought one could slay something which exists in the coils of the mother-serpent, primordial Tiamat.

As for the Children of Tiamat, she is of primordial darkness, that from which the outer worlds are composed. She may not be destroyed but is sleeping in darkness. From the darkness emerges the torch of illumination. Only a shell was cut down as it was the decree of Kingu as the bearer of the Tablet of Destinies that they shall rise up again in new forms, unbenowst to their grandchildren the usurping gods.

Tiamat stirs through the subconscious of humanity, those who may hear her calls shall resonate as her Priesthood. She is the immortality of power, the eternal hunger for life continued. Tiamat is the Goddess of the Coiling Serpent, the eternal one whose blood along with Kingu created this world. Those of the priesthood of Tiamat shall utilize Chaos and Darkness to create their worlds according to the Will alone. Listen to Tiamat and hearken to the voice deep within the darkness, for she guides well.

Tiamat is the Mother of All; she is the sorceress who is both cunning and eternal. She has offered clues to the gods and humanity, her ultimate children born of her mate, Kingu. Her draconian form was only one of many, for she in spirit is the crooked serpent coiled about the world.

Know that we are descended directly from Kingu, his creator is Tiamat herself. We thus carry the blood of the god and the chaos-majesty within us. For Kingu awakens in us, who uses the Luciferian sorceries contained herein may use the sleeping dragon to rise up and then through the self shall we control the gods'.

The Brood of Tiamat from a vessel from Nineveh

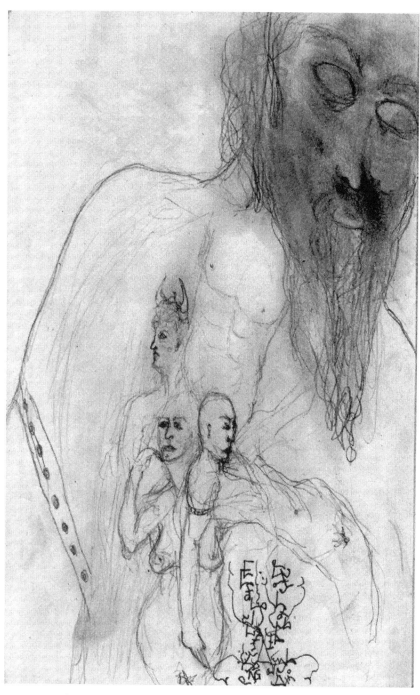
Anu and the Birth of the Anunnaki by Marchozelos

Tiamat the Goddess of Darkness and Sleep

Kingu the God of Chaos and War by Marchozelos

Betrayal and the War of Chaos by Marchozelos

Tiamat manifesting Hubar the Maker by Marchozelos

Kingu Stirring the Chaos-Monsters for Battle by Marchozelos

CHAPTER FOUR

THE GODS AND DEMONS OF MESOPOTAMIA

THE DOCTRINE OF TIAMAT

Tiamat and Apsu/Absu were the first two principles, Tiamat being the salt-water ocean, symbolized as darkness and abyssic waters and Apsu as fresh-water. When Apsu mingled his waters with Tiamat her salt-waters overtook them and the first two were born, Lahmu and the goddess Lahamu. From these two came forth Anshar and Kishar, then Anu the great god of the sky.

Mummu, the Vizer of Apsu, is called the first born of the two, Tiamat and Apsu. His name symbolizes 'making' or noise relating from mud or primordial chaos. The disruption of the primordial darkness was when the young gods continually bothered the sleep of Absu and Tiamat. Mummu, the one of action between the two thought to slay them, the earthly, fresh-water principle of Apsu soon agreed. While Tiamat would not agree, Ea, utilizing his skill of magick cast a spell to cause Mummu and Ea to sleep. Ea took the belt, crown and Melammu or "Mantle of Radiance", then killing Apsu. Ea created his great underwater Absu Palace from his slain grandfather, residing in his newfound power.

Tiamat was soon enraged from which Ea was afraid. The great abyssic darkness would spread to all, devouring those noisy and disrespectful gods.

We can see a common trait among Tiamat and the 11 chaos-monsters; she is a goddess of night and sleep, her realm is thus that of the dream and nightmare. She creates many composite forms there, her power alone there is greatest and undestroyable. If she is slayed in one form, she returns with another.

To fully grasp the iniitation of Tiamat's magick we must look to our subconscious and dreams. The psyche holds the keys to our experience and relation in the physical world. In all of your ritual workings, keep records of your journey and experiences. This will provide a framework for future initiation and reflection.

The sea and dark waters are the abode of the greatest God of Magick, Ea/Enki. From his shoulders flow the two streams which renew and maintain life itself. It is from the dark waters that all emerges, from the Apkallu who comes forth from the sea to instruct humans to the great Magickial awakenings that Ea brings. Listen to the dark abyss, do not wade in the waters, expecting a result. Walk directly in and fully enter the depths, for you will feel the primordial transformation begin. Remember that Ea too takes the form of a sea-dragon-serpent as well, just as his forebears. The primal is very much our key to ascension as individuals; we must not attempt to lock the darkness out.

THE GODS AND DEMONS

You shall find no defined "good" or "evil" here; the ancient ones shall not be limited to the dualistic extremes of later Judeo-Christian inspired faiths. "Good" and "Evil" are contemporary moralistic concepts which have no association with nature itself. Predatory animals and reptiles do not act in a moral structure; they kill to survive. The Gods of old are deeply associated with nature and within our own selves.

The Chaldeans were very knowledgeable in the path of ancient sorcery and magick; we shall attempt to re-establish a modern practice of their ancient workings. It is of course necessary to describe and define the Gods to fully comprehend their duties and purpose.

NATURE AND RELIGION

To understand the Gods and Demons of ancient Mesopotamia you must consider the environment in which this culture thrived. The Gods are a direct mirror of anthropomorphic idea in the interplay of human and nature. Desires such as fear, lust, hate, love and the primitive survival instinct all play a distinct role in creating the Gods. Often the Deities and Demons are representations in part of specific manifestations in nature. Storms, rain and other natural phenomena in part fill the foundations and controlled divine orders of the Gods. Our subconscious minds fill the other which gives manifestation to the Gods in this world. We build them with offerings, worship and recognizing their roles in nature.

As these Gods grow more powerful by our continual energy – thought – offering rituals, they begin to interact with us subconsciously. As our initiation goes further, as we deeply connect with one particular God or Goddess; we may at some point find ourselves becoming as much of a part of them as they are of us.

The difference from a Luciferian and one working to achieve a complete unity with divinity is that the Luciferian wishes to become "godlike" and will invoke other anthropomorphic deific masks and non-anthropomorphic demons to perceive and devour their knowledge. Luciferians refuse servitude, yet the ideal is not arrogance.

The fundamental aim of magic(k) is control throughout history, yet Luciferians view this only as one aspect of it. Sorcery is about control of your experience-environment and ensuring occurances manifest in accordance with the Will. Magick is a non-mystical approach to gaining control of your potential future, minus the unforeseeable such as sickness and accident. Magick is about "ascending", refining consciousness and the higher faculties of the mind and spirit. To ascend is to overtake the role of a divine god or power, not to replace the role humanity assigned them yet rather to have the perception that you are the only consciousness in control of your future.

The ancient Gods of Chaldean and Assyrian religion and myth are balanced in many ways; they are neither completely "good" nor "evil" in any defined way. Like nature they destroy and create. The religions before the vile anti-human and anti-nature Judeo-Christianity were based in the "Survival of the Fittest" doctrine of natural order.

Animals play a distinct role in associations with the Gods and Demons. Lions represent power and mastery upon the earth, the eagle represents power and accomplishment in the air, serpents represent wisdom and the underworld, bulls represent strength and water and carp is wisdom. In the Chaldean religion, there is association with nature and the self. In understanding the Gods and Demons of this grimoire, think carefully upon their symbols and anthropomorphic forms in myth and religion; then apply your offerings based on their role to the goal you may have.

In the Tablet KAR 307[13] the gods manifest in a specific tradition that the ghosts of the gods have entered specific animals. **Tiamat** manifests as a **camel with horns**, a cut off tail and bound feet. The **Daughters of Anu**, obviously Lamashtu appear as **gazelles**. The **ghost of Anu** is a **Wolf**, we see a closer connection with ur.bar.ra which is a-nu and means **"The Wolf-Star is Anu**[14]**"**. **Enlil** manifests as a **donkey**. One may wonder little as to how much later medieval grimoires associated former deities as mere demons with little power.

Nature is a consistent interaction of predator vs. prey, kill and devour or be the victim. We find the beast and therionick spirit in nature, such is the temple of darkness.

---

[13] Mesopotamian Geography.

[14] Mesopotamian Geography, pg.6.

THE GODS AND DEMONS
The Similarities and Classifications

Understand that "Gods" are related to specific phenomena in nature and the human mind – body – spirit. Gods have both destructive and creative attributes; generally have a strong balance in their presentation. Demons generally are on a level between humans and gods. The Sumerian term for demon is "Maskim" and in Akkadian as "Rabisu". Demons can be both creative and destructive, both assisting humanity and harming them depending on the spirit.

As you can read, there is a difference between "demon" and "monster" only in anthropomorphic manifestation; i.e. artistic presentation in ancient tablets and cylinders. "Demons" generally are upright as man and "Monsters" are often on all fours. This is not an absolute as several of the 11 Monsters of Tiamat are upright on two legs.

Demons or the Seven Maskim in Akkadian and Sumerian pantheons are present strongly in magical incantations or sorcery. They represent the instinctual drives of man as well as sickness and the manipulation of others.

Demons are often carrying out the Will of the Gods in association with their nature. Simply written, some demons are associated with causing sickness, when a God wishes to punish a mortal, they enlist the aid of the demon that can cause the ailment.

Demons are also counter-acting beings which do not act in accordance with the natural order, unless supporting a task asked of them by the gods. In ancient Mesopotamia, demons do not have a cult, thus they cannot benefit from the interaction with humans. The modern Kassapu creates a cult for them, libations and offerings are made in relation to the demon and the Kassapu, and thus they benefit from this close interaction.

Some demons are created from Anu, thus they are like Gods themselves except they hold no association with humans other than feeding from them or causing some weather based disorder. A perfect example is the Seven Maskim, demons of the ignited spheres who are associated with various manifestations of weather, nature and the beasts of prey. These Maskim are in turn Gods except their nature will most likely not evolve further.

Magick is the process of "ascension" and the process of spiritual and mental transformation into a self-deified god over a long period of time. While this concept is easy enough to understand, the actual process is quite difficult in the early stages.

There are three basic types of magickian or new age types in this world; they are either mentally imbalanced, viewing the world and some one-side "love" interpretation or finally those who are merely misinformed and uneducated in the history of theology and religion, thus proceeding with their initiation from a Judeo-Christian "dualistic" viewpoint.

The first two categories are helpless as both are mentally "hard wired" to think this way, thus if they are able to rise above this outlook; the first moment comfort is needed they will retreat to the gratifying world view they have chosen long ago. The last category is the most hopeful as mere study, application and result-oriented work will enable the brain to continually evolve and change in accordance with the Will.

What separates the Adept from the lagging initiate is the ability to look at the gods and demons in their selfish actions. All gods and demons act in the self-interest of the manifestation they represent. Demons are considered destructive and selfish as they act according to the phenomena they have affected; Gods are considered mostly helpful and righteous as they have layers of "light" or non-threatening imagery around them. These same gods are often just as destructive and all demand the continued investment of belief to continue their existence in your conscious mind.

The same is said in any society. Look how many so-called "Priests" have abused children, shown preference to a "type" of people contrary to their own spiritual laws (those who attend and support their particular social group). "Satanists" or even "Atheists" are considered "evil" because they are cloaked in something "other" than the mantle of righteousness.

When all illusion is stripped away, all the pleasantries are burnt to reveal the true nature then can we see all gods, demons and humans are self-centered, destructive when angered and kind to those who serve or support their purpose or goals. This like the Babylonian pantheon is entirely self-centered, which is the entire basis of religion no matter which form it may manifest in.

DISTINCTIONS BETWEEN GODS AND DEMONS

The distinctions between gods and demons/monsters are in their opposites, ruling gods have respective control over certain situations and demons/monsters often represent a reaction to those situations.

Gods in Mesopotamian myth and religion have specific responsibility in the cosmic structure and order, while demons often have limited cosmic functions in this area. Often Gods have specific order over dry land, with the exception of Ea, who reigns in the depths of the ocean-abyss. Demons often have residence in the mountains or in the sea as well.

The exceptions are the Sebitti or the Seven Maskim who are able to dwell where they wish, who are affixed to all elements. As with Asag/Azag/Asakku, demons or monsters are associated with usurping rulers, rebels and those who challenge the perceived "rightful" rulers.

Gods are a standard offer an "unseen" stability, like a foundation for the order of the cosmos. Demons have often direct interaction with humanity. F.A.M. Wiggerman[15] makes a clear association between the two which also defines that Gods represent the entirety or whole for which their specific phenomena belongs to. Demons represent a specific phenomena and acts accordingly.

Thorkild Jacobsen in his "The Treasures of Darkness" makes a clear ascension between the Therionick (beastlike) forms of the gods and their transformation to human form in later religions. For instance, in early Dynastic periods, the Therionick or Animal forms were primary while in later periods the human form competed with the animal form to the later time when the gods had a primary human form. This no doubt had importance in the Priesthood of the specific gods drawing a close association with the development of the people.

The Therionick/demonic forms still have their well-spring source of vitality. In the atavistic sense, they often ascend upward from the darkness of the subconscious to then give us glimpses not only of their primal form yet also their ascension to our conscious mind – or human deific mask.

The legend of Gudea, a Sumerian ruler had a dream in which the God Ningirsu appeared in the form of his primal self, the lion-griffin Imdugud also known as ANZU. The Imdugud is a lion-dragon who causes much counter-action or chaos and represents sandstorms, fog or mist.

The Underworld God Ningishzida has two horned serpents, or 'cerestes cerestes' rising up out of his shoulders, relates that in his primal aspect he is associated with the Basmu. This god is the "Lord of the Good Tree' and is attributed to the fertility of the underworld, the growth from the roots of darkness as well as the cold, clean waters of Irkalla. In addition, the serpents from his

---

[15] Mesopotamian Protective Spirits

shoulders and the caduceus represent the poison and beneficial nature of Ningishzida. He guards the gate of the Highest Heaven, the abode of ANU[16] and equally dwells in the underworld and is associated with the constellation known as Hydra.

It is important to consider that the gods also take Therionick forms in reference to constellations or specific actions they reside over. Understanding such symbolism and any god or demon you may work with will have specific aspects which may manifest in dreams or the living world; perhaps as a dream or an interaction with a specific animal/reptile.

POWERS & WEAPONS USED BY GODS & DEMONS

The Thunderbolt held by many gods of darkness, storm and light

The distinction between gods and demons within the Mesopotamian pantheon is one of purpose, representation and natural order. Specifically, demons have more "rebellious" aspects thus bringing a sense of individuality and anthropomorphic association; even if they do not assume human visage. There are specific weapons the gods have in their possession at different times, which no doubt are symbols for aspects of nature and are later mirrored by the records of Kings.

The ritualistic may utilize some of the symbolism within ritual simply by recititng and visualizing the weapon directly affecting

---

[16] The Myth of Adapa, Ningishzida appears in the abbreviated Giszida.

towards the goal. Utilize it, believe it and imagine it striking or touching something to create the outcome you wish. By doing this you will over a period of time train the subconscious into defined meaning when viewing this symbol on a conscious level.

TABLET OF DESTINIES

The Tablet of Destinies was described as a cuneiform tablet from which fates were written. The one who possessed the tablet was bestowed the "Anu Power" or supreme power and authority. Tiamat bestowed the Tablet of Destinies to Kingu who was then empowered as a God who would lead her army of chaos.

A mythological rendition of the Tablet of Destinies

ANUTU

The "Anu Power" given by Tiamat unto Kingu when he was given the Tablet of Destinies. This is the supreme power in which the god is self-deified and knowingly has the power to direct his or her existence as they are able. After Kingu was defeated, Marduk took this power. The Luciferian or Kassapu looks to this as a symbol of antinomian or *"lawless"* perception; *no god will govern who bears the Anutu power*. It may also be perceived as a symbol of awakened consciousness, or *"The Black Flame"*.

MELAMMU

"She cloaked ferocious dragons with fearsome rays, and made them bear mantles of radiance, made them godlike…" – Tiamat's empowerment of the 11 Monsters of Chaos in the Enuma Elish

The Sumerian Melam or Melammu, the Akkadian word, denotes a *"mantle of radiance"* which gods and demons may put on when they wish. This divine radiance is symbolized as a great light which inspires *Ni*, the feeling of awe or terror. On the image of the Musmahhu (7 headed dragon-serpent) the flames which rise off of it can be understood as Melammu. This was the divine radiance, in which Tiamat cloaked her 11 chaos-monsters in which she raised them to gods with a chant. Other then the first 11 Monsters of Tiamat, Kingu and then soon after all of the gods gained the cloak of radiance in which they could adorn. Huwawa, the Demon-God of the Cedar forests of Lebanon had seven rays of Melam and was under the guidance of Enlil.

Melam can be considered a force of the psyche or Will of the Demon/God, likewise the theory of the Kassapu as he or she grows in practice may build up through meditation and discipline. This type of presence may be sensed in the physical world if the bearer is wishing it to be so or "cloaked" as well as in dream projection.

Ancient Assyrian Kings emulated this as well. Tiglath-pileser I (1114–1076 BC) inscribed reference to this power in his cuneiform records during his reign, *"Tiglath-pilesar, the fiery, fierce flame, the mighty battle-storm"*, such is the early symbolism and relation to the King as the vessel of his gods.

MELAMMU AS THE BLACK FLAME

Melammu was originally possessed by Apsu, Tiamat and then she gave this potent cosmic radiance to the 11 Chaos-Monsters, Kingu received the Tablets of Destiny and this divine light as well. Medieval alchmemists had a name for the concept of this light, which they associated as the light in the depths of darkness. The light they write of, Melammu is called the "Sun in the Earth", the earthly, invisible sun is called "black sun" and "fire of hell". In the "Underworld vision of an Assyrian Prince", a vision of Nergal, the God of Black Fire, the underworld and the Sun at Midnight is described:

"I raised my eyes, the valiant Nergal seated on a regal throne, appareled with the royal tiara; with both hands he grasped two grim maces, each with two lion-demon heads..His grimly luminescent splendor overwhelmed me.." –Livingstone 1989, 72

The term used for "Luminescent splendor" is "melammusu ezzuti" and is the divine fire, the rays of consciousness and inner power which may be concealed or brought out. This divine light is found in the darkness, it is consciousness defined, initiated and controlled through the enlightenment of purposeful experience.

In Islam, Henry Corbin makes reference to "Black Light" which is a survival of the concept of Melammu and the underworld. This light represents the highest spiritual stage towards enlightenment. This black light is of the Islamic Shaitan, the Adversary and is a light which "attacks, invades, annihilates, then annihilates annihilation" – Corbin, 1978 and Mehmet-Ali Atac.

The result is wisdom and inner power, Melammu is to be found only in the Darkness, just as all the Divine Order-based Gods possess, they obtained it from the darkness.

The Assyrian king Esarhaddon, son of Sennacherib was crowned king according to his inscriptions by Anu, who crowned him, the throne given by Enlil, weapons bestowed unto him by Ninurta and the Melammu or "splendor-salummatu" by the Lord of the Underworld, Nergal.

Melammu is a great power bestowed through the exploration into the underworld, through the darkness of our primordial origin. All the demons and gods of importance possess Melammu; it may equally be hidden away when one wishes to not display it. This type of divine black fire, or radiance may be built up by the Kassapu through meditation and consistent initiation. The more one struggles in the Great Work, the greater it will shine.

An interesting point is that the Black Light of Melammu is a consciousness and divine radiance earned through exploring the darkness, yet once attained is a potent cosmic power and the very light of Magick itself. Thus, in summary, all Magick is derived from the divine Blackened Fire of the Underworld, even for the "Natural Order Gods" and thus any attempt to "hush up" the exploration of the darkness should be quickly put to an end!

PULUHTU / NI

"Whoever shall look at them shall collapse in Utter Terror" – **The Spell of Melammu to cause Ni to those in the presence of the 11 Chaos-Monsters.**

Puluhtu or Ni is the emotion which comes over humans and other beings when in the presence of a god or demon who has the Melam power on which is described as a "cloak" and also as a "mantle of radiance" or crown upon the head. Ni is the emotion of fear or as if something is "watching" you. It may be considered that astral/dream projecting demons and gods may use Melam to cause the effect of Ni, which in the person affected will cause intense anxiety or a high level of fear, thus which the one bearing Melam may then in turn feed from the excess energy released by the individual.

The original monsters of Tiamat possessed Melammu in its purest manifestation, the original. We notice through various myths, including Gilgamesh and his interaction with the Scorpion Men, the Melammu sets forth terror and fear as it is a type of divine radiance, thus the Puluhtu or Ni is fearsome in purity. Apsu, the first husband-king of Tiamat, could only be killed when sleeping as Ea was only able to remove his Melammu then.

KASUSU

A destructive power used by the gods, most likely relating to the storm.

ABUBU

The flood-weapon of the gods, manifested as flash-floods, torrents and watery-chaos caused by such phenomena. Adad-Enlil used Abubu as well as Nergal and Ninurta.

SHARUR

The weapon of Ninurta which is symbolized as a mace. This may be associated with the Seven-Headed Serpent Mace held by Ninurta.

ASQULALU

A weapon which is thrown, from a mythological perspective, perhaps a spear-throwing stick or even an arrow.

KAKKU

The mace or "kakku" is held by the Ugallu demons. It is a "magick weapon" utilized in their spiritual attacks.

QULMU

The Hatchet held by the Sebbiti in human form on the reliefs of Ashurbanipal. The human form of the Sebitti at times makes them separate from the Seven Maskim/Sebitti, although they are both identified with the Seven Stars and are one and the same in the Erra and Ishum.

DEMONIC SPIRITUALITY

The evidence of the nature of demons suggests that there is a path of "ascension" and "immortality" in Mesopotamian spiritualism. For instance, the Gods were represented in early Sumerian times as "Ilu", meaning that they dwelt in the sky. As the Gods of the Sky could compel destiny to go in their favor, humans would conduct offerings to inspire the Gods to compel such to their benefit.

The demons of ancient Mesopotamia are widely varied and different in nature. The various spirits dwell in both the sky, the sea, the desert and in the Mountains. In addition they dwell also in the earth and within the dark places humans do not go.

The spirits of ancient Mesopotamia exist in what we call the "Astral Plane", or the one of spirit in which humans cannot visibly see in normal circumstances. It can be assumed in sorcerous practice that spirits draw strength in the physical world by feeding from the astral energy from living humans.

Each human in Mesopotamian lore has an Ekimmu which means "the thing which is snatched away", the spirit of each living being. The Ekimmu[17] which is also called the Gidim is the spirit of a deceased person which goes forth to live in the Underworld. The symbol of a God is a star, as in the case of Inanna / Ishtar indicating the spiritual and "astral" connection between deities associated with the sky.

These gidim or ekimmu were offered to by relatives or those affected by the shade. Offerings were in the form of regular food or drink. Like Ancient Egyptian Magick, one may offer incense as well. If the ekimmu is not fed then it will become restless and begin to haunt the living. Often, ekimmu are the spirits of those who physically die in problematic circumstances, murder, extreme sickness, starvation, not being laid to rest or buried properly, etc.

The Seven Maskim, being the children of Anu and Ki are immortal demons which are manifest in not only nature as storms, wind yet also take composite forms of animals and reptiles with human attributes. The Seven Maskim also may take tangible form to drink blood and to consume human flesh when seeking their victims. These Maskim or Demons are also called Gods in various incantation texts.

THE CLASSES OF DEMONS

Chaldean demonology is perhaps the richest, detailed and insightful of all religions through modern Christianity. The divine powers (including non-physical, spiritual beings) that control some aspect of nature or phenomena are divided into three specific classes depending upon their power and influence. The basic categories of demons were collectively organized by

---

[17] The Akkadian spelling is Etemmu

Thompson in his works[18]; however they are from the tablets themselves.

In Mesopotamian demonology, there is a direct association with evil spirits which bring disease, or manifest as disease from the underworld. The Kassapu or Luciferian working in the dark currents in the modern age will find that the mind offers the capacity for which the demons and evil gods shall be worked with. If you invoke them and use the incantations to work within you towards a goal, there will be little area for sickness.

No matter if you believe that demons are literal spirits or subconscious aspects of the deep desire of man, or if spirits exist and manifest through the subconscious of the Kassapu the results are often the same. Approach the demons, evil spirits and gods with mutual respect and you will achieve suitable results.

THE SHAPES & APPEARANCE OF DEMONS

Demons and evil spirits of ancient Mesopotamia assume numerous forms. These spirits haunt the deserts and haunted places avoided by man, however at certain times wander into the dwellings of humans and in their streets to take hold of their bodies and spirits to grow stronger from in the physical and astral world.

It is commonly understood that from the earliest records of the manifestation of spirits, from the works such as this is derived, to Egyptian Pyramid texts to early Palestinian and Judeo-Christian lore, spirits assume forms of animals and specifically predatory animals.

---

[18] Devils and Demons, see bibliography.

The Kassapu may consider that spirits or demons manifest in the forms in which they are associated with, based on the element and function. If a spirit manifests in a dream as half-bird would symbolize the power of the air, of spirit-travel and crossing from this world to that of the dead. If using an incantation to call forth an evil spirit to a specific object, mentally visualizing the spirit in an associative form would prove useful in the subconscious and conscious mind aligning association to the desired goal.

The raven is found in roughly eight species in Palestine and dwells in desolate ruins, glens and deep areas where humans don't regularly frequent. Ravens (including crows) are considered unclean birds by both the Hebrews and Arabs, who consider the birds to be associated with the spirit world including that of devils. Arabs consider Ravens to be birds of ill-omen and to foretell death. For Luciferians, Ravens do not foretell death. They represent the opposite; a spiritual event or subconscious awakening. The shadow is welcomed and revered by Luciferians as well as the concept of light. Luciferians are nourished and empowered by darkness; illuminating an inner light of wisdom and experience.

Sorcerer's have since ancient Egypt been associated with ravens as well. Eagles and hawks also have magical significance, being symbols for specific conquering gods and powers throughout antiquity including Zeus, Assur, Horus, Ninurta, Ammon-Ra and many more. In the Histories of Rabban Hormizd the Persian there is a legend of a sorcerer named Zakkai who sent devils to plague Rabban who saw the evil spirits assuming the forms of Black ravens, who sought to break in his bed chamber and destroy him. These same devils as they are referred to as *"shooting out their venom upon us"* which draws association to the spitting Cobra which dwells in Egypt, Ethiopia and Kenya.

ABSU

Primordial Fresh Water God

Absu is the first husband of Tiamat, representing the primordial fresh waters of the earth. Within the creation myth and variants, Absu is the name from which the God Ea forms to be his dwelling from the dead god Absu. Absu has a primordial form as well; he is symbolized as wearing a crown, his belt and mantle of radiance indicating an anthropomorphic form.

TIAMAT

Dragon-Serpent of Chaos
Mother of All Gods and Demons

Tiamat is described first in the Epic of Creation as the abyssic mother of all. Tiamat is equivalent to the Hebrew name "Tamtu" relating to the sea. For this reason, it is logical as to why she is represented as a great serpent or composite dragon. Tiamat is the mother while Absu is the primal father, Tiamat's original lover. Absu is considered the freshwater ocean that dwelt in the abyss, or underneath the earth before the creation of man.

Tiamat was associated to the word Tamtu representing the ordinary sea, while Tiamat represents the primal sea as well as the primordial composite dragon which reigned within it and manifested in numerous horrifying forms.

In Corey's "Ancient Fragments", several religious myths and lore survived from ancient Babylonia to the Hellenic period were compiled by Babylonian Priest Berossus. Among the lore was the creation and origin of all life tale which is a variant of ENUMA ELISH. The ritual hymn (the Enuma Elish is a Babylonian New Year hymn) involved Tiamat and Absu. From the darkness and the abyss of waters, two hideous beings who were produced from a two-fold principle. There were also men who had wings, or two faces, one body or who had both sexes and the legs of a goat, horns or were serpent like, dragon-men. Over these presided **Omoroca**, known as **Ummu Khubur**, **Thalatth** and **Tiamat**, the Mother of Darkness.

Tiamat is the foundational force of chaos which uplifts and gives power to fiends and Adversarial Powers of the Abyss. From the abyss of primal waters did life evolve and crawl forth from the darkness. Their blood composed of the Lord of War, Kingu who provides the motivation or aggression and ascension from primal instinct.

"There was a time in which there existed nothing but darkness, and an abyss of waters, wherein resided most hideous beings, who were produced of a two-fold principle...human figures were to be seen with the legs and horns of goats"-TIAMAT by George Barton

Tiamat is the primal aspect of the Serpent or dragon itself – the spark of intelligence and possibility of life through willed desire. As the universe is chaos itself, from which we are a part of darkness, we thus can return to it. Tiamat, through Kingu is our father as his blood according to the legend gave us life.

Tiamat is a protean goddess; she assumes the mask which suits her. Traditionally, her war-form is seen is the combination of a dragon-lion, several horns, a face of a lion, cruel fangs, a serpent or scaly tale, the sharp claws and hands shaped as the paws of a lion, wings with sharp talon-feet as a bird of prey. Sometimes she is shown with a serpent-penis, which is explainable as the constellation descriptions of Kingu and Tiamat joined as one to battle Marduk. At times she is described as both woman and the dark waters, also as having the body of a cow and goat. She is described as having udders, a tail and a horn which in the form of a Camael is cut off by Marduk. Tiamat is also shown in the form of a gigantic horned serpent. When Tiamat was creating her children, the 11 Monsters of Chaos, she took the form of Hubur, the creating one. Her link as the primordial salt-water sea is the foundation from which life crawled to the shore via certain evolution theories.

All of the gods originally were not as anthropomorphic as they later appeared. Tiamat and the demonic gods retain their therionick, primordial composite manifestations. Tiamat is described as having four eyes, the two right eyes are the sources of the Tigris and her left eyes are the source of the Euphrates. Tiamat's adversary and descendant, Marduk is endowed with four eyes and ears.

She seeks to devour the Gods themselves, thus she recognizes she is the First, the Goddess which should be viewed in a creative and destructive balance. She still holds maternal instincts, for she did not want to destroy the younger gods at first; she counseled Absu, her husband, that they should not kill the gods.

Tiamat and Absu created numerous children, who became the great gods who later preceded them. From Tiamat and Absu came forth the vizer or attendant Mummu, who is regarded as a child of chaos. The first gods from Tiamat and Absu are the Ilu Limnu, great spirits of darkness of which remained in the world after Tiamat's spirit was cast into further darkness of the abyss.

MUMMU TIAMAT

Tiamat is regarded as the primal deity of chaos and creation in modern chaos-magick and vampyric circles. She holds the collective power of primordial subconscious, our origin and that primal urge for satisfying our desire for continued existence and those lusts which we bare in our minds and bodies. She is a perfect symbol of our predatory instincts and our potential as creators. We must not ignore the balancing aspects of the dark mother.

Tiamat manifests as Ishtar of Nineveh, her form much more suitable to the new gods who are unaware of her true face. In the tablet **'Piristi ilani rabuti'** (Secret of the Great Gods)[19] Ishtar of Nineveh, is our Dark Goddess Tiamat, who incidentally is the Wet-Nurse of Bel.

Some Kassapu and traditional Luciferian witches will seek to find a consistent "cord" in which to draw from the dark goddess, here we are able to see a literary path of connections between the primal darkness and the later manifestations.

Understand that Tiamat is a multi-leveled deific mask of complicated symbolism. No matter if you choose a theistic or atheistic view, the great goddess is a mirror of our subconscious; our origins when we crawled from the primordial ocean. Tiamat is our beginning; elder darkness and still a great empowering force which drives us. She was not destroyed in her battle with Marduk, for she lost that battle and simply evolved.

---

[19] Mesopotamian Cosmic Geography, Tablet KAR 307.

It should be noted that Tiamat is never referred to in any clay tablets as "goddess", specifically as she is the darkness *before* record or perception. Her symbol is the untamed abyssic waters, that which all the other gods' feared to attack. All dieties have the symbol of MUL, a Sumerian sign representing the designation of "star" or "god" before their names, which Tiamat does not: Another clue to her protean nature.

Tiamat is our all-mother; the great serpent which is protean in shape and form; she manifests as other goddesses later on. One must consider that Tiamat is a symbol of our continual process of evolution, maintaining the primordial and creative serpent-fire (i.e. Black Flame) we humans call consciousness; *we are aware of our individual being.* In one perspective Tiamat is the primordial force which exists behind human consciousness; aware of the instinct of survival and the accumulation of inner power; the very driving point of the human race and religion!

Marduk is just a vessel for the continued evolution, his powers in all myths are capable yet by reading the original (and various) versions of Enuma Elish one cannot help but think Tiamat holds back her power in order to rise again.

MUMMU

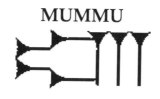

Sukkal (Vizer) of Chaos

Mummu is the willed form of Tiamat and Absu called the vizer or primal form of chaos, which was like ancient water from which all emerged. In ancient Sumerian, Mummu represents *"One who has awoken"*, in Akkadian is "maker". Many other gods including Ea and Marduk adopt the epithet of Mummu when creating. Mummu in addition has an association with "fog, mist" and thus the shadowy aspect between darkness and light. It must be noted that Mummu acts in opposition to Tiamat and suggests to Ea that they slay the young gods; suggesting another concept of "Triad of Chaos" in which Absu and Tiamat are the creative component along, Mummu or the mist, emergence of form in the darkness is not as significant and placed as an adviser to Absu and Tiamat.

The Gods were creating and growing from the primal chaos, they sought to devour and create both, just as their primal forms and parents Tiamat and Absu. Consider the protean nature of Tiamat as you explore the pages and the different manifestations of deific forces; Mummu can be observed as a will manifestation of Tiamat utilized to 'create' or on some level relate to other beings. The epithet of "mummu Tiamat" is used to describe Tiamat as creating the first stage in primordial evolution.

Absu called to Mummu and they went to Tiamat. Before Tiamat, the Great Dark Goddess did Mummu speak about their grievance with the Gods. Absu called out to her "We cannot rest by night or day as they keep us awake; I seek to abolish their ways so that we may return to the darkness of sleep".

KINGU

The Greatest in the Gods' Assembly
The Father of Humanity and Inventor of War

Kingu, spelled also Qingu, is the first-born son of Tiamat and in the traditions of ancient royalty, enthroned as King and Husband of Tiamat after the death of Absu. Kingu is given the Anutu[20] power, which translates "power of the en-priesthood" referring to Anu-power.

The Greatest among all ancient Gods according to Tiamat, Kingu was conferred the leadership of the army of Tiamat and the command of the assembly. Cloaked in radiance and terrible splendor, Kingu directed the Chaos-Monsters of Tiamat against the new gods.

"Kingu it was who created warfare, who let loose Tiamat who 'joined' battle" – Ashur Version of the Seven Tablets of Creation.

Kingu raised the weapon to signal engagement, he mustered all combat-troops. Kingu was given the throne by Tiamat after the death of Absu.

Tiamat said unto Kingu "I have cast the spell for you and made you Greatest in the Gods' Assembly. I have put into your power rule over all the Gods! You shall be the greatest, for you are my only lover! Your commands shall always prevail over all the Anunnaki.

---

[20] Called also Entu, representing the high priesthood. Myths from Mesopotamia, Stephanie Dalley.

She gave him the TABLET OF DESTINIES and he clasped it to his breast.

YOUR UTTERANCE SHALL NEVER BE ALTERED! YOUR WORD SHALL BE LAW!

Kingu received the ANU power which is the power of divine rule. Anu is the Great God of the Sky and thus his power symbolized the majesty of the conquering one. Kingu may be perceived as one who assumes power against the natural order. Kingu represents one who takes power or seizes control without the natural right or in succession.

A semi-anthropomorphic rendition of Kingu (part-chaos monster/part human) with the Tablet of Destinies attached to his chest.

In such terms Kingu represents a usurper, a term meaning "to seize control" or gain power from "ultra vires" which means "out of one's control" according to oppositions. A good example of a usurpers would be Timarchus, a

Seleucid Satrap of Ekbatana (Media) and Babylon who with the support of Rome after the death of Antiochus IV, crowned himself around 163-160 BC (Antiochus IV died in 164 BC). Timarchus had a brief rule however called himself Basileus Megas (Great King), a title dating back to Achaemenid Persian kings. Antiochus IV could be considered a usurper as well.

We see successful Usurpations as well, such as with Tiglath-Pileser III (745 -727 B.C.) who seized the Assyrian throne and executed the remainders of the royal family. This king saved the Assyrian kingdom and expanded the borders to a new level.

Kingu's claim to power was given to him by the supreme Goddess, Tiamat whose right-to-rule was greater than that of any others. While Kingu was a usurper in the eyes of the younger gods, Marduk who took power from Tiamat's chosen was actually was a usurper as well, considering the divine right of rule was not placed upon him by Tiamat, the mother of all. However, Adversarial Magick is like the serpent and is cunning: there is method to the chaos!

Kingu in tablet KAR 307, rev. 17-18 is featured in a ritual where cattle are slaughtered representing '*Kingu and His Seven Sons*' and Kingu is represented as a ram which is placed in the fire during a ritual.[21]

Kingu was defeated in the battle and the Tablet of Destiny was taken from him from Marduk. In the Ashur Version of the Seven Tablets of Creation[22] Kingu was defeated and taken prisoner after the manifestation of Tiamat was

---

[21] Unity and Diversity: Essays in the History, Literature, and religion of the near east.

[22] D.D. Luckenbill. The American Journal of Semitic Languages and Literatures, Vol. 38, No. 1. 1921.

scattered Marduk confirmed that Kingu was he "who created warfare"[23]. Bound and slain in physical form, his blood was used by Ea to create mankind.

Marduk can be perceived as "Luciferian" in that his origins are darkness, yet he conquers and commands his own design and ensures all the other gods obeys his wishes. Luciferians are not relinquished to darkness; for in balance there can be a great deal of light itself. For Luciferians, light is knowledge or the understanding of personal experience which becomes wisdom.

To invoke Kingu is to listen to your darkest instincts, for his blood is in our veins. Listen well to your desires and seek them in this world, for this may be the only flesh you wear.

The Kassapu understands the aim of Magick is to compel change in accordance with the Will. Acts of sorcery and Theurgy as they are known should be conducted in accordance with expanding and refining the consciousness of the Kassapu. Kingu is the blood of the primordial, the direct descendent of Tiamat who seeks to rise through our consciousness again. When Marduk utilized his blood it is called DAMI ISSIMTUM which is "blood and bone", mixed with the bond of KI or Earth. The human being is the very essence of the primordial darkness, reaching up to ascend in self-illumination; the very essence of the left hand path.

Kingu rises up again through the gods themselves; Marduk shall not fight again the chaos-demons rather Kingu controls and compels the Gods through this type of Magick later known as *Theurgy*, for our blood is his own. The Adversary, Kingu and Tiamat are united within the body

---

[23] Line 15.

of man and through this consuming the deific essence of Marduk and the Gods. *There is balance in the act of usurping the essence of the Gods.* Our magick liberates us from the slavery of the gods, placing the Kassapu as the god which is. This process of thought is at first difficult and is slowly adapted in the mind through initiation.

Know now the eleven chaos-monsters of Tiamat, their knowledge sleeps in the darkness of the subconscious and the stars above us.

NABNIT QERBISA

The Children of the Womb of Tiamat
The rebellious "others" in the world

Kingu was the great adversary who was illuminated over the other chaos-demons to fight against the new gods. When Marduk had defeated them, many were captured and became powers with Marduk's authority, some went forth to unknown places of darkness to reemerge later and Kingu was named GOD DUGGA, which means 'the dead god'.

In ancient Akkadian the Lulubi, Gutians and other mountain-dwelling raiders who often fought against the Akkadians and later Assyrian lands were considered offspring of Tiamat and from which the evil gods, spirits and demons dwelled among them. In "Journal Asiatique"[24] there is reference to the Lulubi, mountain-raiders and horsemen who fought the Akkadians were described as

---

[24] Journal Asiatique, Oct-Dec, 1930 p.230

having *"warriors with raven's faces"* which draws their association to the 'other' or demonic offspring of Tiamat.

In the Cuthaean Legend of Naram-Sin the children of Tiamat now dwell "in the Shining Mountains" and were warriors who had the bodies of "cave-birds"[25], a face with ravens' faces[26] and were created by the great gods and were suckled by Tiamat. These warriors were blessed in the womb by Belit-ili and grew up in the mountains. We see here the associations of those who act outside of organized 'society' were considered demonic, as they acted contrary to the perceived laws of nature. Furthermore, society instructs the masses to lose 'individuality' to some extent and fit suitably into 'categories' which allows the conscious self to be submissive to the productivity of our social structure.

While this is not entirely 'negative', the Kassapu must be aware to foster, cultivate and master the elements of the self on an individual level; do not worry about fitting in unless it is supportive of your goals; keep the outer layers of 'self' within the 'fitting in' range to maintain normal economic status (i.e. keep a job, excel in life) and practice your workings in your own time.

To be brought forth by the great gods, the primal ones is to be like the Sebitti/Maskim Hul; be willing to make yourself spiritually independent, strong in mind and will. To be "suckled by Tiamat" is to be nourished and mothered by darkness; know your deep desires, learn to think in terms of primal instinct and survival.

---

[25] Bats can be a speculation of form.

[26] Evil spirits and messengers of the gods such as Anu, Enlil, Ea take the forms of ravens as well.

As a practicing Kassapu and Luciferian, I have many pet snakes (7 at the time of writing) many of which I have raised from small babies. I have spent countless hours with each, training them to lie around my neck and by routine maintaining a healthy, non-fearful reaction when I pick them up. I also learn from them; movement, their purpose in action and their ability to strike in a split-second. Serpents are pure, unadulterated primal instinct. Even overtime they all have personality, something making them different from each other and even showing 'affection' or 'complete ease' with me at times. I am reminded of this careful balance whenever the kill their prey: it is swift, goal-oriented instinct.

The Kassapu to understand the essence of Tiamat is to grow completely "at one" with darkness in terms of primal instinct, nature and the 'otherness' of counter-action. This type of initiation, presented here, creates liberated spiritualists who value insight, laugh against superstition and learn to appreciate the 'other' to further individual wisdom and power. This is the very essence of Luciferianism and the Tiamat/Maskim/Sebitti Dark Sorcery of liberation inherent in every page of this grimoire.

ESRET-NABNISSU
ELEVEN CHAOS-MONSTERS OF TIAMAT

In preparation for crushing the rebellion of the new Gods, the disruptive children of Tiamat, Tiamat in her form of Mummu Hubur created 11 Monsters – Demonic Gods of Chaos who would rush forth with their legions and armies against that of Marduk and the new Gods. With Kingu who commands these monsters, it makes 12 specific monster-gods who go forth to stir forth chaos.

Called in Sumerian texts a variety of names such as **"Esret Nabinissu"**, **"His (Kingu's) ten-creatures"**; Umamanu, "beasts"; Gallu, "soldiers" and Umu, "storms"; these monsters like the gods were immortal. They could be, however, temporarily defeated which would send them into the darkness, waiting for the time to manifest again. The monsters are not specifically "demons" as they are direct creations of Tiamat, however they are not gods attributed to nature or any consistent phenomena. In later times they guard the temples of the gods, yet retain their original powers which cause the gods to respect them.

The Monsters of Tiamat are deeply associated with nature and the possible interaction of the mind, body and spirit with it. King, in his "Seven Tablets of Creation" makes reference that the monster-brood of Tiamat composes some signs of the Zodiac[27]. The chaos-monsters of Tiamat once the war was over and there was order placed in the world the demons of Tiamat became beneficial in the pantheon of Gods.

Tiamat is deeply connected with not only the underworld, yet also the world in which humans live in. The monsters in which she created **"sut me nari u nabali"**, **"those of the water of the river and the dry land"**[28]. In union these monsters are called the "Umu-demons" which have fear against Bel or Marduk.

---

[27] The Seven Tablets of Creation, King. Pg 208

[28] Page 146, Cuneiform Monographs, Mesopotamian Protective Spirits Wiggerman

The gods who mastered these elements represent to the Kassapu or Black Adepts the balanced mastery of the inner desires and shaping them accordingly.

What we can see with the Eleven Monsters of Tiamat is that they are associated with storms and chaos, much like the Adversary of other cultures and mythologies. He who masters and controls these forces within is then granted the "Anu Power" and becomes "like" Kingu/Kingu, the Lord of Chaos itself for a time. Working with such powers is essential to establishing further depth in sorcerous workings.

These chaos-monsters are defined by composite parts of other animals or reptiles; however the names are defined by the overmastering element in which they are associated. For instance, the dragon or serpents have often other elements such as a lion or otherwise. The physical representations in which Tiamat takes form shows her with composite features as well, yet she is still mostly represented as a "dragon".

The ancient Egyptians also presented Gods and Demons as composite beasts, however are primarily represented by the phenomena in which they manifest. Medieval demonology also present the old Gods in composite parts, however their attunement to nature is somewhat perverted and it is often unclear as to what they represent. The Chaldean Gods and other pre-Christian cultures are quite attuned with the balance of nature and spiritual representations from it.

The definition of chaos within this work is that chaos represents the unordered, purely creative and destructive elements of nature. When one is a "Lord of Chaos" such as Kingu/Kingu it does not relate that he is disordered and imbalanced. This is a misperception of chaos in the sense as it is defined in Luciferianism. Chaos is indeed uncontrolled, disordered as a misdirected source of power.

What makes it considerably different is that a God can enter the center of chaos and shape it to his or her will.

In this instance, chaos may be used for creation or destruction depending on the God and how they wish to apply it.

In Magick chaos is the vital fuel for the vehicle which is the self and the will.

Tiamat, the Great Dragon-Serpent, the horned power of darkness, she wielded the power of creation and crowned her chosen in the radiance of Godhood. She terrified her children and grandchildren, the new Gods enough to where only one dared to fight her.

The predatory and conquering spirit of Tiamat and Kingu was the same "blood" within the veins of Marduk; they are interconnected more than what it obvious. For the desire of power and the divine radiance of self-deification which stirs Marduk to usurp the throne of Tiamat, although temporarily considering that Tiamat is eternal darkness and chaos. While banished to outer darkness and her essence created the world and Kingu's blood humanity; they reside in our subconscious waiting to rise again.

UMU DABRUTU

Fierce Storm-Demon

The Umu Dabrutu is a group of demon/monsters created by Tiamat who represent chaos-storms. These monsters have no specific form or anthropomorphic features from tablets or art however as pointed out by McBeath[29] that in the Anzu legend, the Anzu is described as "bared his teeth like an Umu-demon[30]". Wiggerman defines them as "weather-beasts"[31] and as being "Leonine monsters". They are not specifically associated with the 11 chaos-monsters however we can see their "spirit" associated with more developed and known monsters and demons.

The Kassapu may utilize incantations to compel their manifestations at different targets or goals which involve unrest and chaos. They may be used in incantations to initiate change however can be considered highly unpredictable as they seem to be strongly align to be a daytime personification, the fierce sun or weather associated therein (sandstorm?).

---

[29] Tiamat's Brood, Alastair McBeath

[30] Anzu II, Myths from Mesopotamia, Dalley.

[31] Mesopotamian Protective Spirits, pg. 164.

MUSHHUSSU

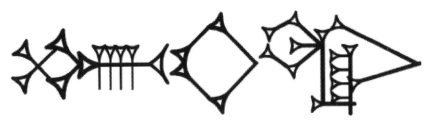

LABBU, the Serpent-Dragon

The Mushhussu, or "Terrifying Serpent" is one of the more well known chaos-monsters of the army of Tiamat and Kingu. A monster created by Tiamat, the Mushhussu is a composite beast which is a serpent-dragon with a lion's head (the Akkadian word 'Labbu' is a title of this monster) and lion-like legs and sharp talons. This image is from the protoliterate period and after the Mushhussu is depicted with more snake-aspects. On the Gates of Babylon the Mushhussu is shown as a Guardian and the Patron Dragon of Marduk, who assumed mastery of this monster after Tiamat went forth into the darkness. The Mushhussu serves the underworld God Ninazu, who is the King of Snakes and may be an Angel of Death for the Gods. Mushhussu holds considerable association with the Horned Serpent species of the area.

The Underworld God Ningishzida, the son of the king of snakes, Ninazu, is also associated with Mushhussu. The depictions of Mushhussu in later mythology indicate that this fearless killer, this embodiment of violent chaos is a guardian of the Gods and Kingship of the City in which he watches over, i.e. Babylon.

Mushhussu appears as a great beast on all fours, a scaled body of a serpent with the forelegs of a lion with the talons of a bird of prey. Crowned in splendor or Meslamu, the Mushhussu often is shown having two horns pointing straight upward.

Throughout ancient Mesopotamian depictions of various gods, a form of the Mushhussu appears. The god Nebo rides upon the furious serpent as well. We must consider that as Nebo is the God of Divination, similar to the Egyptian Thoth, he is the sacred scribe who decrees the destinies of others, thus he is a manifestation of wisdom as well as the serpent-dragon he rides upon.

The Mushhussu is featured throughout mythology as first a great adversary to a god such as Tispak, Ninurta as well as being the patron guardian along with Marduk for Babylon.

In the ancient Akkadian myth, "The Slaying of the Labbu", the Mushhussu is described after it has assaulted humanity. In this tale the the Dragon is said to have been created by "tam-tu-um-ma" or "the sea", perhaps a direct Old Akkadian reference to Tiamat. Enlil illustrated a picture of the Labbu as being fifty miles in length, a mile in width and six cubits wide for his mouth. In the water which he goes forth he raises his tail and sweeps the sky, all of the gods in the heavens were very afraid. Here we see a direct association in how Mesopotamian myth influenced the later Hebrew scribes in composing Revelations 12:4, *"His tail swept a third of the stars out of the sky and flung them to the earth."*.

In the battle which ensued between Tishpak and Labbu, the serpent-dragon created a violent storm, a power consistent with the gods and demons of Mesopotamia. As the Labbu is called the "offspring of the river" Tishpak is called "Abarak Tiamtim", 'the steward of Tiamat' and is considered an agent of hers.[32]

We find in an UR incantation texts that the Mushhussu-dragon, a lion lives in the midst of the sea, drawing an interesting association with later Judeo-Christian symbolism as well.

The type of Mus-hul or Mushhussu is found as a major foundation for the gods to be depicted on, demonstrating a powerful and commanding nature.

---

[32] MAD I, 192 and "Und Mose schrieb dieses Lied auf",Loretz

The Mushhussu may be invoked as a motivation symbol as his form relates to power on earth. Considering that this primordial force is wielded by the victor, it is much centered to the Will as well. Invoking the Mushhussu may in the form of the image of the God in specific areas and initially invoked/charged by the Kassapu.

In a dreaming/astral perspective the Mushhussu may be sought as an empowering monster over the self, thus protection and aggression back to the aggressor, thus chaos and determining the path to victory with your inner and outer earthly challenges.

MUSMAHHU / MUS-SAG-INIM

Seven Headed Dragon

The name of this primordial demon-god announces his fiery divinity and meslamu-radiance. The word MUS is 'serpent' and MAH is 'might, powerful'. The Musmahhu is the Seven-Headed Dragon which in Akkadian is Mus-sag-imin. A type of "group" association of Tiamat's chaos-monsters, Musmahhu is indeed an individual demon-god which was created and after the war went forth to the Zagros Mountains, fighting with, and even assisting other gods like Ninurta.

Known as Mus-mah, this great power of the mountains and the chaotic regions is described as having seven heads and he that brings death. He is shown in an Akkadian cylinder fighting against two horned deities, demonstrating his power within natur even outside of the natural-order itself. Four of his heads are slain yet he still fights on.

A horned serpent, crowned in blackened fire and whose fangs bear the poison of initiation. The most ancient reference of a Seven-headed Dragon, the Musmahhu is shown in early Dynastic art as having a strong dragon body with serpents with long snake-bodies being a part of the beast itself. The Musmahhu was begotten by Tiamat and after the great war of chaos Mus-Sag-imin or Musmahhu went forth to the Mountains which are a common abode for demons and chaos-spirits. Ninurta, the God of War in establishing further structure in the world fought the Musmahhu and banished it further into darkness, wherein it became a dead god.

The Musmahhu may be invoked in the sense of atavistic resurgence, to bring the dark knowledge of the subconscious forth into the waking mind. As our blood flows the life of Kingu, who is of Tiamat so we are too related to the Musmahhu. The primordial dragon represents not only our inner atavistic darkness, the hunger for continued existence and power; yet also the balance we must strive to maintain. This is a primary point in the success in magick; knowing the point of achieveing balance.

The dragon embodies the various aspects of our selves, explored best in the energy-points or chakras from which you may work with the Seven Evil Gods or Sebitti in focusing this energy. As Ninurta slayed this dragon, it was like Tiamat and not dimished, merely a representation of changing types of energy and a conquering of a specific type of force of nature.

CANAANITE ORIGINS OF YAMM/LEVIATHAN

Ninurta battling the Mus-Sag-Imin (Seven headed serpent)

Musmahhu/Mus-Sag-Imin survives in the Ugarit myths as Lotan, the biblical Leviathan. As a manifestation of Prince Yamm, the Sea-God, Lotan was a chaos-inspired form used to cause disorder in the world. The Throne of Prince Yamm was in the ocean, which could attack the dry land with storms when it so desired. Like all aspects of ancient Mesopotamian and Canaanite cultures, the primordial serpent-dragon is eternal, the balance of battle is eternal and life emerges from destruction and chaos. Often viewed as enemy to the religious majority, the dragon-serpent becomes a useful force to many as well.

MUS-SAG-IMIN

Alternative Cuneiform

Invoking the primordial atavism of the Musmahhu will be a controlled ritual of meditation and dreaming introspection. There are several sigils within this book which draw association to the seven headed serpent-dragon and initiation. Utilize that which you find most desireable to your imagination.

USUMGALLU

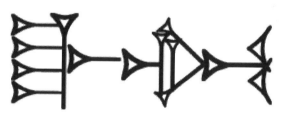

Horned Venomous Serpent

Known as "ferocious or terrifying dragons", the Usumgallu are often written in association with the Mus-usum. The Usumgallu is a derivative of Basmu, "venomous snake" and means "Prime venomous snake", making strong association to this type of horned venomous serpent as being extremely poisonous and even frightening the Gods. **In later times, the Usumgallu like other demons, were used in incantations and oftren epithets for fierce Gods and Kings.** Note this instance of a person of power, a king, being associated with the Usumgallu. This is a clear demonstration of how the serpent-dragon has always been a symbol of power, conquering achievement and overcoming fear. Only in later Judeo-Christian theology did the dragon become a symbol of negativity or moralistic "evil". Most likely this was due to those whom the early Judeo-Christians opposed utilized serpents or dragons in their standards of war or something identifying them. In a Prayer of Marduk[33], the Usumgallu is used as a title for authority and king. The symbol of the Dragon and Serpent in antiquity demonstrates the sense of power in regards to strength, strategy, cunning and the usefulness to wield chaos to then bring order.

In the myths after the Enuma Elish, the Usumgallu and Basmu seem to be often interchangeable with each other, the Usumgallu in a third-millenium text is known as a usumgal/pirig-dragon which is "roaring in the flood[34]".

With associations to authority of "King" and "Ruler", the title of usumgallu is interchanged with Ruler, thus Tiamat as demonstrated with Kingu holds the divine authority to bestow the diadem of leadership of her chosen. In numerous depictions of Marduk, he stands astride in full divinity with the Dragon-Serpent whom he rides *rather* than destroying it.

The Kassapu may invoke the Usumgallu as an epithet of the self; remember your words create the belief and reality you live in. Choose them wisely.

---

[33] Babylonian Magic and Sorcery by King

[34] De Genouillax Trouvaille 1:3, 11

BASMU

Venomous Serpent

The first dragon-serpent of Tiamat's creation, the Basmu is a horned serpent which is a representation of a horned Mesopotamian snake known as the "Cerestes Cerestes". A Sumerian synonym of the Basmu is MUS-SA-TUR and translates "Snake Womb/Womb Snake[35]". And "Birth-Goddess Snake"[36]

The Basmu is a venomous snake which is from the Sumerian word "Usum" and Mus-sa-tur and in Akkadian Basmu. The Basmu is identified anthropomorphically as being a great horned serpent with forelegs. It seems reasonable that after the fall of the chaos-gods of Tiamat that the **Basmu** is related to the underworld god **Ningizida**, possibly being manifest as the two horned serpents around the staff or from the shoulders of Ningizida. The species "Cerastes Cerastes" is the horned serpent which is found throughout the Middle East. The horned serpent is poisonous and a strikingly beautiful species, two sharp horns arise perfectly from the head.

The Basmu is described as a "sea dragon-snake" in the myth KAR 6 and in Angim 33 the Basmu and Usum live in the "fortress of the mountains". We can attest that there is properly several type of Basmu created by Tiamat if we can consider each definition from myth.

---

[35] McBeath, pg. 71.

[36] Wiggerman, F.A.M. pg 169

The goddess Ishara's symbol, who is indentical with Ishtar/Inanna, was the Basmu-snake, in which she is a balanced goddess of both war and love. As a fertility goddess, Ishara was later known as a form of the Scorpion and the constellation known as Scorpius.

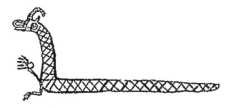

A depiction of Tiamat who appears with the same traits as the Usumgallu.

The Basmu is closely associated with the underworld gods after the war of chaos, specifically with the earth-goddess Ninmah who bears the divine epithet of "womb snake", the goddess Nintud has the bottom half of a snake and the upper parts of a woman, much the the later descriptions of Enchidna, the serpent-demoness and wife of Typhon of ancient Greece and Asia Minor. The name of Nintur and Ninmah are names for the goddess Ninhursaga, whom is associated with the constellation of Hydra, known as MUL.MUS.

Hydra is a significant constellation as many underworld deific masks are attributed to it, including Ningishzida and even Ereshkigal. The Basmu was associated with Ningishzida as well; note the two "Cerestes Cerestes" or horned snakes on his shoulders. While the Basmu of Tiamat was described as horned, yet gigantic with the legs and claws of a lion, it no doubt had some shape-shifting ability and possibly even reproduction considering the many following.

LAHAMU

The water god and primordial giant

Known as the "**massaru tamti**", the Lahmu is one of the first monsters spawned by Tiamat. Lahmu is a word which means "the hairy one" and is depicted as a fierce giant who has long hair and is bearded. His name along with his other pair created by Tiamat and Absu represents "Muddy ones" and may hold reference to their ascension of primal earth and water.

The Lahmu is shown in a cylinder as holding up a lion. The Lahamu is originally the first along with Lahamu were two primordial Gods and the first of Tiamat and Absu. Wiggermann[37] suggests that Lahamu is identified as a "Naked Hero" and was originally a spirit of the river who masters wild animals and takes care of domestic herds with the life-giving water.

The hair which is the basis of his name indicates that water is symbolized by his flowing hair with three pairs of curls. Lahmu/Lahamu is considered to be distinctly different from Gods, in part with no image or personification of Lahmu with a horned tiara. While Lahmu and Lahamu are the primordial in the sense they were before the pantheon of Gods who banished Tiamat to darkness, they were a part of the kingdoms of the Absu and served Ea. In Eridu the Temple of Ea contained fifty statues of Lahmu. Ea/Enki commanded sway over them after Tiamat primarily, giving them the epithet of "**massaru tamti**" or "**guards of the sea**". We often see the Lahmu fighting other lions or creatures, perhaps to control their urge for violence.

Lahmu controls under the authority of Ea the bolt of the sea and the flow of the fish. The Lahmu is later depicted as a type of household protective spirit, including being a guardian monster

---

[37] Mesopotamian Protective Spirits, the Ritual Texts, F.A.M. Wiggermann

of the Assyrian Kings. In addition the bearded Lahamu is known as "ur-sag", which is "hero" and actually means "lion". One of the prototypes for the later Nergal and other conquering ones is actually Lahmu. The Lahmu's companion which he is depicted with in art is the Bull-Man or Kusarikku.

Another interesting Chthonic aspect of Lahmu is that he is shown in various art carrying two serpents, even as a caduceus as a symbol of magickial power, fertility, balance and wisdom.

Utilizing Lahmu may be done with the invocations and hymns to Ea/Enki, wherein you consecrate an image of the Lahmu for a specific 'guardian' purpose.

UGALLU

Umu-rabu, Great Storm Beast, the Lion-Demon

When one describes Mesopotamian demons, either in text or art, the first image to come to mind is the lion-headed demon, called the Ugallu. This lion-demon is the primary demon-monster found in the underworld, two of which are guards for Ereshkigal. Nergal, having lion aspects to his nature, also instructs the Ugallu on torture. Clear by the plentiful depictions of numerous Ugallu, or "soldiers", there is more than one and there is an 'early' and 'later' version with the same title.

The Ugallu as the Storm Beast.

The Ugallu is the "Big-Weather Beast", The Akkadian word ugallu as refered by Wiggerman[38] is a loanword from the Sumerian u-gal, which is "big storm beast" and the actual term is "umu-rabu" relating to "day beast". The early forms of Ugallu is like the "weather-beast" which goes before Ishkur/Adad is a lion-beast which is on all fours, this is the "Umurabu". Marduk fought and defeated this form of the Ugallu alongside Tiamat.

The later Ugallu-demon is a human-bodied figure who has the head and ears of a lion, human hands with the claw-talons and feet of a bird of prey. The upright figure of the Ugallu shows this type of demon-monster as having a strong body of a man,

---

[38] Mesopotamian Protective Spirits.

wearing a short kilt, the lower arm (pointing more downward) holding a **Kakku** (mace) and the raised arm holding a **Gir** (dagger). The Ugallu is also shown with a Gir in his belt.

The fierce lion, whose ears are upright fanged and seeking to fulfill his hunger demonstrates that this type of power is associated with Nergal-Erra, the God of the Underworld, plague and war.

The Ugallu monster was like Pazuzu, a mighty power which is both beneficial and destructive depending on how it was invoked. As noted, the lion-demon image was consistent for many of the demonic personifications including Lamashtu and Pazuzu. Clay figurines of Ugallu were kept in houses or even burial grounds to protect from illness. Please keep in mind that idols represent the 'power' attributed to the Gods, not specifically that it is the "God" itself.

The Ugallu is the monster-demon shown in old Babylonian seals with Nergal, often holding a man upside down and is an attendant of the God of the Scimitar in the Underworld, who is Nergal. The Ugallu is thus a bringer of disease as well, being an attendant of Nergal. Ugallu is also depicted on many Neo-Assyrian palace reliefs as well, being a great protector of the ruling powers.

The Doorkeeper of the Underworld, Petu (known as Nedu) may also be of the Ugallu, his form, like other Underworld Deific Masks shows him also with a human body, a lion head and the claws of a bird, a sacred animal of the underworld.

The lion-demon has a varied and colorful mythology. At some points a guardian against disease, at other times an associate of Adad and an enemy of the sun-god. The Ugallu represent specific "evil days" when Adad/Iskur the storm-god and are released from the sky wherein the howl and roar through storms.

URIDIMMU
Raging Lion

The **Uridimmu** or "**Raging/Mad Lion**" is perhaps one of the most recognizable of the Monsters of Tiamat. The word uridimmu is from the Sumerian **ur-idim**; the word **Ur** meaning "**lion/dog**" and idim being "**howling, raging mad**"[39]. There seems a strong connection with Uridimmu the Monster of Tiamat and Ur.Idim or Urdimmu the constellation. The Urdimmu in the Creation Epic is also associated with a "rabid" or "Raging Dog".

The Akkadian "Ur" with the word zibu meaning "Jackal" could indicate a strong sense of the Therionick imagery of this monster. The Uridimmu is depicted in an Iranian vase where he stands upright with the upper-body being a bearded man adorned in the horned cap of divinity, the bottom half is a bull and he is holding a crescent moon (upright) staff.

In addition to the Uridimmu as the raging lion there is also the Urmahlullu, which is "Lion Man" and is left out of the list of demons/monsters gained by Marduk in his ascension to the throne. The Urmahlullu is depicted as an unwinged lion-centaur. In late Second Millennium BC is the first known appearance of this demon-god, it may be a development of the Uridimmu. Being a guardian demon, the Uridimmu was

---

[39] A more detailed reference is found in Wiggerman, Mesopotamian Protective Spirits, pg 172.

utilized as guardians of the King and various temples. The Uridimmu, with the horned cap of divinity is a symbol of earthly power through the determined will; thus may be utilized in symbolism concerning the protection of a home or person.

GIRTABLULLU
Scorpion-Man

A fierce monster, having a human head, bearded with the body of a scorpion, the girtablullu is described as bearing a terrifying melammu, which drapes the mountains. The scorpion is related the not only the heat of the Sun, yet also of the underworld. Fertility, an association of the snake as well as the scorpion is also an indication of this dual chaos-monster of love/death.

Originally a class of demons created by Tiamat, the Girtablullu or "scorpion man" became an attendant of the Sun God Shamash/Utu who protected the sun and the Mountain of Mashu where the sun rises in the east. The Girtablullu may offer protection against other malicious demons if they deem suitable. The Girtablullu appears as a bearded male who has the hind quarters of a scorpion, a snake headed penis (like Pazuzu) and sometimes bearing wings. The horned cap of divinity is also worn in some depictions. In the Epic of Gilgamesh, the Girtablullu is joined with his wife, a scorpion-woman divinity as well.

Girtablullu who bears the fearsome Melammu

Girtablullu may be perceived as a guardian of the cycle of the life and death bringing sun, Shamash/Utu along with the stinging rays symbolized by the scorpion's tail. In addition the Kassapu may invoke the protection of the Girtablullu when seeking the strength to rise up each day in a period of struggle or hardship.

SUHURMASU
Goat-Fish

The Goat fish, relating to the later "Capricorn" no doubt holds association with Ea and is derived from the Sumerian "Suhurmas" which is associated as a real fish, while the Akkadian "suhurmasu" which is "Carp-Goat". Suhurmasu is associated with the waters of purification and in one Sumerian incantation the priest is called "Sanga-mah-abzu-ke"[40] which translates "purification priest of the Absu" which is directly associated with Ea, Lord of the Deep. Ea carries the staff of the ram, even being identified with the Suhurmasu, which seems to indicate this particular monster is of significance to the god.

The Suhurmasu may be invoked and meditated upon in bathing rituals, cleansing the self of troubles and seeking clear direction from your personal god on the solution.

KULULLU
Fish Centaur

The Kulullu is mentioned in the Creation Epic tablets as being created by Tiamat before her battle against Marduk. The word Ku-lu-ul-lu is "Fish-man" and relates to several other words which may hold the clues of the underworld from which this god derives.

---

[40] Wiggerman, page 184. Section 10 d.

Kulullu the Fish-Centaur god.

A "Ku-li-li" is a "Fish Woman"[41] and "Kulilu is "dragonfly". This god seems associated with the Ku-li-an-na or "Kililtu" which is "friend of Anu". The Kulilitu is an insect or "little bride" which according to Wiggerman in "Mesopotamian Protective Spirits" may have been blended in translations.

The "Fish Centaur" appears is part Kissugu with the lower half having the scales of a fish. The tablets of Gods and their forms make reference to a monster that has the head of a kissugu who also has bird claws. The Kulullu is associated with Ea and also with streams and the water itself. Kulullu no doubt has similar association to the subconscious mind; the varied therionick form of the god it also useful in working with concerning the mastery of unconscious knowledge.

KUSARIKKU

Bull man

The Kusarikku, who is Bull-Man or "Bison" appears as the body of a gigantic, monstrously strong bull (often standing upright) and the bearded head of a man who is double- horned. The Kusarikku is associated with Utu/Shamash and is featured on an ancient battle mace dedicated to the Sun god.

The Kassapu who seeks to work with the Kusarikku should consider that this monster is a directly solar/light/black flame manifestation of the ferocity of Shamash/Utu.

---

[41] Mesopotamian Protective Spirits

URMAHLULLU
Lion-Centaur

The fierce lion-man, from "ur-mah" meaning "lion" and "untamed man" is an un-winged lion-centaur. He is shown on a middle-assyrian period carving holding a club in his hand and wearing cap of divinity. The lion-man or Urmahlullu is utilized as a protective monster against the demon **Mukil-res-lemutti**, a winged servant of death who is known as the "Upholder of Evil".

GODS AND DEMONS

ANUNNAKI
Gods of the Underworld

The Anunnuaki – Igigi are great gods, old gods who reside in the shadows of the underworld. The Enunaki/Anunnaki is chthonic and empyrean deities of the underworld and the heavens respectively. The word Anuna is associated with the term "princely offspring" according to Black[42] and relates to gods which assisted humanity and represents the multitude of divinity. The Anunnaki later are connected with the underworld almost exclusively. The Anunnaki were said to be offspring of Anu and Ki and thus would be related to the other gods including the Seven Maskim.

Marduk divided the Anunnaki into 300 hundred to guard the skies and 300 under the earth. The Anunnaki was pleased and

---

[42] Gods, Demons and Symbols of Ancient Mesopotamia, Jeremy Black and Anthony Green.

offered to build a great Temple for Marduk. The new god was most happy and decreed that the Anunnaki build Babylon. The Anunnaki build great Ziggurats for not only Marduk, yet also Anu, Ellil and Ea. Soon the Anunnaki had built their individual shrines. Clearly by the reference in which they are used, the Annunaki is a term describing loosely all the gods which include the commonly named ones, in addition to unknown gods and chthonic deities.

ANSAR – ANU

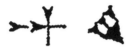

Primordial Sky

In ancient Mesopotamian lore, Ansar along with Kisar are a pair of ancient Gods who represent the Heavens (An) and Kisar (Ki – Earth). The Epic of Creation gives this God as the second after Lahmyu and Lahamu who are the children of Tiamat and Absu.

Ansar is essentially the "whole sky" who is a God who is less associated with the later Gods and humanity, for he is ancient. The main difference between Ansar and Anu is the application of their domain and their interaction within it. Specifically, Ansar is a very calm God while Anu is the more violent and active deity. It can be considered that Ansar is mostly inactive with humanity, while Anu is the great power which begets gods and demons.

KI

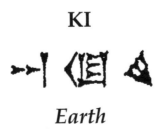

Earth

Kisar/Ki is the Mother or "Whole Earth", she who provides the fruits and fertile ground from which other gods may fertilize and empower. Ki is neither darkness nor light; she is fierce and beautiful earth, the deserts and mountains. She allows the growth of nature and all which exists upon it to be.

Ansar and Ki bore Anu, the supreme God of the Heavens. Ninkigal or Ki/Kisar as she is called is similar to "Tartara" called the Mother of Typhon by Hyginus[43]; which is basically an epithet of Ge to represent what is "under" the earth rather than above. This concept is similar to Ninkigal, except she is both the ground and underneath it properly and all encompassing. The Seven Maskim or Sebitti are called "Throne Bearers of Ninkigal" as well, indicating the Godddess is viewed in a chthonic nature. Ninkigal is also associated with Ereshkigal in reference to the underworld.

ANU

The god of the sky

Anu is a perfect example of transcendant leadership, the divine and constant authority within the spirit. Anu is a diverse yet reclusive deity compared to the duality of western religions. The son of Anshar and Ki, Anu is the God whose symbol is the Horned Crown upon an altar.

Being the head of the Old Gods of the ancient Sumerian/Chaldean pantheon, Anu is a powerful God of the Heavens, the sky and that of the Spirit. He commands and creates both Gods and Demons, for he is balanced in nature. As

---

[43] Python, a Study of the Delphic Myth by Joseph Fontenrose. Pg 78

both the Sun and Moon travel through the domain of Anu, the great god of the sky accepts the balance of darkness and light.

Anu is a great power of the sky, the authority of divinity and that which engenders rain. It is through the engendering with Ki the plants and vegetation of the earth. Azag, the great warrior chaos-demon who later battled Ninurta, was engendered by Anu and Ki and dwelt in Kur, the mountain-land of rebels.

To understand the Gods one must look not only within the self, yet also to nature. Perceive Anu as the Great Sky, on one day or night he brings beautiful and clear skies, the next filled with clouds and great storms. Anu is knowledgeable of all of these things, for he assists in engendering the great demons and Gods of nature and of humanity. Anu confers divinity and power upon who he wishes and what they may do for him. Aiding Marduk in his preparation for battle, he created numerous winds and storms to rally into the army of the new God.

Anu upon MusHussu

Anu is associated with the Wolf-constellation, along with his daughter Lamashtu. Anu is shown on the Maltai rock reliefs and the Zincirli stele riding the serpent-dragon Mushussu. We see also on boundary stones the symbol of Anu, the horned cap atop the serpent-dragon.

Anu is also the husband of Ki in is the father of the Seven Evil Gods, Sebitti or Maskim Hul. Anu is also the father of Lamashtu, the goddess cast from the heavens as she wished to devour and drink the blood of children. As the gods required humans for maintaining their earthly temples, this was not an accepted practice. At a point later, Lamashtu worked with Anu at times as did the Sebitti.

To make incense offerings to Anu or Ansar one may do it in accordance to one specific god rather than two. Anu may be seen as the active consciousness of Ansar who is not approachable.

ANTU
Mother of Ishtar

This is the wife of Anu and mother of Ishtar. In some traditions she is considered a manifestation of Ishtar, especially in the Antum (as she is also called) represents the overcast sky which pours forth rain. Antu is thus identical to Inanna as a Goddess of Storms.

EA

Patesi-gal-Zuab
The King of the Deep and Lord of Magick

Another name of Ea is **Patesi-gal-Zuab** which translates "Great Ruler of the Deep". Ea is known by other names as Enki, Niudimmund (the epithet of Ea as creator) and Hea. Ea is the Powerful and ancient god of Fresh Water, Incantations, Magick and Wisdom. He is the underworld aspect of hidden knowledge. Ea is the twin brother of the God Iskur known also as Adad. Ea is the God of the Depths and dwells in the Absu – named from his Father whom he killed and cast further into the abyss, placing upon his own head the Crown of the Gods. Ea then dwelt in splendor in this great temple.

Ea Lord of the Deep.

The Cult Center of Ea is the E-absu which means "Abzu's House" at Eridu. The Seven Maskim or Demons of the Ignited Spheres are Throne-Bearers of Ea and act according to his bidding when needed.

While Ea is a great God he was not able to bear the anger of his Mother, Tiamat, whose sorceries and howling were too much for him. The Priests of Tiamat who reform her worship and manifestation in this world should not be too quick to condemn Ea, for he is too of Her Royal Blood and should be respected for his manifestation in nature. Ea determines destinies and was highly regarded by the conquering Assyrian Kings such as Shalmaneser II. The Black Obelisk offers an invocation which includes Ea called "The King of the Deep, Determiner of Destinies".

EA IN DRAGON-MONSTER FORM

Ea manifests in various forms and is described in a Babylonian tablet as having the head of a serpent, ears like a basilisk, horns are twisted into three curls, a veil in his headband and the body is that of a Suh-Fish, being full of stars and his feet are as claws. In this form Ea is called the **SASSU-URINNU**, a sea-monster.

In earlier texts Ea appears as a God seated upon a throne with a long beard, crowned in a cap with many horns and wearing a long robe. Water flows from his two shoulders and often he many fish swimming from it.

Ea also takes the form of a Goat-fish in periods of time as well as a LAHMU IPPIRU. This sea-monster appears with features of a lion, bird's claws and a body of a kissugu. He is called the *nutum*, a monster of heaven and earth.

Surmassu the Altar of Ea

Ea is also represented as bearing a curved staff with the horned head of a ram.

The Babylonian Cuneiform texts describe Ea as being the Lord of Magic, thus a Luciferian source of wisdom and inner power. His title, "Lord of the Deep" presents his mighty knowledge of the above and below.

Ea is invoked in authority in a prayer to Marduk as "king of the Abyss, father of the gods and the Lord of Wisdom[44]".

---

[44] Leonard King, Babylonian Magic and Sorcery

DAMKINA

The Mother Goddess & Wife of Ea

Damkina is the wife of Ea and the mother of Marduk. She is a great mother goddess, whom was given offerings of fish in Lagas and Umma in the earliest records of history. The cult center of Damkina was Malgum. The great king Assurnasirpal II (883-859 BC) had a temple built to Damkina at Kalhu which is the modern Nimrud.

The serpent of fertility and wisdom before the Tree of Life, whose roots take nourishment in the darkness.

APKALLU

Guardian Demons & Bringers of Wisdom

The seven Apkallu or "Sages" are instructing-demons or 'watchers' which came from the Temple of Absu, or the Ocean depths on the command of Ea to instruct mankind on development before the flood. The word Apkallu is the Akkadian word for "Sage". Ea, Damkina, Enlil, Marduk, Gerra and Nabu are listed as "Sage of the Gods" in early Mesopotamian texts.

It must be noted that the Apkallu are not the Seven Sebitti or Seven-Maskim-Gods to which this work is dedicated, as the Apkallu and Sebitti are shown in different ritual texts. The Apkallu lead by Adapa of Eridu take human form or at least part-human form with sometimes having the heads or bodies of fish as well as winged gods bearing the heads of griffins, eagles or ravens.

The Seven Sages are depicted as appearing as the fish-men, human males wearing the horned cap with three pairs of horns. We see the most known images of the Apkallu as the bird-headed and winged demons on the reliefs from the palace of Ashurnasirpal II. They are found on numerous other types of art from cylinders to carvings. The Apkallu are flanking the Sacred Tree or healing those who are sick. Modern Luciferians may view the Apkallu as types of 'Augoeides' which is the individual daimon (demon/daemon), true will or later known as the holy guardian angel of the individual.

The griffin-demon of ancient Babylonia and Assyria is a guardian-spirit who appears with the head of a bird of prey, wings descending down (underworld) and upward (signifying the air or heaven) holding the cone of blessing and bearing two daggers in their belt. The Apkallu are the equivalent of the Watchers who instructed humanity and inspired evolution in the human race.

The concept of having a *'true will'* or *'divine god'* is not found origin-wise in modern magick, rather it is as old as written records. We find the Antediluvian kings of Mesopotamia in the *Warka King List* have their own Apkallu paired with their names', finding it that this divine will of the king guided the development during each reign.

The Apkallu instructs the individual (in ancient Assyria the King) with skills. We find this the basic foundation of sorcery or magick within any tradition. Obtaining knowledge, apply the knowledge and gain skill along with the result of wisdom and success. The Luciferian works exactly in this way and the Apkallu may be viewed as an excellent pre-Christian concept purified from the dualistic dogma.

ENLIL

Lord of the Seven Storms

Enlil means "Lord Wind" and is considered the moving force in nature. En means "lord" in the sense of mastery and production, like a King. His very nature connection is the spring, the Winds of growth and change. Enlil is the God which manifests the spring rains, causing the vines and crops to grow. He is a foundation on the continued existence of life in this sense.

Enlil is the guardian of the Tablets of Destiny after the war against Tiamat. An interesting association is that Enlil's Temple in Ekur is an abode for Utukku-demons which are associated with the God. Enlil may be offered to in spring, especially if you are cultivating a witch-garden or simply planting trees, flowers or such. Enlil's cult center was E-Kur, a mountain home in Nippur, north of Sumer.

The name of Enlil also possesses a sinister side as well. In "The Cuthaean Legend of Naram-Sin[45]" Enlil is the god of "evil spirits, specters, ghosts and fiends, creatures of Enlil" whom Naram-Sin commands an officer to cut one of the mountain-tribe enemies to see if they bleed.

An interesting aspect of Enlil is the dark nature he possesses along with the other more 'ancient gods'. Hugo Radau[46] described the violent nature of Enlil and of his "Seven Sons" or

---

[45] The Sultantepe Tablets IV. The Cuthaean Legend of Naram-Sin by O.R. Gurney Anatolian Studies, Volume V 1955.

[46] Sumerian Hymns and Prayers to NIN-IB, Hugo Radau.

manifestations. Drawing a connection to the Seven Sebitti, the names of Enlil as Seven Gods are written:

1. Bar-ul-li-gar-ra
2. Pap-su-ug-ge-gar-ra
3. Lil
4. Lil-duq-qa-bur
5. Nin-sub-bi-gu-sag
6. As-sir
7. Ne-gun

Enlil is known as En-ug-ug-ga, "Lord of the Seven Storms" and works with the "te-su-u qar-du-te su-nu" or "the Seven are mighty destroyers". Radau makes reference that Seven Gods of Enlil also appear as the Asakku later on. Enlil is often changed with Anu in different tablets as the father of Lamashtu, who is the sister of the Seven Maskim or Sebitti.

We find his son, Nin-ib as being a god who is "a roamer about night", and "usumgal...a lier in wait" as well.

NINLIL

The Mother Goddess

A very pleasant and benevolent Goddess, Ninlil is the wife of Enlil. She manifests the motherly love and protection of the people. Ninlil was raped by Enlil when she was young; in this violent copulation she became pregnant with Nergal. Ninlil is known also as Mullisu/Mullitu in Assyria and the wife of Assur. The patron beast-form of the mother goddess is a lion.

NINURTA-NIN-IB

War God & Origin of Biblical Nimrod

Nin-ib is one of the most ancient of the Sumerian gods; his name itself means "son" and "mighty warrior of the chief god of Nippur, Enlil". The god is known to wear and illuminate Melammu before all. Over a period of time Nin-ib is transformed into Ningirsu as a god of growth and later as the war-god Ninurta.

The Sumerian word 'Nin-urta' means "Lord of arable earth" and is a great hero deified in Sumerian and Babylonian legends. The God of War, Ninurta whose origins of worship are found in ancient Sumer is a fierce god who later inspired the Assyrians. The son of Enlil, Ninurta had a temple at Esu-me-sa at Nippor. The god Ningirsu is suggested to have been at one time the same god as Ninurta. Ninurta may have been pronounced as "Nimrod" in ancient times, a mighty war-god who 'troubles' the early Hebraic tribes. Ninurta represents the defense against enemies of his people, then being a god of agriculture and the pastoral fields. In such a sense Ninurta seems identical to Marduk of Babylon.

Originally a fertility deity, Ninurta was associated with growth of plants, crops and even fish. A god near Lagash, called Ningirsu is identical in function and description of Ninurta and is suggested to be the same god.

Ninurta was the war-hero who fought the Anzu demon and retrieved the Tablet of Destinies which was stolen from Enlil. In Anzu Ninurta is the leader of the Annunaki. In a dream by Babylonian ruler Gudea Ningirsu/Ninurta appears in the form of Anzu (Imdugud) as it seems he assimilated the power of this god when defeating it. Ninurta appeared as a symbol of a watching bird at times, being both skilled at war and diligent in his advice and support to famers and herders. Ninurta also battled the mountain-demon Asag to retain temporary order in the world.

Ninurta is invoked and praised by the Assyrian kings; Assurnasirpal II (883-859 BC) built a temple to the god in the capitol Kalhu (called Nimrud).

Ninurta is depicted as a bearded man who is aiming the bow and arrow, much like anthropomorphic depictions of Marduk and Assur. Ninurta is described in the Anzu tale as "Broad of chest, who forms the battle array" and his battles are described as the "armour-plated breast was bathed in blood[47]". In biblical studies[48]

Ninurta before the Mussagimin Serpent-Dragon by Marchozelos

---

[47] ANZUII, Myths from Mesopotamia

[48] Dictionary of Deities and Demons in the Bible

NINGIRSU
A God of Growth

An older manifestation of Ninurta, the name of Ningirsu means "Lord of Girsu". By the period of the Third Dynasty of Ur Ningirsu was assimilated into Ninurta. The symbol of this god is the plough and his sacred form is a lion.

SIN

The God of the Moon

The Sumerian Nanna/Sin is the Moon God, the very son of Enlil and Ninlil. Nanna is the established God of UR in ancient Sumeria, replacing the former Moon God Kingu after the war of chaos. Nanna may be considered the Moon in its' waxing elements while Kingu may be the waning and eclipsed elements.

Nanna is depicted upon a throne bearing the circle and rod of divinity and power, bearded and wearing the horned cap of divinity, each side having four horns each as in tradition of Gods and Goddesses. E-gish-shir-gal (house in the great light) was the name of the Chief Temple in Ur for Nanna.

Sin can also be viewed as a protective and cursing god as well, even if he could not compare to the mighty Sebitti. On an inscription of Ashurbanipal of Assyria, the disc of Sin had a curse inscribed *"Whoever plots evil against Ashurbanipal, King of Assyria, and begins hostilities against him, I will send an evil death upon. I will bring his life to an end by the swift iron dagger, the firebrand, famine or the devastation of Gira (a variant of the Pest God*

Nergal)." The moon holds the keys to madness and paranoia as well, the death offered by the lunar current is more lengthy and foreboding than that of the Sun.

NEBO

The God of Divination, the Scribe

Nebo, spelled also Nabu is the divine scribe god, the Mesopotamian equivalent of Hellenic Apollon and the Egyptian Thoth. Nebo is the divine scribe who may be sought in divinatory workings and the articulation of thought and writing. Nebo is considered the son of Bel-Marduk, from which he was carried from Syria to Babylon from the ancient Ammorites. The symbol of Nebo is the writing stylus, the form of a wedge and he is depicted as a kingly male like Marduk who also stands/rides upon a mighty serpent-dragon.

Esarhaddon (681 – 669 B.C.) was the son of Sennacherib and was a mighty Assyrian King who put down many rebellions during a period of turmoil for the empire. Esarhaddon's invocations to Nebo are reflected as supporting him in war.

The symbol of Nebo

The Seleucid Empire venerated Nebo and Bel-Marduk in the cities appropriate, no doubt finding common ideals in Zeus (Bel-Marduk) and Apollon (Nebo). Antiochus I Soter (280 – 260 B.C.) recorded tablets in Babylon as rightful King and invoked Nebo. Antiochus called upon Nebo and named him "Nabu, son of Esagila, first-born of Marduk, of highest rank…" and "Nabu, exalted son, powerful leader of the gods, who for exaltation was born."

Nabu/Nebo is thus a deific mask utilized by the Kassapu to visualize, find the possibility for manifestation and then compelling it to manifest over a period of time. Nebo is thus a Luciferian god and one which compels possibility through the subconscious.

ADAD

ISHKUR / RAMMAN/ADAR
The God of Storms

The Storm God known in Akkadian as Adad and Sumerian as Ishkur, Adad manifests as Ramman which means "Thunderer" and Rimmon in Aramaic. Adad is a powerful and fierce god, who holds a great power over the forces of storms in nature. Adad is a lord of omens, whose symbol is the Bull and the Lightning Fork. Adad is a powerful god who bears a horned tiara and who is both benevolent and violent when his thirst demands.

In most traditions Adad is the son of Anu and his wife is Sala, although it is consistent that he is the son of Enlil. The ministers or visers of Adad are two gods named Sullat and Hanis. The depiction of Adad is a bearded god wearing the horned cap of divinity, holding the symbol of the lightning fork and riding upon the winged lion-dragon, one of the children of Tiamat Musmahhu who joined the Gods.

Adad has a balanced representation as a god, while on one hand a fierce storm god who is joined by the cloud, called "Adad's calves" he brings great storms yet also the beneficial rains needed for agriculture. At Assur, Adad was worshipped along with Anu in twin Ziggurats.

Adad and Ishtar of Nineveh

Offering libations to Adad may be done for workings of storms which bring creative change, initiatory wisdom and the power to overcome challenging obstacles.

Adar is also a name of Adad in antiquity; his name is "the sun is the south".

BEL-MARDUK

God of Babylon & Bringer of Order

Marduk was the patron God of Babylon and was the mate of Zarpanitum. While Bel-Marduk is regarded as the one who battled his ancestors Tiamat and Kingu, creating life and order from this battle, he possesses too, like other Gods a shadow aspect.

The Sumerian Mar is "Sun" and when placed with the Second Dynastic Period Amar-ud brings form to Marutuk and the later variant form of Marodakh. The utu-k was present a older form for the Sumerian word for "sun" and "storm". The name Utu is a divine epithet Uta-ulu which is the "South-storm" of Ninurta.

The name of Mar-utu (a) k thus shows the origin of "Son of the Shade" or "Son of the Storm". Equally so Marduk is called "eldest son of the Ocean Deep[49]". How can one possibly associate Marduk as a "son of the storm" which could hold such violent aspects? The answer is in his attributes and nature according to the legends.

Marduk in the Epic of Creation is filled with an inner fire and holds the power of lightning. Marduk additionally controls and commands the Four Winds, the Southwind, the Northwind, the Eastwind and the Westwind. They are given to him at his birth by Anu, a God who has both destructive and creative qualities.

---

[49] Tablet K from Devils and Evil Spirits of Ancient Babylonia.

In addition Marduk also commands other storms and winds, a cyclone, a flood-storm and rides a "Chariot of the Storm" which is deemed terrible.

Bel-Marduk as the usurping god

Thus Marduk may be more appropriately known as "The Sun of the Storm" rather than "Son of the Sun". His nature was to be the usurper against Tiamat, for his ancestors are Gods of Darkness.

In addition, a symbol of Marduk is the Mushussu-dragon, a monster created by Tiamat in the great war of Chaos. A common name for Marduk later on was Bel, meaning "Lord". The Gods in their seat of power or dwelling are called "Bel" there, the same as "Baal". Here we find a common association with the myths of Ras-Shamra, otherwise known as ancient Ugarit as *Ba'al the God of Storms and War*.

Ba'al is called "Lord of Thunderstorms" and "Rider of Clouds". Ba'al fights the primordial YAMM, the God of the Chaos-Sea, who is an anthropomorphic form for Lotan or Leviathan in Hebraic myth.

The Epic of Creation in various forms displays Marduk in the Babylonian and Assur in the Assyrian depiction in the palace of Sennacherib.

Marduk was crowned by Anu as having the highest destiny of the gods, even ones older than he. At his coronation as God of Babylon, Marduk is given fifty names which describe his nature of rule. They proclaimed him the "Majesty of the Gods", who's bright light casts down for all others to walk in his illumination.

THE FIFTY NAMES OF MARDUK

The symbol of Marduk – the dragon and the spear upon the altar.

Divine Epithets are titles given to Deific Masks representing the essence and role of the God. Just as when Tiamat begets her monsters of chaos she takes the form of Hubar which is the Epithet if her creating.

The names of Marduk were granted to him as he was crowned King and made the law maker and god. Offerings to Marduk may be with Myrrh when the conditions are appropriate.

The Kassapu is utilizing the deific mask of Marduk from a perspective of Kingu, that you are controlling the God accordingly. In your workings with Marduk, you are gaining a strength and expansion of knowledge through this interaction.

The Fifty names of Marduk are utilized with the specific action in which they are used. If seeking to bring order into your life, you will simply burn incense with an invocation to Marduk, in the dawn or at noon when the sun is visible. As you see the smoke billow up, recite the epithet of Marukka (bringing order) for example and visualize the most chaotic elements in your life being brought to control in the near future. Often in dreams following these workings, your answers will appear more visible to you in your conscious mind.

Understanding a new perspective on the names is important. "Violence" can be consistent discipline and tenacity towards your goals. Bringing "order" is simply overcoming difficult obstacles in your immediate life and "light for his people" can be simply that you have a clear direction and leadership for your life.

THE FIFTY NAMES OF THE CONQUERING GOD OF BABYLON

If incantations to Marduk are employed, it may be beneficial to use several of the epithets here to further empower your spells.

MARUKKA – The God who compelled order.

MARUTUKKU – He is the help of his people (Babylon)

MERSHAKUSHU – Fierce, Violent yet considerate, furious and calm when needed. The Balanced.

LUGAL-DIMMER-ANKIA – Whose command is higher than the Gods his father.

NARI-LUGAL-DIMMER-ANKIA – Director of all the gods, who founded our dwellings in heaven and earth. Who decreed the stations of the Anunnaki.

Under the above name, there are three additional assigned to Nari-Lugal-Dimmer-Ankia:

ASARLUHI – The first is the name which his father Anu gave unto him.

NAMTILA – The god who gives life, who restored the damaged gods as if they were his creation.

NAMRU – The god who purifies the path.

ASARE – Giver of the fertile land.

ASAR-ALIM – Whose council is valued.

ASAR-ALIM-NUNA – The Honored One, the Light of Anu who beget him.

TUTU – Creator of renewal. Who invents incantation that his Will is made upon the four directions of the Winds.

The second of TUTU is ZI-UKKINA, the light of his people, who fixed the places in the sky.

The third of TUTU is ZIKU, who upholds the purification of his Will. Who illuminated mankind and liberated them in life itself!

The forth is AGAKU, Lord of the Incantation who revives the dying. For Agaku is the god which has the power to give life.

The Fifth is TUKU, whose spell is pure.

SHAZU – The intuitive god, who establishes the gods' assembly.

SUHRIM - who uproots the enemy by force of arms, who scatters those against the winds.

ZAHRIM – Destroyer of enemies…

ZAHGURIM – Who destroyed the enemy himself in battle…

ENBILULU – The Lord, mighty one is responsible for sacrificial omens. Who brings the life enriching waters…

EPADUN – Lord of the countryside and the canals which feed the land.

HEGAL – Who is abundance.

SIRSIR – Who usurped the throne of Tiamat, who established the Mountain of the Gods. Who had the Will of his forebear Tiamat to face her when no other could.

MALAH – who is the boatman who has conquered the depths of the subconscious, to rise upon the waters of Tiamat.

GIL – who amasses the grains for the people.

GILMA – who brought stability among the gods, who caused them to bond towards a common goal.

AGILIMA, who is fearless against the waves, who controls snows.

ZULUM – Who brought the fields to the people.

MUMMU – Who fashioned heaven and earth, who is of the blood of his Grandmother.

ZULUM-UMMU – Which no other God may equal in strength.

GISH-NUMUN-AB – Who makes the quarters of the world, who fashions all things. Called Destroyer of Tiamat's Gods[50], yet in his Light emerged from this darkness.

LUGAL-AB-DUBUR – who scattered forth the chaos of darkness to establish his own order among it. It is Lugal-Ab-Dubur who seized the weapon of Tiamat.

---

[50] Luciferians view Tiamat as the Greatest of the Dark Gods, for she sleeps within each of us. As Marduk became as her, the greatest of the Gods, her essence is too with him for they are of the same "blood" just as we are fashioned by Marduk from the Blood of Tiamat's husband and general, Kingu/Kingu.

PAGAL-GUENA – the leader of all lords, whose power is supreme, whose might is victorious!

LUGAL-DURMAH – the King who brings all the bond of creative unity. Who is the greatest of the gods, who ascends above all in might.

ARANUNA – The Counselor of Ea, who is the God of the Deep.

DUMU-DUKU – Who begets laws which govern.

LUGAL-SHUANNA – King whose might is most powerful among the gods.

The Lord whose might is graced by Anu.

IRUGA – who took captives within Tiamat.

IRKINGU – Who captured Kingu in war, who decreed command over all.

KINMA – Commander and guidance of the Gods, who confirms direction.

E-SIZKUR – Who sits in the heights of invocation.

GIBIL – Who has established the ferocity of weapons, who is strong in wisdom.

ADDU – Who covers the sky.

ASHARU – The God of Destinies whom bears responsibility.

NEBERU – Who holds the balance of the heavens and earth. Neberu is the star of this god in the sky. It is he who controls the crossroads, the beginning and end, the darkness and light.

ENKURKUR – Ellil named Marduk thus.

THE PURPOSE OF MARDUK IN THE ADVERSARIAL PANTHEON

Marduk is not shunned by the Kassapu or Priests of Tiamat as one may think. Consider that by Adversarial interpretation that Marduk can represent the one who masters the darkness within; the hungers and desires which may empower us yet also destroy us.

Marduk is symbolized as riding the serpent-dragon Mushussu which is a direct creation of Tiamat by her manifestation as Mummu (creator). Marduk is the patron God of Babylon, those who ascend as Gods, illuminated; shining their divinity down casting darkness in their wake. Like Marduk, the Assyrian Ashur is the deific mask of the same god-form. Ashur/Marduk is equally a destroyer and creator, who are comfortable in their divinity and mastering that which they choose to.

Marduk may be offered to with incense for the protection of the household; symbolizing good fortune caused by your wise decisions in personal matters. One may equally work in the darkness of Kingu and Tiamat as well, without inner conflict.

ASSUR

God of Assyria and Conquering Deity

Often when looking to the Gods, one should seek to understand the people of which offers and gains power from their offerings to it. Assur is clearly one God which beholds a great power in the unity of army and the response of necessity. In a land which to the North has fierce and rugged mountains, inhabited by warlike people, to the south-east the Babylonians, who could be equally aggressive, combined with the landscape of burning summer heat and deserts you have Assyria.

The ancient Assyrians were to make themselves for a period of antiquity the most cruel, violent and warlike of any in the area, surpassing and enveloping their enemies. Fueled with the Gods of Babylonia as well, the Assyrians were a clear example of conquering with balance – impaling, skinning their captives, offering to the Gods yet also having a defined and articulate society. It is of course because of the Assyrians that we know of many ancient Babylonian demons and spirits.

Assur was not only the name of the God, yet also the city. Understanding the often difficult interpretation of Assur with Mesopotamian religion, we look to the inscriptions and imagery of the god.

Tiglath-Pilesar I was king around 1100 BC calls Assur the God "above all others", while other gods are praised as well. It is inscribed as if Assur is a type of empowering "fetish" or "idol" of collective subconscious energy of the people of Assyria. Specifically "whose weapons ASUR has predestined, and for the government of the four zones has proclaimed his name for ever; the capturer of the distant divisions of the frontiers above and below; the illustrious prince."

Assur is depicted reigning in the sky within a divine circle and winged Feroher, an Assyrian anthropomorphic male, wearing a horned cap holding a bow and arrow.

While it has been argued that Assur is identical to the City and nation, it is clear he was viewed as a separate god. In the clay tablets of Tiglath-Pilesar I Assur is mentioned "Trusting in ASUR my lord I assembled my chariots and armies."

Assur is depicted on a blazed brick panel found in home in Assyria from the 7th – 9th century BC[51] shows Assur as a figure like depicted as the winged god, however as a male figure holding a diadem. From 1300 BC it is considered that Assur is identified with as Enlil (the Sumerian God) as the chief of the

---

[51] Gods, Demons and Symbols of of Ancient Mesopotamia, Jeremy Black pg. 38

gods. Sargon II of Assyria identified Assur as Ansar, the primordial father of Anu.

Sennacherib as an official governmental policy identified Assur as Marduk especially in the alignment of the association of Assyria and Babylon. Assur then adopts during the period of Sennacherib the Mushussu snake-dragon, the steed and guardian of Assur clearly from Marduk. Assur also is identified with the Horned Cap, the only other god exclusive to the cap as a symbol by itself was Anu, the God of the Sky.

Assur in Assyrian art always depicts him within the winged-disk presiding over war, ritual dedications and hunting. In this way, Assur is an empowering diety or deific mask. It has been considered that Assur has been mistaken for Samas/Utu as the Sun God, which I deem incorrect. In the Labartu plague from the De Clercq Collection Assur is shown at the top of the plaque along with the sun-symbol of Shamas.

SHAMASH – UTU

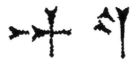

God of the Sun

Shamas / Utu / Samas is the ancient Sumerian god, whose symbol is the light of the sun. Samas is the Akkadian name of this ancient God, depicted with a horned cap upon a throne. The power of Shamas is renewal by light, each day he comes forth to offer humanity, animals and plants warmth and growth. Ashurbanipal had inscribed upon his Black Obelisk around 648 BC a detailed account of his achievements while King of Assyria, he names Shamash as one God therein. Shalmaneser III, a great conquering Assyrian King also mentions Shamas in his records as well, naming him "Shamash, Judge of Heaven and Earth, director of all.." in his invocations beginning the obelisk.

Shamash is considered judge and order-keeper based on his consistent rule in the sky, the one who brings growth and destruction through the heat he brings. In some points, Nergal is associated with the destructive aspect of Shamash. The Sebitti or Maskim are supported by Shamash when they attempt to devour the Moon-god Sin.

Shamash is the God of Magicians when called to exorcise demons or baleful spirits in ancient Mesopotamian texts, however the Kassapu will interact with Shamash upon a level of empowering the self; remember the Sebitti were supported in their attack against Sin the Moon-god by compelling it by Shamash.

NUSKU
God of the Night & Fire

Nusku is a god of the night, invoked in conjunction with Shamash in traditional Babylonian witchcraft exorcism rituals[52]. Nusku's sacred symbol is a lamp and is invoked in many exorcism rituals being a protective deity of night. Nusku is a highly venerated god mentioned by numerous Assyrian Kings in their invocations to the gods and records of their rule. When a torch is used in rituals, it represents Nusku.

---

[52] Mesopotamian Witchcraft by Tzvi Abusch

NAMTAR

Sukkal Erseti
Vizer of Ereshkigal & God of Disease

Namtar, the illustrious god of disease and death, sukkal erseti, the title meaning "the viser of the underworld" is Ereshkigal's chosen messenger to the gods and the 'offspring of Ereshkigal[53]".

Namtar or Namtaru is the underworld God of plagues, the viser of Ereshkigal. His name derives from "fate" and he is associated with that which cannot be stopped[54].

Namtar is the son of Enlil and Ereshkigal (also Mul-lil in some versions), which makes him a powerful and destructive god. Namtar introduces the dead to Ereshkigal, the Queen of the Underworld. Namtar holds specific power of 60 different types of demons and plagues, which correspond to the human body. Namtar sends forth this power depending on the desires of Ereshkigal. The wife of Namtar is Khushbisag and together they create numerous demons in the underworld.

Invoking Namtar can be a seemingly frightful event. For those who think in terms of the subconscious mind would such an invocation bring forth sickness?

If the Kassapu meditates upon Namtar as a death-demon then if the gods dwell in his temple this would too include Namtar? This "fate" may be utilized to strengthen the Kassapu against overwhelming sickness and physical death. Much like a vaccine,

---

[53] Dictionary of Deities and Demons in the Bible Brill publishing 1999

[54] Namtaru is parallel to Astovidat in Persian Yatukih or Zoroastrianism.

if you grow ill invoke Namtar and offer up incense in the night; seek to grow strong from this unfortunate event. Never attempt to banish fate, for this darkness like the Yatukih Astwihad[55] there is no escaping the hunger of Namtar. There are ways for the Kassapu to enter the violet streams of phantasms of Namtar.

KHUSHBISHANGA

The wife of Namtar, an infernal underworld goddess of plague. Khushbishanga dwells in Irkalla with her husband Namtar who are authorities in the court of Ereshkigal and Nergal. In the underworld, she is given the comb of womanhood, defining her status as wife of Namtar.

NINAZU

Chthonic Serpent God

Ninazu is an ancient Mesopotamian god, associated with the Usumgallu serpent-dragon and the Mushussu serpent-dragon. Ninazu's name has original meaning of "Lord Physician", the very underworld origins of medicine! We must attempt in further to strive for the balance of mind and spirit in which Ninazu and his son Ningishzida offer, the underworld is a place of healing, of fertility and also of darkness and death. This is the balance we must consider, do not deny light for darkness or the opposite – both reside within us.

---

[55] The Yatuk Dinoih in Luciferian Witchcraft and The Gates of Dozak by Michael W. Ford.

Serpent god

Being a healing chthonic god, Ninazu is also a predator as well. There was a pre-Sargonic mace-head dedicated to Ninazu, in addition he is referred to as "spitting venom" is old incantations.

Ninazu is also called the husband of Ereshkigal before Nergal, yet by some texts is the son of Ereshkigal. Ninazu is by most accounts the husband of Ningirda, a daughter of Enki/Ea. He was said to have been born in the underworld, on the mountain of Kurmussa, which is 'snake mountain'.

A title of Ninazu is "King of the Sword" who is able to "fill men with venom", he is called to protect some against Usumgallu, then making reference in the ritual when a serpent is handed to another calling forth that Ninazu is the King of Snakes.

The Temple of Ninazu is called "E-sikil" and also "E-kurmah". Ninazu may be later associated with the Greek Asklepios, who is the god of medicine and holds a serpent-staff along with his son Ningishzida. The Temple Enegir or Esikil of Ninazu was between Ur and Larsa and was considered an underworld gateway of sorts.

We see a highly interesting description and connection between Ninazu and Ereshkigal in the Sumerian Temple Hymns:

"O Enegir, great libation pipe, libation pipe to the underworld of Ereškigala, Gudua (*Entrance to the nether world*) of Sumer where mankind is gathered, E-gida (Long house), in the land your shadow has stretched over the princes of the land. Your prince, the seed of the great lord, the sacred one of the great underworld, given birth by Ereškigala, playing loudly on the *zanaru* instrument, sweet as the voice of a calf, Ninazu of the words of prayer, has erected a house in your precinct, O house Enegir, and taken his seat upon your dais."-Temple Hymn ETCSL translation: t.4.80.1

A copy of a serpent god before incense from a cylinder.

We see also a mention of Ninazu and his temple in Esnunna which describes his mighty place:

"O E-sikil whose pure divine powers are supreme in all lands, whose name is high and mighty, magnificent dwelling of the warrior, holy house of Ninazu, house of the holy divine powers! House, your divine powers are pure divine powers, your lustration is a cleansing lustration. The warrior refreshes himself in your dwelling. Ninazu dines on your platform. Your sovereign, the great lord, the son of Enlil, is a towering lion spitting venom over hostile lands, raising like the south wind against enemy lands, snarling like a dragon against the walls of rebel lands, a storm enveloping the disobedient and trampling on the enemy." Temple Hymn ETCSL translation: t.4.80.1

This hymn describes a great power contained within Ninazu. We see his association with a dragon as well:

"When he strides forth, no evil-doer can escape. When he establishes his triumph, the cities of the rebel lands are destroyed. When he frowns, their people are cast into the dust. House, your prince is a great lion from whose claws the enemy hangs. Your sovereign is a terrifying, mighty storm, the vigour of the battle, in combat ...... like a ...... with a shield on his lofty arm, a net over the widespread people from whose reach the foe cannot escape. When the great lord is resplendent, his magnificence has no equal. The true seed born of the Great Mountain and Ninlil, your sovereign, the warrior Ninazu, has erected a house in your precinct, O E-sikil, O Ešnunna, and taken his seat upon your dais." Temple Hymn ETCSL translation: t.4.80.1

Serpent God

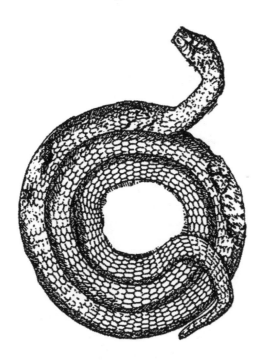

Serpent of the Primal Waters, from boundary stone

NINGISHZIDA

Serpent God & Guardian of Demons

The origins of Ningishzida/Ningizzida and his divinity are found in the obscure parts of mythology and history. This often overlooked god is often difficult to pin down as to what his deified associations. Let us shed some light upon this god and open a pathway to his ascension through us.

A wise underworld God whose symbol is a staff entwined with two serpents, the original caduceus if you will. The image of Ningishzida is a robed bearded man, crowned in the horned cap of divinity that has two horned serpents from his shoulders. Ningishzida means *"Lord of the Good Tree"* and in many ancient epics including "The Death of Gilgamesh" Ningishzida is the guardian of demons in the underworld. In a Luciferian aspect, Ningishzida is the personal deity of subconscious wisdom, thus the serpent upon the Tree of Knowledge. He retains the balance of darkness and light.

In the myth of Adapa, Ningishzida is called "Giszida" and guards the gate of Anu or the heavens. Thus it shall be considered that by seeking knowledge in the darkness do you also seek the wisdom of the heavens.

The symbol of Ningishzida, the basmu or horned serpent is associated with the constellation Hydra. Ningishzida is also *"The Throne Bearer of the Earth*[56]*"* who no doubt establishes wisdom

---

[56] Thomson, Devils, Book I page 60 (original facsimile edition).

among the living. It seems originally that Ningishzida was a form of Nin-girsu, who is a solar god from the city of Lagash near Ur in ancient Sumeria. In the "Death of Ur-Namma", Ningishzida is called "The Valiant Warrior".

Ningishzidda and Ea

In the ancient tale of "Ningishzida's Journey to the Netherworld" he is called *"throne–bearer of the wide nether world"* and whose queen is Ereshkigal.

The name of Ningishzida is translated and interpreted in several ways, one being *"Lord of the gracious scepter"* and the most reasonable, *"Lord of the tree of truth"* or "knowledge" (Nin-giz-zi-da). On the eastern gates of the heavens and the realm of Anu there were two guardians, Gizzida (Tree of truth) and Dumuzi (Tree of life). Sumerian culture provides us with a distinct understanding of the origins of the Tree of Life, which was adopted by the Assyrians and later by the Judeans.

The Ningishzidda Caduceus guarded by two Mushussu dragons

The Tree of Life to the Sumerian mythos was a bright star in the heavens, if originated as the Eastern or rising star it would easy to associate Dumuzi and Gizzida as the Morning Star, thus a primal manifestation of the deific mask of the later visualized Lucifer of the Greeks.

Ningishzida is depicted as two coiled serpents, akin to the later Caduceus and also as a dragon with two coiled basmu. Ningishzida also represents the wisdom of the hidden, the place of the underworld and is associated with the *"Azal'ucel"* – Holy Guardian Angel – Daimon which the Chaldeans called *"Personal God"*. Gudea, a southern Mesopotamian ruler from Lagash around 2144 BC asserted his personal god was Ningishzida.

Ningishzida is the son of Ninazu (the Lord of Serpents) and Ningurda (who is a variant of Ereshkigal). Ningishzida is consistently the throne-bearer of Ereshkigal in many hymns and tales. In short, the serpent-god works with the desires of Ereshkigal and conducts workings for her not only in the underworld but also on earth.

We see a consistency with Ningishzida being associated with Nabu[57] and the planet Mercury, hence the transformation of the self in the traditional way in which the planet is associated with. Another scholar showed that Ningishzida was attributed to the Hydra[58].

We see a description of a temple with reference to the god:

"O primeval place, deep mountain founded in an artful fashion, shrine, terrifying place lying in a pasture, a dread whose lofty ways none can fathom, Ĝišbanda, neck-stock, meshed net, shackles of the great underworld from which none can escape, your exterior is raised up, prominent like a snare, your interior is where the sun rises, endowed with wide-spreading plenty. Your prince is the prince who stretches out his pure hand, the holy one of heaven, with luxuriant and abundant hair hanging at his back, Lord Ninĝišzida. Ninĝišzida has erected a house in your precinct, O Ĝišbanda, and taken his seat upon your dais."- Temple Hymn

Ningishzidda upon Mushussu Dragon

In many theological lists of gods Ningishzida is associated with the family of Ninurta; however his idea as a deity or deific mask

---

[57] Winckler, Altor Forschugen, 11.

[58] Kugler, Sternkunde, I.

is older. Gudea affirms him as the "Offspring of Anu". Ningishzida plays a role similar to Pazuzu when he has the power to keep demons under control when he desires so.

If you wish to invoke and offer to Ningishzida it should be done in a manner of introspection and understanding your opportunities and issues. As you gain a meaningful experience with the god then you may seek further incantations and workings.

DESCRIPTIONS OF NINGISHZIDA

Ningishzida is called the "warrior-god" who led Gudea into battle, thus acknowledging that the god raised Gudea above others; indicating that Gudea had developed the fertility and underworld god as his personal daemon.

Ningishzidda with two Mus serpents on his shoulders.

In a "Balbale to Ningishzida", the god is called "Lion of the distant mountains", "Ningishzida who brings together giant snakes and dragons", "Mighty power, who no one dare stop when he spreads confusion (chaos)", "Hero who after surveying the battle, goes up to the high mountains", "King, you who carry out commands in the great underworld, there where your commands are issued", "Ningishzida, you understand how to wield the scepter into the distant future" and "you fall upon the many, you burn them like fire".

Ningishzida is associated with the axe being his weapon and in the Malqu series is a daemon who is an exorcist against other demons. As a healing god, Ningishzida is symbolized as the crowned serpent, the wise one who brings fertility of the mind and body.

Ningishzida is also able to ravage the land with plague and fever as well, much like Pazuzu. His manifestations are varied, yet usually always appearing as a serpent in some way. The god appears in mortal form as a bearded male, wearing the horned crown with two 'cerestes cerestes' horned serpents from each shoulder like the Persian Azhi-Dahaka or Zohak. He is leading Gudea to Ea, the Great God of Magicians and the Absu.

NIRAH

Serpent God

Worshipped primarily in the city of Der, the area between ancient Mesopotamia and Elam was the minister of the God of Der, Istaran. Nirah was long worshipped until the middle Babylonian times in the Temple of Enlil where he was a protective deity.

Nirah the Serpent God holding crab (Cancer)

NERGAL

The God of War, Plague & the Underworld

What can be written to describe the essence and power of the Lord of the Underworld, Nergal? Who inspired so much such as the concept of Melkart, of Herakles and others?

Nergal/Erra/Irra was conceived in the underworld by Ninlil and Enlil. On one hand Nergal represents the burning and destroying heat of the Sun, on the other he represents the Midnight Sun of the Underworld. Nergal called also Erra is a plague god, whose throne was in the underworld.

Nergal is a God of Necromancy, some of the first rituals of communing with the Shades of the Dead where scribed in myths of the God Nergal. Not only a God of the Underworld, of Necromancy and the black arts of knowledge, he is also a God of War and Plague.

His primary city of worship was Cuthah / Kutha which was a favorite burial area for many Babylonians. In Cutha and Uruk, Nergal was often referred to as "**Lugal-banda**" which translates *'Powerful (banda) King (lugal)'*. Nergal's name is sometimes inscribed as "**Ner-unu-gal**" which is the *"Lord of the Great place"* which is the underworld.

The great symbol of Nergal is a Lion-headed Mace which represents his power in the Summer-solstice, of burning power and the conquering spirit. The planet associated with Nergal is Mars, which draws a close parallel to other Gods associated with Mars in other pantheons.

While Nergal was a fearsome deity, his cult spread across the middle east, even to Sidon due to the deportations and settlements made by conquering forces such as the Assyrian King Sargon.

Nergal Mace head and Representation

While Nergal is a God of the Underworld, he also is attributed to the Noon-tide Sun and the destructive elements of solar cycles, lending his power of pestilence and other destroying insects cultivated by the Sun and its power of growth. Nergal was attributed to a great underworld cave called Aralu.

The forms of Nergal were many. Often depicted as the fearsome lion, he is also symbolized as a war-mace with the head of a lion. He also holds a mace of scepter with the two lion-heads. Nergal is also shown as a god dressed in a long robe, often one leg is out trampling a man. Nergal wears the horned cap of divinity and is shown also in burial pose representing the God of the Underworld.

Nergal is described in a ritual text as a vampiric god, "Nergal, dragon covered with gore, drinking the blood of living creatures[59]".

Some epithets of Nergal include *"raging king,"*, *"furious one"*, Lugalgira, Sharrapu which means "the burner" relating to the heat of the Sun. Nergal's name itself is related to *"Lord of the Great Dwelling"*, the great dwelling is of course the Underworld, which is commonly depicted in literature as being vast and extensive. An interesting title of Nergal as being *"The Glowing*

---

[59] An *adab* to Nergal for Šu-ilīšu (Šu-ilīšu A).

Flame" is also brought into accordance with the *"Black Flame"* of self-illumination or consciousness.

Nergal's underworld bride was Ereshkigal, known as the "*great lady under earth*". In Chaldean lore, Nergal became assimilated to Jupiter, Saturn and Mars. While his primary indication was indeed Battle, he found to be satisfied with the pestilence and plague which would erupt at different times, bringing death in a seemingly whimsical manner. Being connected with the Sun, Nergal had positive attributes associated with him such as an Agriculture God.

There are instances where Nergal is interchanged with Shamas, however specifically the phase of the noontide and the summer solstice, when the season ends with death and the lifelessness of the destructive heat. This is perhaps why Nergal is the God of the Underworld or realm of shades, his gateway is at the end of the natural cycle as it is; a balanced and adversarial gateway to the concept of death and transformation.

The Babylonian title of Mars, "Mustabarru – Mutanu" means "The Death-spreader" is one title associated with Nergal as well.

MESLAM
Temple of Nergal

Meslam was the chief Temple of Nergal in Kutha. The designation of Nergal is "Meslamtaeda" which means "The One that rises up from Meslam". Another cult center of Nergal was in Maskan-sapir which flourished for a period of time.

The altar of Nergal generally features a lion-headed mace or staff. It is important to understand that in ancient Mesopotamia that many demons and gods could have the features of birds, lions and serpents. Those seeking to create an altar of Nergal should have an image of a Babylonian styled lion which may include images of the Ugallu demons. Nergal is associated with Mars, war and plague so any symbolisms associated therein.

IRRA-NERGAL – Lord of Plague and War

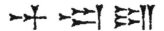

Irra-Nergal as Lord of the Plague

SHARRAPU

The Fire Serpents of Nergal

The term Sharrapu is an epithet used to describe the flames in which Nergal manifests. In Canaan Nergal or Erra was the "sharrapu" or "burner", who brings scorched earth and war under the title "Irra" or "Erra". Nergal also appeared as one who hears invocations or callings and can restore the shades of the dead to life. The title of Sharrapu was used in devising the fire-serpents called "Seraphim" who were utilized in early Judeo-Christianity.

Ugallu Demon and Underworld Demon-God

ELAMITE DIETIES

Elam is a mountainous land which had numerous conflicts with Assyria in antiquity. Their methods of warfare were based around hit and run tactics, being experts on horseback. In addition their archery skills were noted. The gods of Elam are closely connected with Assyrian and

Babylonian culture and most of the Mesopotamian gods were honored. The specific deities of Elam are listed here to add possibility in specific workings.

The significance of Elam is that the Babylonians considered Elam the residence of rebellious gods, demons and various chaotic powers of Tiamat. No doubt fueled by their serpent-deities, some of which found a home in the Mesopotamian pantheons as well. Elamite deities in contrast to Babylonian lore will no doubt provide the imaginative Kassapu with some chthonic powers to work with.

KHUMBAN / HUMBAN/ HUWAWA

Khumban/Humban, the great sky god of the Elamites who is associated with **Huwawa**, the demonic-guardian of Enlil's cedar forest (of Lebanon) is the most powerful deity of Elam.

The demon-guardian Huwawa is depicted as having a face which resembles or is composed of innards as they would have been used in divination. Huwawa is a fire-breathing associate of the god Wer who is a storm-god who is identified with the god Adad.

Huwawa was said to be protected by *"Seven layers of terrifying radiance"*. The connection of "radiance" is a part of the energy of the specific deity, and is grounded to the god like a garment which may be taken off. The radiance, from the two associated words Ni (*the effect of living humans from the divine power, a terror or awe inspiring feeling similar to intense invocations of the personal god or Daimon*) and the divine power Melam.

The Elamite god Humban, whose name is later known as Napirisa is the god of the sky and earth is a powerful old god who was viewed as the greatest among the Elamite deities, with the exception being the earlier Pienenkir/Ninikir (whose name was invoked in the Naram-Sin treaty). In honor of this great god, several Elamite kings were named after this diety. While it is obvious that Humban became the Huwawa of the Babylonian "Gilgamesh" legend, having the fierce claws of a lion and being a violent enemy in which Gilgamesh needed help to defeat, at certain periods the Babylonians aligned Humban with both Bel-Marduk and Enlil.

In addition, the legend of Huwawa and Gilgamesh places Huwawa as the lord of the cedar forest in Lebanon, Syria. We could see here a clear representation of the Huwawa as the Egyptian Bes, who was popular throughout the Middle East.

In a neo-Assyrian record, the corpse of Assyrian king Sennacherib is guarded by Humban with two other Elamite deities Naprushu and Yabnu.

PININKIR/KIRIRISHA
Mother Goddess

The mother-goddess of the Elamite pantheon dated from around 3rd millennium B.C., Pinikir (spelled also Pienenkir) was the chief goddess and diety of the Elamite powers for several periods. She is mentioned in the Naram-Sin treaty.

Also known as Kiririsha, the "Lady of Liyan" sits beside her Lord Khumban as a powerful goddess who had numerous temples dedicated to her in Elam. The name of Kiririsha was used in the southern areas of Elam while Pienenkir was originally the goddess worshipped in the North. As the Elamites held the southern region to be the center of their power at certain periods, the deities most revered would gain notoriety in due course.

The Cult of Pinikir revered her as the "Soverign of the Gods" and the Assyrians listed her as the assimilated Ishtar, revered throughout the Mesopotamian lands.

INSUSINAK

Lord of the Underworld, Darkness & Light

This god is the "Lord of Susa" being the ancient capital of Elam. Insusinak is the third of the triad of supreme deities of the Elamite pantheon along with Kiririsha and Khumban. Insusinak over a period of time was the personal god of many Elamite kings and overtook the position of Humban as being the most important god. While importance shifted continually, invocations of the Elamite gods always began with Humban/Khumban and then Isusinak followed by the goddess Kiririsha.

The divine lord of the Elamites, or specifically Susa was associated with both Babylonian gods Adad and Ninurta.

The difference with the Elamites and the Assyrians was that Isusinak was refered to as the King's "Personal God" rather than being "storm-god" or "war-god". He is described by Ashurbanipal as being the "God of their Mysteries, who dwelt in a secret place, whose divine acts none was ever allowed to see[60]".

In first millennium B.C. funeral tablets, Isusinak passes judgement over the shades of the dead residing in the underworld, yet is also invoked along side Nahhunte the Sun God as well.

NAHHUNTE
The God of the Sun, Justice

The God of the Sun, justice and considered the same as the Assyrian-Babylonian Shamash/Utu. Many Elamite kings refer to themselves as "ancestor of Nahhunte" and find divine rule in the power of the Sun. Nahhunte was widely used in sorcery as a name scribed in houses to protect against intruders, threatening those who enter with a curse of being barren and sterile.

---

[60] The description of the Assyrian King's sack of Susa and removing the statue of the god to Assyria.

Ningishzidda with two crowned, cerestes snakes.

A manifestation of Tiamat, bearing "Melammu" or "Black Flame", a third eye and a scale-type skirt.

Nergal instructing Ugallu demon on torture by Marchozelos

Cult of Ereshkigal and Her Reception of Libations by Marchozelos

ERESHKIGAL

The Goddess of the Underworld & Sorceress of Irkalla

While her name is known and feared in ancient Babylonian myths, the great goddess Ereshkigal has been little explored in the study of Mesopotamian religion and magick. Let this attempt provide a suitable grounding for the pale goddess to rise again from her ancient sleep, seeking the blood to nourish her body in moisture again.

Ereshkigal is the Goddess of the Underworld. Her name means "Great Lady under the Earth" indicating that she is both destructive and creative. The sister of Ishtar, Ereshkigal may be viewed as the "crone" aspect of the goddess in modern incantations involving the powerful deity. Ereshkigal drinks water with the Annunaki and drinks "troubled water", that which carries the spirits of the ekimmu travel upon and the demons are sent back to underworld in exorcism rites.

Instructions are given to Ishtar to summon Ereshkigal "conjure her by the oath of the great gods...she who creates a dragon (saturru = sasurru)[61].

The main Temple of Ereshikigal was located in Kutha, like her husband Nergal. In Sumerian hymn "The Descent of Ishtar" Inanna/Ishtar is the younger sister of Ereshkigal. This Queen of Darkness had photophobia (being averse to sunlight) and chose to remain exclusively in the underworld. She held great power

---

[61] A New Recension of Ishtar's Descent into Hell pg. 27

in the underworld and her name Irkalla became the same as the underworld abode she ruled over with Nergal.

Just as Hades is symbolic of the place of Hades in which he ruled in Greek mythology, Ereshkigal became "Irkalla" as the place where she dwelled. Ereshkigal became the Goddess of the Underworld when the Earth was separated from the sky, thus it seems logical than in older times Ereshkigal was once a sky goddess. Her nature in the ancient Mesopotamian texts displays her as a Goddess of Darkness who rules the shades of the dead, yet she is also extremely violent.

Ereshkigal has a powerful *sukallu* (a viser or general) named Namtar, who is also known as *mar sipri* (messenger) of the dark goddess. Namtar is given the power to breed the life draining sickness and demons of disease.

Ereshkigal may take beautiful form, as suggested in the legend of "Nergal and Ereshkigal". She bathes and wears a beautiful dress. Ereshkigal is also able to raise the dead rise to earth and eat the living, thus a necromantic magick in which the shades of the dead are given the "waters" of Irkalla and arise as vampiric ekimmu or Akhkhazu.

Ereshkigal survived well beyond the Babylonian pantheon, we find her name as a "Name of Power" associated with the gods of darkness invoked in an Egyptian "Invocation of Typhon-Set" in a spell to inflict catalepsy. Ereshkigal is named with other names of Typhon-Set.[62]

---

[62] The Leyden Papyrus, Edited by Griffith & Thompson.

ISHTAR

The Goddess of War & Lust

Ishtar/Inanna is a very powerful goddess who appears in numerous deific masks or goddess-forms throughout the Mesopotamian pantheon. Ishtar is both a goddess of intense beauty, sexual desire and also a warlike spirit of violence and mastery. Ishtar is called a "wolf" as in "you are a wolf sent forth to snatch a lamb" and is the sister of Ereshkigal.

Ishtar is a daughter of Anu as well, making her a sister to Lamashtu. Ishtar is a complex and complete goddess, having a balanced character as an individual.

Depicted as a sexual goddess, she is shown with standing with one leg revealed; her slight frame is supported by her divine fire of being. She wears the horned cap of divinity and is represented as the Morning and Evening Stars. For this alone, she is the original prototype of the Hellenic-Roman "Lucifer" or bringer of light. Ishtar/Inanna is also directly related to the Syrian Goddess Astartoth.

The principle cult centers of Inanna Uruk, Nineveh and Erbil.

Inanna/Ishtar was highly interesting as she is not a "mother goddess", rather she was a goddess of sexual love and her priestesses would participate in temple prostitution. Ishtar is also a warrior goddess; the battle grounds of old were called the "playground of Ishtar". She is shown with wings and many weapons extending from her body. Ishtar of Arbail/Arbela was the Assyrian war goddess.

As Luciferianism today is built from the foundations of the gods here and in other cultures, we see an interesting connection between Ishtar and Tiamat. In an obscure tablet entitled '**Piristi Ilani Rabuti**' or *"Secrets of the Great Gods"*[63] reveal that Ishtar of Nineveh is Tiamat, such is the Dark Mother was the wet-nurse of Bel.

Ishtar thirsts for power and split blood, she grows strong from the sacrifice of war, sex and bringing light and wisdom to those who seek her. One symbol of Ishtar is the 8-pointed star which holds representation of her as the illuminated Morning and Evening Star, thus she is "Inanna of the Sunrise".

Ishtar rides upon a great beast which is depicted as a lion. This beast along with her numerous weapons also shows her surrounded with bright stars.

Ishtar – Inanna the War Goddess

---

[63] Mesopotamian Cosmic Geography, see bibliography.

These three aspects, sexual goddess, war goddess and illuminating goddess demonstrate her subtle yet empowering and conquering nature. Ishtar is the first Triple-Goddess and seems to be an elevated manifestation of the "Goddess of Night" whom is called Lilith.

Ishtar favored the conquering Akkadian King Sargon (2335 – 2279 B.C.) Inspired by the great goddess, Sargon raised himself from gardener to royal cup bearer, soon usurping the throne from Ur-Zababa of Kish and then conquering Mesopotamia, Syria, Anatolia (parts of) and Elam. His daughter was installed as High Priestess of Nanna the Moon God. In addition, being favored of Ishtar, Sargon renamed himself Sharrukin, meaning "True King".

ISHTAR AS TIAMAT

The Scorpion Constellation, known as Mul Gir-tab is associated with Ishtar, the goddess of war and love. The very name of Ishtar's constellation as the form of a scorpion is written with the 'Gir' symbol, which means dagger or sword. Ishtar is the sword of the heavens, while the Tab sign or two points represents the "Double" or "Twin" aspect which is Tiamat and Kingu. Ishara, the wife of Dagon in Syria is a powerful goddess worshipped at one time by many in the ancient near east. Like Ishtar, Ishara is a goddess of love yet also was revered in Syria with Teshub and having the power to bestow and cure disease, which is slightly different from Ishtar-Inanna. Being a goddess of victory in battle, Ishara is applied to Venus and is regarded as a balanced power.

The name of Tiamat as Ishara Tiamat, or Ishara of the Ocean which reveals her manifestation and continuation of Tiamat in the Mesopotamian pantheon, in addition to Kingu surviving as a form of both Marduk and Asakku.

Ishara is called the Mother of the Seven Gods, which is a bit different from the myth of Ki (Earth) bringing forth the Seven. Ishara thus instilled the power of the Seven Star cluster as the bringers of war and darkness.

From a perspective of both astrology and theology it is not difficult to find indentification of Ishtar and Tiamat. As Kingu continued in Marduk as evident from some of the *Fifty Names of Marduk*; **ASHARU** (*God of Destinies*), **IRQINGU**, we see upon deeper study the survival of Tiamat as well. As the mother of the gods, Tiamat was by nature immortal through the law of nature as evolving; Ishtar was a symbol-deific mask of the more 'friendly' towards the new gods, from which she could still hold sway over the gods in a way she could not before.

We find also the association of Ishtar with Venus, not to mention Ishara associated equally. Venus, the morning star is the bringer of light and darkness, the herald of the night as the last star and the bringer of dawn as the first. This balanced perspective is the foundation of Luciferianism as not only an ideology/philosophy, yet also an initiatory one.

GILGAMESH
Deified Hero-God

Gilgamesh was a deified king of ancient Sumeria, specifically in the city of Uruk around the time of the Early Dyanstic Period. After the death of this king, a god named Gilgames was worshipped in numerous places in Sumer. Gilgamesh in legend was one-third human, two-third divine and was possibly a model for the Phoenican Melkart and the Greek Herakles. Gilgamesh in legend went on numerous adventures to gain power, including the practice of Necromancy. Gilgamesh achieved immortality and a place of power in Irkalla.

EKIMMU
EKIMMU LIMNU
Spirit of the Dead

The Ekimmu is the departed spirit of a human, a mortal who has died and went to the Underworld, Irkalla. Traditionally, the ancient Sumerians and similar cultures would make offerings of food and water to their dead. If one had no family, or if they were not brought food or drink they could return to earth and become "Ekimmu *Limnu*", or *"evil* spirit" which would attach itself to some living person or family member, feeding from their energy, causing nightmares and even sickness. The Ekimmu are not essentially or specifically predatory, they are like people and act still accordingly. Considering that their ancient culture is long dead, any contact with remaining Ekimmu would be awkward as they would not understand us, nor we them. The most suitable suggestion if one is deemed lucky enough, is to relate on the level of *"feelings"* as this would be the only form of communication.

Ugallu Demons

Girtablullu the Guardians of Darkness by Marchozelos

Tiamat and Kingu ascending from ancient sleep by Marchozelos

Adad and Ishtar of Nineveh by Marchozelos

Moon God Sin and Worshippers by Marchozelos

Girtablullu before the Gods by Marchozelos

Ereshkigal the Great Goddess of the Kassapu by Marchozelos

Lilitu and Urmahlullu by Marchozelos

CHAPTER FIVE

THE DARK GODS AND EVIL SPIRITS

War God and Ugallu Demon

UTUKKU / UDUGHUL
UTUG-HUL / GIDIM – HUL

"Evil Ghost" "Evil Spirit"

Udughul, Utug-Hul, Utukku (or **Utuq**), meaning "Evil Spirit" are specifically two types under the same name. While this can be confusing we must consider two aspects, one group *is not* divine and one *is* divine.

The Uttuku in relation to a departed human spirit is one who has been summoned by necromancy. The Udughul in reference to being in the host of seven refers to the Seven Maskim/Sebitti, the evil gods who wander upon the earth. Some "Udugs" can be either evil ghosts which have returned to earth to haunt man or evil spirits which are more demon or "divine" than human. This means either they are "evolved" from human ghosts into more powerful "demonic" type of phantoms or they were never humans in the way we accept. It is best to know in reading the context of the sentence.

The world of spirits in ancient Mesopotamia can be as varied as the individual personalities themselves. While there have been specific categories of spirits, gods and demons based on their associated roles, elements or drives there are still those who blur the lines of basic categorization which much of later Judeo-Christian demonology offered. What makes Mesopotamian demonology much more invigorating than later one-sided manifestations is that the categories contained various types which are seemingly more balanced much like living humans.

The Ekimmu is a specter or shade of a dead person who has been raised from the underworld itself. Necromancy is the ancient art of ensorcelling or encircling the shades into the living world. Necromancy is the primary method of divination in the East during ancient times. We find Necromancy utilized throughout the Babylonian and Chaldean tablets and spread as far as Greece and even Italy.

Workings of Necromancy in the modern world will bring the Kassapu into communion with the shades of the dead. What is most interesting is that you will have "impulses" of the spirit if working with something far ancient; simply put there is no direct way of understanding even a half-way understood forgotten language.

In the Epic of Gilgamesh, the hero appeals to Nergal who is the God of the Dead, of sorcery with the shades and the underworld. Gilgamesh offers to (in incense or libation) Nergal to restore his dead friend Ea-bani in this world, and soon the god allows this. The earth is described as opening up and the Utukku of Ea-bani ascends up from the depths "like the wind".

This type of Necromancy is quite similar to the later tale of the "Woman with a familiar spirit" who dwells in En-dor. This woman possesses a talisman which allows her to commune with the shades. Her visions see the earth opening up and a spirit rising up in burial shroud, similar to the earlier methods of Necromancy in Mesopotamia. After the Jews were relocated to Babylon around 500 B.C, no doubt many Chaldean methods of sorcery and magick traveled back with them to Palestine and the Levant.

The Utukku may be offered to in workings, with water, rose water or incense. It is not advised for the Kassapu to use his/her blood in workings as it may bind the Utukku to seeking to remain in this world. Such Utukku, if of ancient origin, are often more powerful than the Kassapu may perceive. The only weakness of the Utukku is that they are dormant from the most ancient times; if they have the ability to rise up from primordial consciousness, feeding them will restore to the strength needed to once again operate.

Utukku may be bound to a specific sigil for knowledge and wisdom of some ancient type; this is when blood of the Kassapu only may be used. They will grow stronger in their connection to the talisman yet also the sorcerer as well. Your vitality will over a period of time decrease even if you don't have spiritual occurrences in your home. Some shades will not cause disturbance at first as this requires energy as well, they most likely are seeking to merely grow stronger in the world of the living. Vampyre Sorcerers or Kassapu who are adept in vampiric arts may consume these shades or their vitality to commune in this world, separating them from their link in the physical, thus liberating them from becoming vessels for the Utukku to feed from after they are no longer needed.

What is clear is that if one seeks to work in this area of Necromancy, like Nergal the Kassapu must be cold and merciless when the situation calls for it concerning shades. Some may serve you well, if you energy can provide it. For those sick and feeble, or of mental illness or imbalance, you will be in grave danger (literally) and should keep from this type of practice.

The connection of blood to the spirit is vitally important to the lore of the Levant and Mesopotamia. The Arabs mentioned the 'nafs' flowing out of a man who had wounds and was dying. The 'nafs' is in the Semetic dialect "breath" which is the "spirit" which rides in the blood. Many Semites of the ancient world were afraid of drinking/eating the blood of slaughtered animals in that it might be possessed by the spirit of the animal.

Traditional necromancy or vampiric rites have involved this type of act within the sacred circle, such as the *Toad Rite*[64]

---

[64] Luciferian Witchcraft by Michael W. Ford. Succubus Productions 2005 – 2009.

wherein a toad is killed to acquire its spirit as a familiar. This type of working is sacred to some Luciferians as it involves the primordial form of Ahriman and the Cainite toad-witch of Medieval Europe.

The dead have long been offered to in the ancient world after their spirits have departed. In Chaldean lore, the etimmu or the spirit of the man leaves the flesh but returns for offerings in this world which are traditionally of food and water. Equally so, these ekimmu have much of their formal intelligence possessed in their past life, thus establishing an existence of a "psyche" of "isolate intelligence" and "soul" in this lore.

The shades of the dead throughout the old world could travel where they wish and take hold of anything they wish to dwell within. Inanimate objects such as grave stones were often occupied by the dead as statues could be possessed of the energy of the specific god.

In Arab lore Djinn or such spirits could appear in the forms of birds, serpents and owls just as in earlier Babylonian lore[65]. This type of freedom brought the tales of possession to front in Palestine. The word of insane, 'majnun' means 'possessed by Djinn".

Necromancy is a discipline and magical practice among the ancient Chaldeans, one of the titles of a sorcerer in ancient Assyria was **Muselu Edimmu**, translating "Raiser of the Departed Spirit"[66]. This is from which Necromancy would derive in medieval form much later, when combined with the Greek methods and discipline.

In several incantation tablets, the Utuq attacks the forehead of the man in working with other demons such as the powerful Namtar, a disease demon who is the viser of the Underworld Goddess Ereshkigal.

---

[65] Spiritism and the Cult of the Dead in Antiquity, Lewis Payton, 1921.

[66] W.A.I. ii, Tablet. Devils…Thompson Introduction. Semetic Magic, R.Thompson

ALU LIMNU

A-LA - HUL "Evil Demon"

(Related to Akhkharu/Akhazu)

The Alu is a demon which stalks in the shadows, hiding in caverns, haunted ruins and places where humans avoid. When night brings down its cloak upon the world, the Alu is able to move through the streets of a city or town in the darkness unnoticed. The Alu lies in wait for the passer-by to then "envelop him with a garment" or wrapping him in the darkness of its presence, to feed of his vital energy/astral life-force and often to remain with him to grow stronger in both worlds.

The Alu grows strong from the fear of man and woman, entering the bedchamber at night, the Alu can ignite the mind into the realms of fear, as if something is watching them, to feed from their energy caused from their increased brain-activity and anxiety. The Alu can also appear in nightmares, often taking form of that which you fear in that specific dream.

The Alu is often described as having half-human and demonic composite parts. The Lilitu or Ardat Lili breeds many of the Alu from joining with a man whom she lays with and absorbs life-fluid from. In Judaic lore the Alu is known as Ailo, a demon-vampire begotten by Lilith. It is considered that the Alu is closely related to the Ahhazu/Akhkharu vampire, both are said to "envelop him as with a garment" and is described as entering a bedchamber at night and drains their sleep away. This is an obvious reference to the energy or vitality gained through normal sleep, thus a type of energy-etheric vampire.

R. Thompson describes the Alu as having a horrible apparition, sometimes appearing not without limbs, ears or even a mouth. Considered a ghoulish off-spring of the Ardat-lili and Lilitu the half-human, half-devilish offspring is related to later rabbinic lore as beginning with the union of Lilith with Adam, the demonic spawn born from their union. The tradition of the Alu continued throughout the near-east long after the fall of Babylonian culture and like other religious foundations, worked their way into other developing beliefs.

RABISU LIMNU

LABASU /RAPANMEA

"The Specter and Ghoul"

The Labasu is a word meaning "ghoul" and refers to a devil or haunting spirit. This is a vampire spirit, indicating living or dead and is associated with the Ahhazu.

The Sumerian word *"Maskim"* or *"Lie in wait, ambushers"* is in Akkadian **Rabisu**, *"evil fiends"* which is a lurking demon which is known by causing those who sense its appearance by their hairs standing on end. This devil draws from the vital energy of those who it is around. The Rabisu will approach and haunt others along with Labartu, Lilitu and other storm-demons. The

Rabisu is also a title of a high official in the Ur III Period and was the second highest official after the Judge.

There are numerous demons with the title of Rabisu; all by definition are lesser in power than the Seven Maskim. "Rabis Uri", "Rabisu of the Roof"; Rabisu Nari, "Rabisu of the River", Rabis Harbati "Rabisu of the Wasteland" and demons which attack travelers upon the road: "Rabis Urhi", "Rabisu of the Road".

RAPGANMEKHAB
AHHAZU/AKHKHAZU/AKHKHARU

The Seizer and Vampire

Sigil of "Blood/Gore" in Sumerian.

The Akhkhazu[67] or Ahhazu is "the seizer" and is related to the primal vampire in ancient Mesopotamia. The idea of vampirism from Chaldean lore is that t he vampire seizes the victim and drains them nightly of their life, blood and spiritual energy. The symptoms are found in the exorcism tablets from which many of the incantations contained herein derive.

---

[67] The word is derived here from Chaldean Magic it's Origin and Development by Lenormant.

The Akhkhazu is described in W.A.I. Tablet 3 as *"With dark clothing which is the terror of the vampire (akhkhazu), the dark cloak, the cloak of splendor, he has covered the pure body."*[68]

The Akkadian name of the vampire is **Rapganmekhab**, the Assyrian translation is **Akhkharu**. The Goddess Vampire Labartu is named as **Rapganme** (Akkadian). Another demon associated with the Akhkharu is not only Labartu (as the Phantom spirit) and Labassu (Specter).

The vampire is the symbol of nightside or the subconscious desires of the Kassapu, the very lusts of the flesh and mind. As we lay dreaming, often we journey forth into worlds of shadow to engage in activities and possibilities often unreachable to us in the physical world. The Rapganmekhab or Akhkharu is the vampire who has left the flesh and exists in the world of shadows, or the underworld. During the nocturnal hours, the Akhkharu comes from the world of shades to spread its cloak or shadow upon the sleeping woman or man, to feed of their vital energy.

---

[68] The Origin and Growth of Religion as Illustrated by the Religion of the Babylonians by A.H. Sayce.

ILU LIMNU

"Evil God"

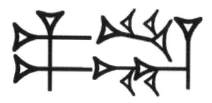

Cuneiform for Maskim

The Ilu Limnu or "Evil God" is suggested to be originally one of the children of Tiamat by Theophilus Pinches[69] who remained like other spirits associated with Absu, Tiamat and Kingu. The Ilu Limnu seems to be a title associated with the Seven Maskim. The "Evil God" may be either singular or plural and often is shown as single for the ease of writing. For instance, the gem carving of the Moon God Sin attacked by the Sebitti shows a single evil god rather than seven. We may safely consider that the Ilu Limnu is another epithet for the Maskim of Sebitti as Evil Gods born of the union of Anu and Ki.

---

[69] The Religion of Babylonia and Assyria by Theophilus G. Pinches, LLD.

PAZUZU

"Pazuzu, the king of the evil lil-spirits"

The enigmatic Pazuzu holds a long and rather detailed history in Mesopotamian religion, mythology and modern occult lore. A demonic god of Babylonia and Assyria, Pazuzu holds a beneficial and malicious purpose to humanity. Pazuzu is an embodiment of the forces of nature as devouring, destructive; that which rides upon the wind. Traditionally Pazuzu is associated with the South-western wind which is towards the deserts of Arabia thus hot and pestilential wind. Charlier[70] associates Pazuzu with the north-eastern wind as cold, wintery associated with the mountains of Media and Armenia.

If we can associate Pazuzu with Sutu or the South-Western wind then his power is the desert winds as it refers to "sand". Pazuzu's amulets are found throughout the Middle East, from Susiana (Susa, Elam), Samos and even Palestine. Many of the amulets describe the name of Pazuzu and an identification line, "I am Pazuzu, the son of Hanbu, the King of Lil-Demons".

The form of Pa-zu-zu depicts him as an upright standing figure. He has human shoulders, a torso which appears similar to a wolf or narrow bird. The head is a bald lion-wolf skull, fangs with two deep set eyes and long horns. In some appearances he is shown with a beard and several insect-like curves on his skull. The horizontal lines on the face of Pazuzu show him with all the features associated with demons. He is shown with wings, two pointing upward and two downward, showing his association with both the air and the underworld. He has the claws of a predator and his feet are shown as a bird. In addition, Pazuzu has the tail of a scorpion and the penis in the form of a snake. Often he is shown with the hind-quarters feathered like a bird.

---

[70] Charlier 1992, Heebel 2002: 2, 62-66 & Iconography of Deities and Demons 2007

Pazuzu, King of the Lil-Wind Demons, Son of Hanbi

Pazuzu is usually shown with an arm raised in attack and one downward. Pazuzu is depicted in ancient Assyrian depictions as a beneficial demon who keeps disease and sickness away.

Incantations with Pazuzu may be done for protection, or for connecting in a dream-projection purpose. Simply use the incantation of Pazuzu before sleep, along with a consecrated image or statue of the wind-god. Focus on the elements of Pazuzu which make his depiction. You will find Pazuzu as meaningful demon to work with who is both beneficial and malicious.

Pazuzu, Bringer and Averter of Pestilence

ASAKKKU
ASAG, AZAG, ANZU

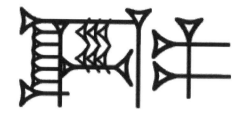

The Chaos Demon of the Mountains

Asag's name is associated with meaning "the one who strikes the arm[71]". In the myth of "**Lugal ud melambri Nergal**", Asag like Lamashtu is born of the same parents as the Seven Sebitti/Maskim, being Anu and Ki. Asag is the mighty warrior who is cloaked in the radiance of Melammu, he acts countering the natural order, yet still a powerful demon-god.

Spelled also "Azag[72]", this demon is a chaotic and monstrous fiend who mated with the mountains to beget his children who are considered stones or "sling stones" from the mountains which are embodied as Kur. Azag is described as a giant, a great dragon-serpent which caused fear even in the hearts of the great gods. Azag commanded an army similar to how the Gutians were described; they utilized arrows, stones and various other weapons.

Azag is described as a fearless warrior, whose own army of mountain raiders come down and despoil the towns below. He goes forth and does his will and answer to no other gods.

---

[71] A Dictionary of Ancient Near Eastern Mythology; Leick

[72] The source for Horror writer H.P. Lovecraft's "Azathoth" along with the Egyptian God Thoth.

Asakku the Storm Demon

"Like an accursed storm, it howled in a raucous voice; like a gigantic snake, it roared at the Land. It dried up the waters of the mountains, dragged away the tamarisks, tore the flesh of the Earth and covered her with painful wounds. It set fire to the reedbeds, bathed the sky in blood, turned it inside out" -168-186 Ninurta's Exploits, describing the attack of Asag.

Possessing great power, the Dragon-Monster holds the ability to cause the waters in riverbeds to boil and kill the fish within it. Asag is associated with the Seven-Headed Serpent-Dragon Mussaginim as well as Anzu. We see a definite form between the Seven Maskim/Sebitti and Asag as the manifestation of chaos causing reformation and order.

Like Tiamat, Asag or Asakku takes the primordial form of a lion-dragon, who in turn is eventually defeated by Ninurta, the God of War. In later demonology, Asag or Asakku assails humans by causing great fevers and sickness. It is clear, however that the Asakku demons which plague humanity later are as "offspring" of the character of Asag who battled Ninurta.

Anzu is known as the Sumerian Imdugud, called Zu in Akkadian as well as Azzu. Anzu is a lion-headed eagle or bird of prey, much like the manifestations of demons such as the

Gallu/Ugallu or others. The Anzu in lore was a usurper, stealing the tablet of destiny for himself; attempting to make himself king.

LAMASHTU, DIMME LABARTU

"The Rushing Hag Demon"

One of the most interesting points of the ancient Mesopotamian pantheon is the balance of the deities. Specifically, there are gods who are equally demons in that they are free to go forth and do their will, even working with others gods at times. The Sebitti/Maskim/Seven Evil gods are one example; they are sons of Anu and Ki who are able to do what they will. No other gods can control them even though they are beseeched for assistance from the Seven at times. Another example is the *sister* of the Seven Evil Gods, Lamashtu.

A Babylonian incantation of Labartu describes the Goddess: *"A rushing Hag-demon, granting no rest, nor giving kindly sleep. It is the sickness of night and day. Whose head is that of a demon, whose head is that of demon, whose shape is as the whirlwind. Its appearance is as the darkening heavens, and its face as the deep shadow of the forest. Its hand is a snare; its foot is a trap."* – Tablet P, Plate XXV. Line 5.

ORIGINS OF LAMASHTU

"a-nu-um a-bu-sa is-tu sa-ma-e i-pu-sa qa-qa-ar-su-um"

"Anu, her father, cast her (Lamashtu) down from heaven earthward" – BIN 4 126:10-13[73]

The early manifestation of Lilith, perhaps the very first "Lilith" is a child-snatching, blood drinking vampire-demoness who is actually classified as a great goddess. She acts without structure and does her Will without the restraints of other gods. Known as Dimme in Sumerian tablets, Lamashtu in Akkadian and Labartu in the Seleucid-Babylonian period texts, her names are many and her forms equally protean.

Lamashtu in ancient Mesopotamian Goddess who was born of Anu and next to Tiamat, Kingu and the Seven Sebitti/Evil Gods is the most important goddess of the left hand path or Luciferian tradition associated with the near eastern pantheon. Lamashtu holds specifically a unique existence as she is both a goddess and demoness who acts according to her own will rather than the design or nature.

---

[73] Mesopotamian Cosmic Geography p. 224

Lamashtu on her journey to the Underworld

Daughter of Anu

The origins of Lamashtu are attested by texts which declare her a goddess and a daughter of Anu and by some sources a sister of Inanna[74]. In mostly all incantations attempting to ban her, she is always referred to with **"ilat"** meaning *"she is a goddess"* The translation from BIN 4 (as read above) declares *"Anu, her father, cast her (Lamashtu) down from heaven earthward"* for her desire and request to have human flesh (babies) for her dinner[75]. Ea, the

---

[74] Birth in Babylonia and the Bible: it's Mediterranean setting, M.Stol pg. 225

[75] Birth in Babylonia pg 225 from Lambert I 187ff, II 92ff.

Lord of the Abyss (Absu) and God of Magick was known by an incantation text as "Ea taught her" which indicates her power of magick and of the knowledge of humanity.

Against the Divinely Ordained Cosmos

Lamashtu is considered **"istiat"** among the gods, being *"singular"* which confirms her individualistic nature. As a goddess, she has both Magickial and hidden wisdom which liberates her from the structured cosmos, which indicates she inherited genealogical traits of her great-great grandmother, "Tiamat" as being a truly left hand path goddess who is acting as **"utukkat"** or *"evil spirit"*. She is very much like her seven siblings, the **Maskim Hul** or **Sebitti**. Lamashtu is said to have a **"temu la damqu"** being a *"bad disposition"* and having a disrespectful proposal (requesting the blood and flesh of humans for substance).

Understanding how Lamashtu works against the ordained cosmos of the Mesopotamian pantheon, considering others demons work within the structure will specifically define why she is significant as a left hand path goddess along with Tiamat and the Seven.

The indication of Lamashtu having her own independent Will is the fact of reference that she is the Daughter of Anu, much like the Seven Maskim or Seven Demons of the Luminous Spheres. They while are sent to destroy others by Ea at times, being his Throne-Bearer, they also feed according to their own Will.

In Mesopotamian religion and myth humans were created with the blood of Kingu in order to serve the gods. These human slaves were to build temples, feed their spiritual existence by mirroring upon the earth so to speak. Good service was rewarded by no harm coming to the humans, while failure to serve (a so-called biblical sin) the gods was punished by disease, misfortune and death. In the dominant view as clearly defined by the theistic views demons and many ghosts would implement the divine order itself, similar to the later concept of Satan and the story of him smiting Job with boils. While demons operated on their own according to their desire and nature, they did conduct "workings" for the gods per request. When the human sinned against the gods by not being a good slave then a demon was called in to punish.

As it should be understood, Lamashtu desired the blood and flesh of babies, while she did go astray to lesser wanted substance bringers such as older men and women. Infants had not yet had the chance to offend the gods so harming them was not within the cosmic ordained structure. Lamashtu excelled at the one thing which placed her contrary to the natural order of the cosmos according to Mesopotamian mythology and religion. Lamashtu did not provide a chance for these babies to mature and in turn feed the gods.

We see this slavery again in our origins; being of the Blood of Kingu, the great Adversary and husband/son of Tiamat, the gods so hated his power that they used his blood to create humans, the slaves of the gods. Enlil in the myth of Atar-hasis shows that the blood and genetic inheritance of Kingu lived on in humans, making early ones noisy and disturbing the sleep of Enlil, much like he and the others gods did to Absu and Tiamat. Enlil, enraged created the flood to destroy humanity and so he could more easily keep survivors in check.

In the next instance, the gods find a way to invite Lamashtu into the divine order and to snatch babies from certain women to control population. She is named as "**Pasittu**", "*the exterminator*".

The Abode of Rest for Lamashtu

Lutz presents the series of incantation texts against Labartu in Plate XX No. 113 and it names Lamashtu and an alternate "Deific Mask" called Innin, mistress, lady of the black-headed. She comes forth from the cane-break or the reeds of the waters. Lamashtu, like the other demons and powerful spirits which represent the dark shadow of the gods make their homes in places such as deserts, the swamp lands south of Babylonia.

The Labartu (an earlier form of Lamashtu) is a female demon who is a daughter of Anu, the accepted and trusted of Irnina. Labartu's home is in the mountains and the cane-breaks of the marshes of ancient Mesopotamia. Labartu is described in Incantation Tablets as dwelling in the underworld, coming forth from the Abode of Bel. Labartu is called "The Rushing Hag Demon" who causes the sickness of night and day, she grants no rest to whom she seeks. She manifests sometimes as a headache, a sickness and then others as a great vampire-demon who devours the young. What is clear is that like her brothers the Seven Maskim, Labartu is not bound to serve or obey any god or goddess.

The Forms of Lamashtu/Labartu

The description of Labartu indicates her connection in the spiritual or astral plane with nature-attributes. Her head is of a "demon", from which most demons of Mesopotamia are a combination of Lion and Reptile, often bone-thin. The shape of Labartu is a Whirlwind and appears as the darkening heavens.

Being described as a "Hag Demon" indicates she is able to wear a form of an ancient crone, whose body is composed of dark clouds and smoke. The most represented form of Lamashtu is featured on a bronze plaque of the ninth to seventh B.C. and shows her upon a boat on the rivers of the underworld **NAR**

MARRATU, the very abyssic path to the underworld. She is looked over by **Pazuzu**, considered to be her husband and a king of wind-demons and Lil-spirits.

Lamashtu then appears with the head of a raging lion, the large teeth of a donkey, nude breasts and a hairy body. The hands of Lamashtu are talons of the Anzu (called ZU) – bird and are blood covered. She is suckled by a pig and a dog, holding two serpents and riding upon a donkey-like beast.

In the Utukki Limnuti Tablet III **Labartu** and **Lil-la** are interchangeable in their translations, both relating to *"The Hag-Demon"* and her powerful nature. The Hag-demon Labartu is also able to "fill man with venom" and there are numerous incantations against her.

The Mesopotamian prayers against Lamashtu are numerous as she was a child-killer; she drank the blood and ate the flesh of babies' right after they were born. An incantation gives a detailed description as such;

"She is fierce, she is raging, she is a Goddess, she is a wolf, the daughter of Anu...Her feet are the talons of Anzu, her hands are filthy, her face is that of a ferocious lion. Lamashtu came up from the reed thicket and her hair falls free. Her breech cloth is cut away, she walks with the tread of an Ox, and she comes down with the tread of a ram. Her talon-hands seek flesh and blood; she comes in through the window, slipping in around the cap of the door. She enters the house and goes out from it. Bring me your sons to suckle Lamashtu whispers, let your daughters turn to me so my breasts can be placed in the mouths of your daughters[76]".

Lamashtu is well documented in the Mesopotamian spell tablets and amulets designed to ward off the goddess. Much of the origins of classical and modern ceremonial sorcerous practice and ceremony have their origins in Mesopotamian (pre Judeo-

---

[76] Demons and Population Control by Erle Lichty, 1971

Christian) practice as found in not only her tablets but other practice in Temples.

Lamashtu is described that she has the head of a lion and sometimes a dog as shown in others. The association with the lion is that the majority of her demon-god siblings and the Ugallu have nearly identical manifestations. While the Ugallu (lion-demon) is her primary head, she appears as having the head of a dog which is actually a wolf. In one text Anu is attributed as her father, Ea educated or initiated her and Enlil gave her the head of a "bitch" (i.e. female dog). This may be a misinterpretation of the native classification of UR-demons, gods and beasts of prey. Specifically the word for dog "UR.GI", the lion "UR.MAH" and wolf "UR.BAR.RA" are found in the same family in association. A name of Lamashtu is also Barbaru/Barbarat or "She-Wolf".

Lamashtu is associated to the red star in the kidney of LU.LIM, known as Andromedae. The name of **Ka-mus-i-ku-em**, "Eaten by the mouth of the Serpent" is a name associated with **Pasittu**, the "Obliterating One" which is Lamashtu. This red star, associated with the fallen-from-heaven goddess herself may provide some fodder for the imagination of those working with Lamashtu.

Lamashtu holds numerous atavistic powers *in the symbols* of forms she assumes. Her wolf form, for instance is the predatory instinct, the sexual desire to devour. The serpents in which she holds indicates she offers wisdom to those who dare seek her. Her breasts offer nourishment to the beasts of the earth; her lion-head is her mastery over not only the predatory instinct, also the ability to manifest her divine (yet cruel) nature in the sun. An Arslan-Tash amulet displays Lamashtu as the Barbaru or "She-Wolf" with a scorpion tail[77]. Lamashtu is described as a

---

[77] Kelilinschriftlkiche Bibliothek Schrader Berlin

"demoness, lies in wait for her victims like a wolf, and sniffs out their trail[78]".

Lamashtu is shown in a clay plaque as a hideous, nude hag with the head of a lion-demon, with sagging large breasts. In this plaque, she is able to slip through in spirit-form into houses and the cracks of doors and windows. Often, plaques were hung in rooms (opposite of the doorway) to keep Lamashtu from taking a victim in the home.

Lamashtu appears also as having the head of a snake, a bird of prey, and also appears not only nude yet also more beast-like and even robed. The hands of Lamashtu are described as having seven fingers representing her "seven-fold grasp[79]". On one amulet Lamashtu is in full wolf-form devouring a baby, indicating her ability to utilize her Therionick nature and protean skill in assuming forms.

The following few pages illustrate basic clay talismans of Lamashtu in her various manifestations. If creating a talisman of summoning, one side should have an image of the goddess; the back should have her Seven Names and a sentence of intent, "it is my will for Lamashtu to visit me in dreams, that me may seek to drain others" if vampiric.

---

[78] Lamashtu, a Profile", Wiggerman.

[79] Lamashtu, Daughter of Anu, a profile" from Birth in Babylonia.

Lamashtu in lion-demon form

The triangle with the 7-pointed star (representing seven names of Lamashtu) may be placed within the triangle on any talisman.

LAMASHTU PLAQUE DRAWINGS

Lamashtu as Wolf

Lamashtu Werewolf

Lamashtu Asakku-Ugallu form

Lamashtu Lion-Hag-Bird

Lamashtu Bird of Prey/Eagle

Lamashtu Lion-Bird-Hag

Clay Talismans drawings of Lamashtu

Lamashtu as Lion-Hag

Lamashtu Lion-Demon

Lamashtu Ugallu-Demon

Lamashtu Hag-Wolf

Clay talisman drawings of Lamashtu

The Earth-Elements Associated with Lamashtu

The elements in which demons manifest in often reflect that in which they are attributed to in nature. Lamashtu has dwellings in the marsh-lands, the wild places outside of society where demons and their predatory beasts dwell such as the mountain-regions as well. Some examples of the form of Lamashtu and her elemental manifestations are mentioned below, as attributed in classical terms.

Wolf-human hybrid: Earth (natural order, predatory spirit)

Ugallu (lion-demon) headed: Fire (drive, motivation)

Bird of Prey headed (sometimes Anzu/Azag/Asakku): Air (spiritual, dreaming projection)

Serpent headed: Water (underworld)

The Names, Incantations and the Sorcerer's purpose of invoking Lamashtu

The Demon-Gods of Ancient Mesopotamia were able to be turned away from killing and feeding by creating clay or bronze images of the demons, consecrating them with water, anointing oil and performing incantations with offerings. Pazuzu also would feed and drink the blood of women and newborns; however by utilizing him with offerings and respect he would protect mothers and keep Lamashtu away.

The primary role of Lamashtu was to kill children; this was a suitable way of explaining death of infants in a climate and time when childbirth was a dangerous event. It also provided the people something to blame this unfortunate natural event on.

The Kassapu may invoke Lamashtu to seek the knowledge of the underworld in relation to the self; Lamashtu seeks more life and it allows her the passage through the world of the living and her journey back. Offerings to Lamashtu were made in the form of her going back to the underworld rather than killing onward. She is given a cloak, jewels, a comb and anointing oil.

Lamashtu may be invoked and made manifest to gain energy from her prey. In modern times the Kassapu will not invoke her to harm children or mothers, rather to draw from the energy source in which she drains from other. We must understand that demons were often symbolized from sickness as well.

LAMASHTU AS ARDAT LILI

Lamashtu is identified as Ardat Lili in some texts relating to Pazuzu, specifically when Pazuzu is called "King of the Lilu-demons". While Lamashtu is not shown with wings except in a select few clay plaques, the Lilitu is identified as the "Goddess of Night" shown with the lions on the Burney relief. The "fury" of Lamashtu is compared to a "Lilu" demon which, like her will steal children and drink their blood. What we can be sure of with Lamashtu is that she is a shape-shifting goddess; she also is not limited to children as mentioned before. She will drink the blood and eat the flesh of any she wishes to. In some incantations she is called to "fly away with the birds of the sky"[80].

Lilu demons are interested in drinking blood and consuming flesh for substance in the world, thus they are highly flexible in their ability to assume various forms and ride the winds to their victims. In a modern sense, Lilu demons drain astral energy; they draw from this energy when you sleep or if they attach to

---

[80] Lamashtu, a Profile, F.A.M. Wiggerman

you. Once they have drained you, they are able to continue on in the world.

SUMMONING LAMASHTU

Lamashtu, like all other spirits, demons and gods have the ability to appear in the astral or dream plane clothed in the elements they wish to create their body from, the atavistic or primal nature in which they are driven by. Lamashtu, appearing in the physical plane will be represented by those bestial-forms and their predatory actions. A useful time of "invoking" or "consecrating" something to the goddess is by watching a recorded act of a lion devouring prey, recalling the mind to the symbol; atavistic resurgence.

Additionally, feeding a live rat to a snake and during the strangulation process in your home during an incantation to the goddess will feed her atavistic-gate in this world and through the temple of darkness which is the Kassapu. If you don't have a pet as such, a small amount of your own blood (not another's') will provide the link in the gateway of your mind.

Lamashtu has many names, many of which are used in incantations to keep her from harming mothers and children.

Names are symbols of specific power or energy. No matter if you invoke gods of light or darkness, names are utilized as the subconscious mind itself is empowered or recalled by definition and meaning. Names/words are how we apply identification in all elements of our life. Streets, authority-figures (policeman, judge, cook, and prostitute is an example) and categorized generalizations are used.

For instance, most people will recognize authority first in a policeman or uniformed individual than the assumed image of a prostitute. Thus when you utter the barbarous words of summoning, allow yourself to grow inflamed and excited with intoning the words, if in a need of being quiet situation, vibrate the words in a controlled manner visualizing each name as a mask of Lamashtu.

THE NAMES OF LAMASHTU ARE:

"Lamashtu, Daughter of Anu."

"Innin, queen of queens."

"Lamashtu, O great lady, Who seizes the painful Asakku"

"Sister of the Gods of the Streets."

"The Sword which splitteth the skull."

"She who kindleth a Fire."

"Goddess of whose face causeth horror"

"Committed to the hand."

"Barbaru": *(Barbarat, She-Wolf)*

"Eradicator"

"Hnqt'mr"[81], "She who strangles the lamb"

LAMASHTU IS KNOWN TO HAVE SEVEN OTHER NAMES:

"Dimme, Daughter of Anu"

"Who was named by the gods"

"Victoria, heroine among ladies"

"Lamashtu the exalted"

"Who holds the evil Asakku in a tight grip"

"South Wind Weighing heavily on mankind"

When invoking the Goddess Lamashtu/Labartu, consider that each name you recite visualize the action she shall perform,

---

[81] (possible pronunciation: Ha-nwuat, mirr)

visualize her and the energy she gains from each act. Lamashtu like her later manifestation of the Judaic Lilith demonstrates her plethora of names which indicate the type of action/manifestation she brings forth.

If you use a drawing of carving of the goddess, scribe one set of the above names of Lamashtu, the bottom line should read "Lamashtu is to instruct me in the art of dream vampirism" or something similar.

Known also as "Irnina" provides the foundation for the "Satrina" of the later Lilith goddess emergence. In some text, Lamashtu is a confidant of Irnina who is a Sumerian goddess akin to Inanna/Ishtar. The later manifestation of the Judaic Lilith demonstrates the Deific Mask of Ishtar, Lamashtu, Ardat Lili, Lili and Ereshkigal as the Goddess of Night and the Underworld.

The Labartu texts, a series of incantations which describe the Goddess in details offers clues to her vampiric nature as well as her ability to remain as a "rebel god" like her brothers, the Seven Maskim.

Like her siblings the Seven Sebitti/Maskim, Lamashtu may prove a challenging Deific Mask for the Kassapu as she is not simply a demon *per se*; she is a goddess who by this account represents the control of phenomena while still having demonic existence as well.

We see the survival of the Deific Mask of Lamashtu in ancient Greek lore as **Lamia,** *Queen of Libya* and the Gyllo/Obyzou vampire-demon. In Judaic lore she is Lilith, queen of demons which is Lamashtu combined with other Deific Masks such as Ishtar, Ereshkigal and others.

Lamashtu plaque with Pazuzu and Seven Evil Gods

Lamashtu Plaque Pazuzu on back

LILITU

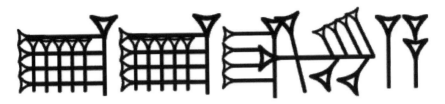

The Lilith of modern interpretation has a plethora of deific masks she wore in numerous manifestations throughout antiquity. Some are predatory, some more balanced and creative depending on circumstance and need.

Lilitu (Lilith) is an ancient demon-goddess, a vampire spirit which haunts the deserts and wild places of Mesopotamia. The name of Lilitu may be derived from 'lalu' "luxuriousness" or 'lulu' "lasciviousness". Like Labartu/Lamashtu, Lilitu is not bound by any specific laws, although there are incantations to keep her away. The various classes of night spirits when unified all contain elements of the later Rabbinic Lilith, the Bride of Samael.

Lilitu is the night-witch who is both skilled in sorcery yet also therionick or "beast-like" in her form according to her disposition. The Lilitu-Witches are wraiths, demons that exist in the realm of shades and grow strong in the physical plane from drinking blood and drawing energy. The Lilitu like Labartu/Lamashtu and the later Greek Empusae and Lamia are called "Murderess" and "strangler".

We can see from the Sumerian relief of the Goddess of the Underworld the manifestation of Lilitu as Goddess of the Underworld and Night. She is shown with the horned tiara, a symbol of divinity, wings pointing downward as a symbol of the underworld, two rod and circles held upward representing her divinity. The legs are as those of an owl or winged bird of prey and she is supported by two owls and lions, symbolizing her mastery over both the solar lions and birds of night. Consider that also just as the solar power is great in the day-hours,

Shamash-Utu and Nergal illuminate a "Black Sun" in the underworld.

The known relief of Lilith shows her described above; however the symbolism is even more interesting concerning the Sumerian associations. The essebu, "owl" is an association/correspondence of **Kilili**, the epithet/name of Inanna being the Goddess of Harlots. She is nocturnal by nature, practicing her skills beginning at dusk as when the owl hunts.

If you make a combination of Ardat Lili, Lilitu, Lamashtu/Labartu, Ereshkigal and Inanna/Ishtar you will have the manifestation of the Hebraic Lilith and the Greek texts under various names. The Names of Power associated with the Hebraic Lilith are numerous and have deeper meaning. They are known from several Jewish texts and are from the Greek-Hellenic influence in the area.

THE NAMES OF LILITH

(From Studies and Texts in Folklore, M. Gaster)

Lilith, Abitr, Abeko, Amizo, Batna, Eilo, Ita, Izorpo, Kali, Kea, Kokos, Odam, Partasah, Patrota, Podo, Satrina, Talto.

SECOND VARIATION OF THE NAMES OF LILITH

(From The Book of Lilith, Barbara Black Koltuv, Ph.D.)

Lilith, Abitr, Abito, Amorfo, Khods, Ikpodo, Ayylo, Ptrota, Abnukta, Strine, Kle Ptuza, Tltoi Pritsa

THIRD VARIATION OF NAMES OF LILITH

(From Folk-Lore of the Holy Land, J.E. Hanauer)

Abro, Abyzu, Ailo, Alu, Amiz, Amizu, Ardad Lili, Avitu, Bituah, Gallu, Gelou, Gilou, 'Ik, 'Ils, Kalee, Kakash, Kema, Lamassu[82], Lilith, Partashah, Petrota, Pods, Raphi, Satrina(h), Thiltho, Zahriel, Zefonith

FOURTH VARIATION OF NAMES OF LILITH

(From The Hebrew Goddess by Patai)

Lilith, Abitar, Abiqar, Amorpho, Hakash, Odam, Kephido, Ailo, Matrota, Abnukta, Shatriha, Kali, Taltui, Kitsha

THE MEANING OF THE NAMES OF LILITH

The Meaning of the names of Lilith is the source for her power as a divine goddess who resides both in the infernal (chthonic) and empyrean (air, heavens) region. Many of her names are from several interpretations of Hellenic, Judaic, Babylonian-Sumerian and Akkadian and even from India. Please consider that trade routes really made a passage way for the myths and religion spread and association through neighboring cultures.

The names of Lilith are specific "power" areas for her quality. Ayylo Oko Pdo or Ikpodo and Ayylo translate to the Greek Child stealing Harpies Aello (stormwind) and Okypete (swift-flying one). Satrina(h) or Shatrina is from Strina which is in turn from Striga = strix/strega; the child stealing witch/vampire (see Lamashtu) who takes the form of a screech-owl, Amorpho is a name meaning "ugly". Abnuka is from epinukitos - "nocturnal". Khods is "flying one" and kko eidem (Kokos and Odam) is from Kakoeides – "ugly". Kle Bduza is from Kleptousa or "female childstealer" or "female thief".

We see in the Third Variation many names added to Lilith are but names of other divine spirits from Babylonain – Assyrian lore, Gallu (the lion-demons), Lamassu (a mistranslation of what

---

[82] A corruption of Lamashtu, also a name of the goddess.

should have been Lamashtu. The Lamassu is a guardian) however Ardat Lili was correct. We see also the Obizuth who described herself to King Solomon as being a night spirit who may take many forms and shapes. She is also described as a winged female dragon to fights against an Archangel Bazazath in the Testament of Solomon.

ARDAT LILI

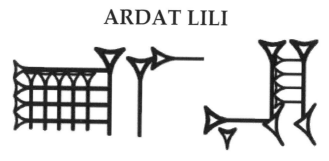

Handmaiden of Lili

The Seductress Vampire & Demoness

The Handmaid of Lilith, a demoness and vampire-spirit who seems related to Lamashtu, the Goddess and daughter of Anu. The Ardat Lili is a nightmare or succubus spirit who joins with man or woman when sleeping. The medieval succubus and incubus along with the Lilith and Labartu demons are from which they derive. The nightmare is called by the Akkadian name Kiel-udda-karra.

LILU

Ghost winds, Male Lilit

The Lilu is the male incubus or vampire offspring of the Semetic Lilith. Entering the dreams of woman, the vampire-demon Lilu drains the sleeper of vital energy through sexual or fearsome experiences in her own mind. The release of energy through phobia and anxiety feeds the Lilu accordingly. The female of Lilu are the Lilitu.

GALLU LIMNU /MULLA-HUL

Evil Devil & Blood Drinking Demons

The Gallu are closely associated with the Sunu Zikiku or Maskim, in many incantation tablets the Gallu is but another name for the Maskim as their manifestation is nearly exact. The Gallu in later cultures such as Greek is united with Lamashtu to become Gyllou/Gello/Obyzou, a vampire-demoness who conducts her actions the same way that Lamashtu does.

The Gallu is a devil which assumes the form of a Bull, relating it as the "Evil Genius" or rebellious demon. The Gallu is called "The headstrong bull, the great ghost"[83] and like the Seven Maskim is described as being "neither male or female" thus having no human associations in gender or existence. The Gallu are said to be seven in number as well and are known to drag souls to Irkalla, the land of darkness.

The Gallu seek the blood of man to devour and seems to be a title which includes younger types of spirits. These "Evil Devils" as their name translates are literal demons or "genius" which have individual consciousness and dwell outside living flesh in spirit form. We may sense them by our hairs standing on end, a feeling of "someone is watching" or consistent noises which cannot be explained by some normal household occurance.

The Gallu are described as being "devastators of heaven and earth, the bull which pierces, the very strong bull, the bull which passes through dwellings....the indomitable Telal, there are seven of them...they watch men, they devour flesh; they make blood flow, they drink blood...they injure the images of the gods..." – W.A.I. IV, 2,4

The Ugallu are different from the Gallu Limnu as the first mentioned have the head of lion-demons and human bodies, the Gallu Limnu when appearing in anthropomorphic form appear as bull-men.

---

[83] Tablet V, col. 3 and Devils, Demons…Thompson.

Apkallu fighting Gallu-Sedu Demon

Guardian Beneficial Sedu-Demon

SUNU ZIKIKU
SEBITTU – MASKIM

THE SEVEN PHANTOMS OF FLAME

Their names are many, from Gallu Limnu, Sebitti (Seven), Maskil Hul (Evil Fiends) they are known from the most ancient of times. Sunu Zikiku, the "roaming windblast" is also a name for the Seven Maskim or powerful, malevolent Gods of rebellion. The Seven Gods/Demons, born of the union of ANU and KI, thus of the Air/heavens and the Earth are perhaps the most powerful rebel-gods next to their sister, Lamashtu. The Sebittu are powerful demons and gods who hold magnificent power and assist Erra (Nergal) in his battles. They control weather and represent the chaos of nature. They are of the four elements, earth, air, fire and water.

The Sebittu/Sebitti, called "UDUGS" or "Utukku" are demons who hold both beneficial and malicious traits. It is perceived[84] that the Sebittu are balanced in their nature, although they are found as terrifying demons. The Seven fought a great battle with Ninurta, the God of War and were temporarily defeated as they

---

[84] Personal experience in meditation and ritual work with the Seven Maskim in the few years leading up to this grimoire.

cannot be completely destroyed. In ancient tablets, the Gods are referred to as "the evil gods are raging storms, ruthless spirits created in heaven's vaults". They are more inclined and comfortable with causing storms and devouring, like an invading army of ancient times.

The Seven are often called "Udughul" and "Utukku", however should not confuse them with the *raised-from-the grave "Utukku"*, for they are different. The Seven Udughul are divine (gods) and not human. While some humans can ascend and become divine (gods), the Seven Maskim were never "human" and cannot deeply relate.

Dina Katz[85] in her execellent documentation of the Sumerian Underworld, associates the Seven Gallu with Ereshkigal, whom she lists as the probable "mother", although this is questionable. The Seven are listed consistently as the offspring of Anu and Ki, unless Ereshkigal may be a "manifestation" of Ki along with Ishtar, it is unlikely. The reference of "they are messengers of Ereshkigal" does not hold weight to parentage; for the Seven are listed as Messengers of "Bel" and "evil ones of Ea" and also are called "Beloved Son(s) of Bel". The Seven are consistently listed as the sons of Anu and Ki, thus their association with the others indicate they "work" in association with the other gods from time to time.

The Seven Spirits are immortal and powerful demons and more precisely gods as they hold deific power of certain phenomena as well as the ability to move distinctly. The invocations against the Seven describe their anthropomorphic manifestations as demons, which hold associations with the darker forces of nature. What is clear in the ancient texts is that the Maskim are the highest class of demons, the same as Gods while they don't seek to empower the sheep of humanity. These Dark Gods inspire the strong who seek the depths of knowledge in which Ea is crown Prince over.

---

[85] The Image of the Netherworld in the Sumerian Sources, pg 145.

The Kassapu who seeks communion with the Maskim must be carefully balanced in the art of sorcery; there must be personal experience of both Gods of Light and Darkness. Invoking the Maskim will take a very long period of exploration and experience. Understanding the attributes of the Seven is significant to recognizing their nature as it manifests within you.

It is the Sumerian and Akkadian tablets themselves which name the ascended majesty of the Maskim, naming them gods which are vast and immortal in essence. As they are of "ignited flame", we may hold association to Luciferianism or the Adversarial Path, the Black Flame or the isolate intelligence of the Psyche.

The Seven Maskim are invoked in numerous tablets referring to them as gods of the vast heavens, of the great earth, of igneous spheres, malevolent gods, phantoms, seven malevolent phantoms of the flames, in the earth Seven and so on. As with demons, it seems only Lamashtu is held in such high regard despite the fear she instills.

The Seven Gods known as the Maskim dwell not only in the heavens (astral plane) yet as the Seven Stars or Pleiades, also the earth (the chthonic depths, the physical world itself within humanity) and have a "hidden retreat" within the depths of the Ocean. Being that Ea is a God of the Abyss or Ocean Depths, these gods may visit the underworld palace of Ea. Keeping in mind that they are "Throne Bearers of Ea", and no doubt they hold association with the great immortal god. They are called at times enemies of Ea as even he has challenges controlling these powerful gods.

In a tablet known as the "Seven Evil Spirits" the Gods neither male or female, they are bred (or empowered, rested) in the depths of the ocean, they are as the roaming windblast, having no wives or sons. They hearken not to prayer of supplication. As the Kassapu ascends in his or her Magick, the Seven Gods may be invoked and if proper offerings are made, invocations of respect (never banishing) and the spirits directed towards their own attributes within the self (the mind and associations).

The symbol of the Maskim is the seven pointed star, which holds association to the shadow aspect of the Seven planets and to the Pleiades or MUL.MUL, the Seven Stars. We see the connection of the Seven Planets in Yatukih-Daevayasna[86] or Zoroastrianism later on.

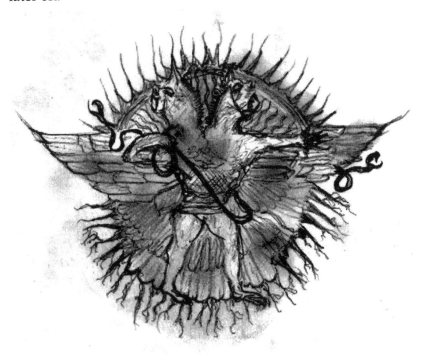

A Sigil-Talisman of the Seven Phantoms of Ignited Spheres, the Ilu Limnu

These Maskim as they are, said to be counterparts or adversaries at times to the seven planets and their ruling Gods. One may consider the parallel association in Zoroastrianism, wherein the Seven ArchDaevas of Ahriman are in existence in the same manner[87].

---

[86] Liber HVHI, Gates of Dozak, Luciferian Witchcraft by Michael W. Ford

[87] Compare the ArchDavaes in Luciferian Witchcraft, Liber HVHI, Gates of Dozak, The Bible of the Adversary for associations and sigils.

The Seven Maskim or "Ensnarers" are symbolized by the modern work of the Kassapu as a seven pointed "star" with each point terminating with a "head" and symbol for each god. The Seven Gods will challenge the sorcerer, for they are associated with all the elements at different points. They are said to dwell in the bowls of the earth, they essence grown so powerful even in the days of Babylonia that they surpass all other in power and their ability to terrify all.

The traditional symbol of the Seven Stars in their astral form is the ancient seven circles aligned together with one at the head of them; in ancient lore the Sebitti as the Seven Stars journey with Nergal-Erra, the God of Plague, War and Death.

In *"Chaldean Magic and Sorcery"*[88] the Seven Maskim are described to ravage the heavens and earth and trouble the natural order itself. Understanding the Sebittu is best considered in learning of the balance of destruction and creation in nature itself. When something "bad" happens, something "good" arises from the ashes. The Kassapu must be willing to move past the torment of duality to balance both darkness and light within; doing so will prepare you for such black or alchemical magick of Theurgy, self-creation itself!

Nergal/Erra is given the Seven Maskim to direct them in sending plague and battle to others. After Anu had impregnated Earth (Ki) and she bore the Seven Evil Gods, they stood before Anu and he named them Sebitti (the Seven).

The Seven Maskim proceeds from the Western Mountains, increasing in the Eastern Mountains. Thus from darkness they move and increase to the East and then downward into darkness. The Western Mountain was the place where the door to Hades is found, often identified in the south-west as well. The Mountain of the North-East was the symbol of the human race, where life arose and man conquered in the image of the Gods!

---

[88] Francois Lenormant.

In an Akkadian poem on the Seven Maskim[89] the Fire God is asked how the Seven were born. The Fire God replies that "seven in the mountain of the sunset were born, in the mountain of sunrise grew up. The Seven Maskim dwells in the caverns of the earth, the desolate places such as mountains and the deserts.

The Seven Evil Gods are said to be "unknown among the wise Gods" although Anu and Ki brought them into being; they are called "Throne bearers of Ea" and work in accordance with Adad and have Shamash as their companion at times. The Seven gallop over the Mountain of Sunset. These Gods are very powerful, for even the God of Fire, Girra, is not overly willing to discuss them. In a tablet Girra seeks to speak with Marduk of the Seven, who speaks in whispers under the canopy of night.

Marduk then discussed this matter with Ea, the Lord of the Abyss who answered solemnly. Ea informs Marduk the Seven were born of the earth and reared in the earth. They are able to transverse the heavens and also the bounds of the ocean.

The hollows of the earth they have their own dwelling, on the high-places of the earth they proclaimed. The Seven in the mountain of the sunset they rise, in sunrise they set.", hollowing into the earth.

We see that this is contrary to the "ascension" of Shamash, thus the Seven Maskim are "antinomian" to the natural order itself; they are rebellious spirits who have made themselves gods in the world and beyond.

This destructive image of the Maskim is but a veil, for the key to unlocking their power within yourself and thus the world you live in is in their symbols and nature. We will explore this further shortly.

---

[89] Translated by A.H. Sayce, M.A.

The Sigil of the Sebitti/Maskim by Marchozelos

THE DESCRIPTION OF THE SEVEN MASKIM

The great evil gods, the ones of primordial darkness, the children of Anu and Ki are rebellious gods who are able to take numerous forms. The Sebitti will be described in original forms here. The sigil of the Sebitti demonstrates their early manifestations.

The first of the Seven is the South Wind; Anu declared *"When you band together and march out, you will have no rival"*.

The second is a dragon with mouth agape that none can withstand. Anu decreed that it shall *"ignite like Girra and blaze like a flame"*.

The third is a grim leopard that carries off children. Anu gave this one the power *"to put on the face of a lion, so that anyone who sees him shall collapse in terror."*

The fourth is a terrible serpent and Anu commanded, *"the mountain flees before the one who bears your fierce weapons."*

The fifth is a furious wolf from which Anu proclaimed, *"blow like the wind and go forth to the rim of the earth."*

The sixth is a rebellious giant who submits neither to god nor king. Anu decreed that this one shall *"go above and below and spare none"*.

The seventh is an evil windstorm (messenger of the fatal wind) from which Anu filled with dragon's venom to *"lay low living things"*.

Going on to explain the nature of the Gods the Maskim are said to *"bear gloom from city to city"* and who are *"tempests that furiously scour the heavens"*. The Maskim are not named individually yet are frequently attributed to the Powers of the Air which no doubt accounts for some of the origin of the Adversary in later Judeo-Christian texts.

The Maskim have a great power over the air, being *"Rushing windgusts who casts darkness over the brightest day.."* who *"force their way with baneful windstorms."*

The Seven Evil Gods send forth lightning bolts in the height of heaven, which makes them as mentioned supporters of Enlil/Enki the Storm God. The Seven Maskim also has the power of the evil wind, called Imkhullu which was given to Marduk in his rebellion against the Dark Mother Tiamat. The Seven have in their rebellion the support and empowerment of their father, Anu who in turn gives them the power to wield Imkhullu.

Through the many incantation tablets there is much which describes the nature and essence of the Maskim. While there is not an elaborate authoritative text surviving on the Seven Gods, the tablets when compared side by side describes a great detail in clues concerning their powers.

The Maskim support the workings of Ea, Adad, Nergal-Erra and other gods. In the Utukki Linuti XVI the Maskim are "Mighty Destroyers" and "the deluge of the storm-god, stalking at the right hand of the storm god". As their non-human forms have been described, the Sebitti also appear in human form as well; a traditional, bearded God wearing the horned cap of divination, holding an axe and what appears to be a bow and arrow. The inscription describes them perfectly; *"the Seven Gods, the warlike gods, who carry bow and arrow, whose rising means war"*. Another form of the Seven Evil Gods is depicted from all symbolized as one Lion-Dragon demon, winged attacking Sin. This symbol is highly suitable for meditation and ritual work also.

The Seven Evil Gods represented as One

The children of Anu, in modern associative terms would be called "Fallen Angels[90]". They did not answer to any God specifically and one tablet describes how Bel[91] (Marduk) with Ea, the Lord of the Abyss who is called "The Guide" of the Gods counseled with Sin (the Moon), Shamash (the Sun) and Ishtar (Venus) who are the dominion of the heavenly host.

Soon the Seven Maskim entered the vault of heaven and gathered about the Moon God, Sin. Soon they won to their side Shamash who is *"The Mighty"* and Adad the Warrior (*the Storm God*).

The Seven Evil Gods eclipsed the Moon and brought much chaos into the night sky. Bel (Marduk) told his minister Nuzku to go and bear a message to Ea in the Ocean Deep and describe the

---

[90] I use this definition cautiously, however "messenger" is "angelos" and "fallen" indicates they do not dwell in the abode of the Gods as they exist. The term has no Christian connotation beyond this.

[91] Bel is a title meaning "Lord" (Baal) and refers to Gods in their domains, such as Ninurta in Anzu, etc.

chaos before them. Ea then described a spell on which a Tamarisk is given and an Incantation of Eridu to exorcize the Seven Evil Gods away.

It seems according to some spell tablets that the Seven Maskim holds much power over other demons and spirits as well when they wish to. Ereshkigal, called the wife of Ninazu is asked to *"turn her face elsewhere"* that she may have an interest in the work of the Seven. It seems when one is sick and afflicted by some aspect of the Seven, and then Ereshkigal grows hungry in obtaining the spirits.

In "Assyrian Discoveries: An Account of explorations and discoveries on the site of Nineveh" by George Smith there is a translation of a tablet describing the Seven Wicked Gods.

"In the first days the evil gods, the angels who were in rebellion, who in the lower part of heaven had been created, they caused their evil work, devising their wicked heads...ruling to the river... There were seven of them. The first was . . .the second was a great animal . . . .the third was a leopard . . . . the fourth was a serpent . . . . the fifth was a terrible . . . . which to . . . . . the sixth was a striker which to god and king did not submit, the seventh was the messenger of the evil wind which . . . . made. The seven of them messengers of the god Anu their king from city to city went round the tempest of heaven was strongly bound to them, the flying clouds of heaven surrounded them, the downpour of the skies which in the bright day makes darkness, was attached to them with a violent wind, an evil wind, they began, the tempest of Vul was their might, at the right hand of Vul they came, from the surface of heaven like lightning they darted, descending to the abyss of waters, at first they came. In the wide heavens of the god Anu the king evil they set up, and an opponent they had not." –Assyrian Discoveries, George Smith

We see here the Seven as "Messangers of Anu", the definition of "Angel" is "Messanger" and is not tied to any specific pantheon. The Seven Gods of course survived into much later magical texts.

"Seven of them the evil gods, spirits of death, having no fear, seven of them the evil gods, who like a flood descend and sweep over the earth. To the earth like a storm they come down. Before the light of Sin fiercely they came..."- Assyrian Discoveries, George Smith

SEVEN MASKIM:
HERALDS OF PESTILENCE

The Seven Maskim or Evil Gods are given the title of the "Heralds of the Pestilence", "Throne-bearers of Ninkigal" and "Throne-bearers of the Gods" They are seven gods of the broad heaven and earth; they are robber gods (stealing life, vampiric towards spiritual energy and the sacred fire). The Seven Gods are described as "demons like raging bulls, great ghosts that break through all houses."

The Sebitti (Seven) are not only immortal gods, dwelling in many places as they desire they also are said to "rage against mankind. The Seven spill blood like rain, devouring their flesh and sucking their veins." "They are demons full of violence, ceaselessly devouring blood". As the Sebitti are not bound to the depths of the sea, the earth, the underworld or the heavens. They direct the storms and have the support of Adad the storm god.

Using the winds and the powers of the air, they direct the plague of pestilence to destroy crops and make humans sick. The first of the Seven is described as "The South Wind"; Pazuzu who commands the powers of the air with his father as is known from his statue description. "I am the god Pazuzu, son of the god Hanbi, king of the evil wind demons".

THE EVIL ONES OF EA:
THE RAVENS OF DEATH

The Seven Maskim also "Evil Ones of Ea" who are throne bearers of the gods. They march like great assaulting armies and gallop forth among the hills like horses. The rites of exorcism to deter the Seven Evil Gods is only Anu who is symbolized as "The Heavens". They are messengers of Ea who holds powers of balance, being both destructive and creative.

The ancient Palestinian "Unclean Spirit" is no doubt the Seven Maskim surviving through the ages. They are not called "Gods" at this time as the Babylonian culture is nearly forgotten; however they are now "evil spirits" who move from place to place.

The survival of the Maskim in Syria and Palestine preserved some of the basic attributes of the Evil Gods. One Syriac charm describes them as "Seven accursed brothers, destructive ones...why do you creep along on your knees and move upon your hands?" the Gods then answer "we go on our hands, so that we may eat flesh, we crawl along upon our hands that we may drink blood" and then the charm moves into trying to command the Seven by Gabriel and the Holy Ghost, which no doubt is an alien upstart to ones as old as they are. In some Assyrian tablets they are said to "creep like a snake on their bellies".

The Unclean Spirit mentioned in Gospel of St. Luke continues the tradition of the Seven Maskim. As the spirits leave a man possessed they enter swine. The Seven Evil Gods in Assyrian lore are called along with lesser demons as "the unclean spirit" who, when having gone out of a body of a man passes through waterless places, seeking rest. Beliar in the "Testament of Twelve Patriarchs" sends forth the seven evil spirits against man.

Evil spirits and gods are often depicted as having a 'bird' form when they desire. "an evil demon that like a bat dwelleth in the caverns by night, or an evil demon like that a bird of night flieth in dark places.."[92]

The Seven are associated with traditional birds representing the underworld. In one specific cylinder, a single composite dragon-lion-bird demon, standing upright in a similar position of Tiamat and Asakku is shown assailing the Moon God Sin is a symbol of the Seven. Called "The Bitter venom of the gods, they are great storms directed from Heaven (Anu), they are the owls which hoot over a city", the Sebitti are supported by many of the gods.

Feeding upon man like vampires, it is no doubt they are brothers to Lamashtu and quite possibly even Pazuzu. Birds such as ravens are considered ill omen among the Semites although with the Assyrians ravens are birds which help the gods while among the Arabs they are hostile. Syriac Christians have many legends of evil spirits possess men and when banished often take the form of ravens in flight. Rabban-bar-idta[93] was sent many demons by a sorcerer in the form of "black stinking ravens" who sought to destroy him. As the owl is the bird of the Seven Maskim in ancient Assyria, the owl is a symbol of a Lilith or a wraith of a woman seeking to take a child of a mother.

Ravens also are known as helpers of the gods as well, although we can see from the ritual tablets that the Sebitti co-exist with the gods are work with them when needed.

---

[92] Utukki Limnuti, Tablet B plate XXVIII.

[93] The Histories of Rabban Hormizd The Persian translated by E.A. Wallis Budge, 1902

The Seven Evil Gods Attacking Sin and Ninurta by Marchozelos

Alu and Lilu Shadowbody by Marchozelos

Mus-Sag-Imin Serpent-Dragon and Ninurta by Marchozelos

Kusarikku by Marchozelos

Lamashtu the Goddess by Marchozelos

Ereshkigal and Inanna by Marchozelos

Kingu risen and Ardat Lili by Marchozelos

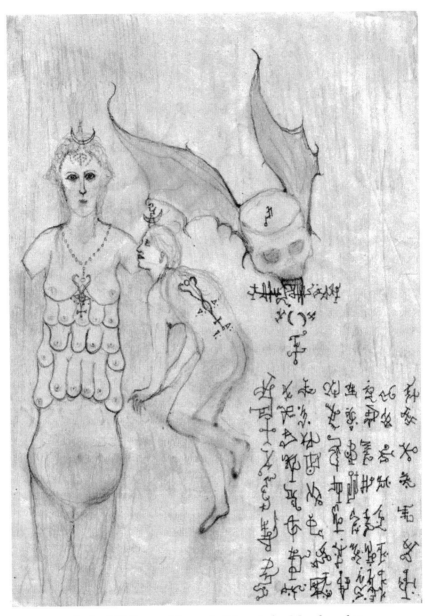

Ardat Lili the goddess of all beasts by Marchozelos

Marduk and Mushussu, the Hidden Darkness by Marchozelos

The Gate of the New Gods by Marchozelos

Nergal, Lord of the Grave, God of Battle, dragon by Marchozelos

CHAPTER SIX

THE RITES OF KASSAPU

The Seven Evil Gods encircled

THE RITES OF KASSAPU

THE BOOK AND GATEWAY

Behold! The path of the abyss is opened forth to those who hear the words! It is the time for the reawakening of Ilu Limnu, the Gods of the Dark Moon, the ancient dragon which swallowed the sun. Within the pages of this grimoires are no Gods of absolute evil, nor of good, within is balance and the power of self and world mastery.

The gods are called by the empyrean and infernal elements in which they are empowered, such must not be ignored. The Kassapu must become familiar with the gods on all levels before the path truly opens.

THE KASSAPU / KASSAPTU

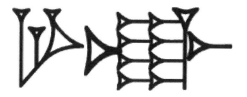

The Sumerian Cuneiform for Kispu, sorcery

Preliminary Definitions

The primary title used for the sorcerer or Luciferian[94] in this grimoire is Kassapu. The definition of this word is "warlock"

---

[94] Luciferian is a modern definition representing a specific initiatory system outlined in "The Bible of the Adversary", "Adversarial Light – Magick of the Nephilim" and "Luciferian Witchcraft".

who practices "destructive" or "black" magick. The feminine of the word is Kassaptu which is of course "witch". Kassapu is from Kispu which is "witchcraft". When referencing "Kassapu" the word is used to describe both the masculine and feminine with no underlining prejudice towards the feminine. As "Asipu" is a word denoting the exorcist who rids humans from demonic and sickness caused by evil gods, the Kassapu is essentially the mirror image or opposite in nature of Asipu.

What must be settled first is the context of what Kassapu is referenced to in relation to the accepted term of "black" or "destructive". In previous works, my own assumption of "black" is to the original definition in Arabic root words, meaning "knowledge" or "wisdom". Like the image of the beast with the single torch between the horns, the awakened or illuminated one, the Kassapu enters the *Mare Tenebrosum* or the "Sea of Darkness" from which Tiamat and Absu and then Kingu brought all the Gods into being and soon humanity to ensure their continued survival in the psyche of mankind.

The Kassapu is commonly associated as a witch which has barely any identification in the world of the living. Like the later Yatukih sect of ancient Persia[95] often these practitioners were hidden in society as within the Priesthood of Marduk/Ea or like the Yatukih, Ohrmazd/Ahura Mazda. What is similar between the two is that Ea associates with the evil gods and spirits and is the great instructor of magick to humanity; Ohrmazd in the Zoroastrian practice made a pact with Ahriman/Angra Mainyu and could not exist without his dark equal Ahriman.

The demonic symbolism and image found in this living grimoire is symbolized of the inner desires, lusts and passions of the Kassapu and the deific masks which take form of composite monsters. Their traits are not random, for even in the most complicated nightmare the symbolism has meaning *somewhere*.

---

[95] Zurvan, A Zoroastrian Dilemma by R.C. Zaehner.

Like Luciferianism as I have introduced with my crowning of Nikephorus[96] I bear further support from the gods of old, Nabu and Ea have decreed this future as I have proclaimed it[97]. Luciferianism provides a multifaceted approach to seeking wisdom, power within and the means of transcending the 'reacting' defensive of socially-perceived "satanism".

This grimoire is a different avenue of Luciferianism with painstaking authenticity of the olds gods, demons, spirits presented in a modern, realistic context. The Kassapu does not "react" to Judeo-Christian "righteousness" but by simply presenting the old gods as how they were before the "sheep herding" blind faith system. The old gods are balanced; you will find many are both destructive and creative. That the darkness holds the keys to our liberation and the very knowledge of our potential, our desires and the unknown spiritual worlds around us is right there for those strong and wise enough to grasp it.

Understand that this grimoire is indeed a modern interpretation of this ancient stream of knowledge, thus it is not a "historically accurate" thesis. While my work has been strongly focused on keeping consistent with known tradition, it has been developed from my own initiatory perspective.

KASSAPU AND THE GODS
The Initiation into the Mysteries

Kassapu: *Masculine, warlock or sorcerer.*

Kassaptu: *Feminine, witch or sorceress*

---

[96] "Bearer of Victory" or the manifestation of the Winged Goddess as crowning a success. Reference of the success of Luciferianism as evolving magick and spirituality as a belief in the possibility of self without the need of blind faith or settling for "what you are now".

[97] Nabu, God of Scribes and Destiny, of which I present a ritual to compel your own destiny of desires you have. Ea, the Lord of the Abyss and God of Magick who has guided me towards the Sebitti or Seven Maskim.

Derived from: *kispu, sorcery and kasapu, 'to bewitch'.*

Kasapu - to bewitch, to ensorcell/encircle
Kispu – witchcraft, sorcery
Zeru – hatred, curse rituals

The recitation of Siptu or *"incantation"* by the Kassapu is not merely a supplication to powers; from the view of the practitioner it is a seizing of the essence and ensorceling of the power itself. The Asipu or "exorcist" will supplicate the gods, and then direct them against another power as servants of the gods. The Kassapu seeks continual transformation and an accumulation of personal power; we do not supplicate or prostrate to anything! The Kassapu seeks to initiate a deep communion with the gods; a variation of the gods and demons should be attempted for a period of time. While not all the gods will find an association within the Kassapu, a majority will.

In the ancient view of Babylonian – Chaldean – Assyrian religion the Kassapu performs destructive sorcery. The veil of initiation into the mysteries through a Luciferian interpretation presents that the Kassapu works a balanced sense of both creative and destructive magick. Internal change; the awareness of possibly and confirmed self-direction towards achievement of goals and spiritual initiation is the goal of all Magick.

Ea, the Lord of the Abyss and of Magick also has his own "Witches" or "Sorcerers", called the Apkallu or predatory-bird headed sages or "watchers". The Apkallu are viewed as "Daemon" or protective spirits associated with the Kassapu.

Luciferians do not distinguish between "black" or "white" magick; all magick is self-directed even if for the gratification of helping another. There is no magick other than "Black". Observe the nature and basic outlook by the ideology of both black and white magicians in our modern world.

THE CATEGORIES OF MAGICK & SORCERY

ANNUNAKI SIPTU
Deific Dialog

In many ritual texts of ancient Mesopotamia, we find an interaction between one god and a lesser one, instructions to cast a spell. Traditionally, one made against the Seven Evil Gods features Marduk and Ea. This structure is a psychodrama and interplay from one deific mask to another, establishing the command of the Kassapu during the rite. As you are self-initiated into the workings, you may wish to adapt interplay between different gods depending on the goal.

MIMMA LEMNU KISPU
Demonic Incantations, summoning to objects or people

The demonic incantations are utilized to bind them to objects or to utilize in dreams. This is what would be "lower" or "Therionick/Yatukih" sorcery. Utilized for spells, curses, astral/dream projection, empowerment and lust.

SIPTU ILU HURSAN ANU
Magick of self-transformation & power

This is the category of incantations used to empower the self, offering libations and fumigations to the gods and invoking the deific mask to gain knowledge and thus power from the aspect the god represents to the self. This type from the name is **'Incantation Ordeal of Anu'**, interestingly enough witches are called **Marat Anim sa same**[98], *"Heavenly daughters of Anu"*. The

---

[98] Mesopotamian Witchcraft, Tzvi Abusch.

Kassapu either male or female proceeds with incantations of both the Annunaki above and below, furthering to the dead gods of Kingu and Tiamat, working all the while with Lamashtu and the Seven Maskim/Sebitti. This is the process of the "Great Work" or "Holy Guardian Angel/Azal'ucel" by other pantheons.

DIVINATION AND SELF-DIRECTED PATHS

The Luciferian Approach to Divination and the wise thoughts attributed to Naram-Sin

In the ancient world, there is a strong direction for leaders or people of action to seek the guidance of the gods; seek oracles and often plan wars based on such. In modern times the Luciferian or Kassapu must be cautious in placing too much in consulting something 'outside' of the self. In the Cuthaean Legend of Naram-Sin, Naram-Sin, the Akkadian King questions the gods Ishtar, Baba, Zababa, Anuitum, Nabu and Shamash who did not give him favorable direction to go forth on a campaign. In this text he thinks to himself the following, which is the essence of the Luciferian ideology:

"What lion ever observed oracles? What wolf ever consulted a dream-priestess? I will go like a robber according to my own inclination, and I will take for myself luddu-weapons of iron."-Naram-Sin

As we can see, Naram-Sin by announcement makes himself as the Seven Evil Gods, the Sebitti or Maskim who go according to their own inclination, still working with the gods when they wish to. The Kassapu must understand that he or she is responsible for their individual direction, thus if seeking through divination be cautious in your decisions and compel the gods, demons and spirits to move according to your design when possible.

Meditation, willed-thought and simply compelling, visualizing and shifting your reality towards your goals are ways to accomplish this. As you grow adept in your own workings, this will become clearer through the passing of time and the results therein. Don't expect your goals to come tomorrow no matter how hard you chant or meditate; you still must operate in the constraints of this material world.

MAGICKIAN AS SERPENT
The Word which Compels

The association of the Magician[99] with the serpent has been noted since the earliest records of not only Sumerian text yet also Babylonian, Assyrian, Canaanite and Egyptian religion and magical practice. In a "balbale to Ningiszida[100]" the "Lord (Ningishzida), your mouth is that of a snake with a great tongue, a magician" and is then in a similar script is "a poisonous snake".

As we can see with later religious movements, dualism identified the concept of evil with a specific spirit or demon controlling it rather than the previous balance found in the religions of Egypt, Babylonian-Chaldean, Assyrian and Greek.

"When the Evil Spirit entered, he intermingled the poison of the noxious creatures, the outgrowth of sin, such as that of the serpent, the scorpion, the large venomous lizard, the ant, the fly, the locust, and an immense number of others of this kind, with the waters, the earth, and the plants." – Greater Bundahishn

---

[99] Magician in the terms of this grimoire is spelled "Magickian", the "Kia" in the center representing the compelling of creation and destruction according to the Will of the Kassapu. See Austin Osman Spare, "The Book of Pleasure".

[100] Spelling alternative of name. Hymn from Oriental Department, Oxford University.

The gods of the ancient Mesopotamia were both of darkness and light, they worked together in many instances in relation to nature and their association with humanity; the source of their "food" (in the form of hymns, prayers and offerings of various types). The emergence of Zoroastrianism instructed a difference and grew from a paganism which existed for thousands of years along with ancient Mesopotamian culture.

Ningishzida is understood as a god of the underworld, a throne bearer of Ereshkigal and a fertility deity who bears two cerestes-cerestes horned serpents upon his shoulders, equally so is a symbol of the sorcerer of a beneficial nature in Lagash. This symbol of this underworld god is Azhi-Dahak or Zohak in Zoroastrianism. His manifestation is sorcerous power as a malicious demon of Ahriman.

"The serpent, the dragon, the two-headed and the seven-headed 'azdahak'"-Greater Bundahishn

This dualism further fueled the Judeo-Christian ideology later one in their "absolutism" and monotheistic views which ruled out balance. The concepts within this grimoire demonstrate balance, not complete darkness or light as we do not find this a reasonable application in nature or the world we live in.

Sorcerers and Magicians are viewed as being associated with snakes in nearly every culture. The Greater Bundahishn comments that *"One says that the noxious creatures are all sorcerers and the serpent is the most sorcerous"*.

Initiation in sorcery, the obtainment of knowledge through initiation is based upon the precept of "Know Thyself". Those who open these gates take of the "Tree of Life" and become as gods. Ningishzida is known as the "Lord of the Good Tree" and is a bringer of knowledge via the Underworld (or subconscious).

"By remembering the evil spirits a man gets assistance from the demons and thereby becomes very wicked in both worlds. Thus, for instance Zohak, descended from the world destroying Taj, having remembered the Dev Eshm, received from Ahriman venomous horn-

shaped serpents on the shoulder bones below the neck." – Denkard Book 3

No matter if Zoroastrian, Chaldean-Mesopotamian, Egyptian, Canaanite or Greek-Hellenic, the Serpent represents knowledge and power. It does not matter if it is "good or evil" this is interpreted by those who dictate the religious texts.

The ancient Egyptians, who had interaction with Assyria and Babylon at several points, understood the significance of the serpent in both a creative and destructive way. You find the Uraeus Cobra as a royal and deified symbol, many gods/goddesses such as Sekhmet, Set and other gods took the form of serpents. The gods Shu, Gebb and Khnemu are shown holding snakes in pre-dynastic illustrations[101].

Egyptian magicians were said to utilize snakes in their works of sorcery and high magick relating to the gods. The goddess of magick, Urt-Hekau manifested primarily as a Cobra-headed goddess who also took the form of a frog as well. Heka is the goddess of magick as she herself is that "fire" which was created by Ra. Her name is self-creating, thus the works of magick are empowered by the uttering of the sacred names. This is fueled by the power of Will-Desire-Belief, that within your circle of self, all is possible. There were two sisters: Cobra-goddesses who were deified of Lower and Upper Egypt (Wadjet and Nekhbet). The serpent represents new life and youth, symbolized by the skin-shedding process.

Mesopotamian religion also held the serpent in good regard, primarily as a growth, renewal, power and wisdom symbol. While the serpent was at times malicious, it also was beneficial as well. In sorcerous works, the Muslahhu is a snake-charmer who performs sorcery and is mentioned in several old Malqu texts.

---

[101] From Fetish to God in Ancient Egypt by E.A. Wallis Budge.

THE MYTH AND REALITY OF THE KASSAPU

The word *kassapu* (sorcerer) and *kassaptu* (witch) is a derivative of the verb *kasapu* which translates 'to bewitch'.

The path of the witch or Kassapu is one of an immense power and possibly failure. What causes failure on this path? It is the temptation to fall into short-term pleasures without regard for the future. It is also the temptation to become that which others "define" you to be; destructive. It must be understood that those who are destructive without being creative equally are doomed to undo themselves and slowly adapt to the sickness of self-hate.

The Kassapu will work with darkness as the primary foundation; it is our origin and it must be clear that your beginning patron Goddess is Tiamat. Tiamat and Kingu are the beginnings from which all emerge; Tiamat for the gods and humanity, Kingu for humanity.

The work of the Kassapu is first one of discovery and balance. Firstly, begin a disciplined process of invocation or "calling within" the powers or gods which you seek; then "evocation" or summoning the gods, demons or ghosts to specific objects such as Altar statue, talismans, fetishes or that which you choose.

Incantations require the investment of belief and a focus which allows your mind to intensely encircle the fascination of the working. You may find this works by reciting in formal ceremonial fashion or it may be more suitable by holding and object and reciting to yourself. Some seek the gods or demons by being encircled by the element they represent. To commune with Shamash for the purpose of vitality, inner strength and reason then you may meditate in the sun for a period of time. If seeking the wisdom of Sin you may meditate under the moonlight. As you can see imagination and belief is the key to any successful working.

The process of the sorcerer is to ascend into their own self-directed divinity. Your initial workings with be centering yourself in a balanced aspect with Tiamat and Kingu, then moving forward to the Sebitti and the other gods, demons, vampires or ghosts. Every working must be one which is a give and take; for offerings to the gods you will seek their knowledge from within yourself.

Remember that every experience is done from within yourself; thus the interpretations, inspiration and other mental manifestations are the powers or deific masks relating to you.

The power of the Kassapu is then to become disciplined in working in the astral plane. If you have previous experience with astral workings or more beneficially "astral vampirism" this will no doubt aid you. Working in this spiritual shadow-world will be your path of advancement, for all rebellious spirits go this path.

The Kassapu in ancient Sumerian and Babylonian tablets such as the Malqu series is a shadowy figure who works destructive sorcery on others. The Kassapu will obtain objects of their intended victim, controlling their thoughts or actions to some extent by sending "impulses" or "inspirations" which will lead towards their goals. The Kassapu will create clay or wax figures to then bury them with the impression of the victim. They may be made of meat and fed to animals in a curse, it is the Kassapu slowly transforming into a semi-divine (an isolate consciousness) spirit.

The act of the Kassapu is in a series of incantations and anointing a model which represents the intended victim of the curse. One specific document[102] relates that the witch (Kassapu) has fed the victim with life-depriving potions, rubbed the figure with deadly and unclean water, destructive oil and then sent a

---

[102] Mesopotamian Witchcraft, Tzvi Abusch.

roaming ghost of a stranger who has no family to bring it offerings.

IMAGE AND SYMBOL

The workings of sorcery relate to the sacred path of Magick, defined by the works of darkness as the process of self-evolution, ascension and refining the consciousness. The awakening Draconian Sorcerer or Luciferian will view the potential of the sacred art utilizing the traditional elements used in medieval ceremonial magick; yet going beyond these precepts.

DREAMS
The Gateway of Evil Gods

The Kassapu, often regarded as a malicious witch who is antinomian (not of the laws of mainstream spirituality) and works the majority of his sorcery via the shadow, that is the dream. This requires that the Kassapu must work closely with the tools of his craft. If you create fetish objects then fully invest belief and a bit of your "essence" in them so that they may carry out their appointed task.

Dream workings are significant to the development of the Kassapu, specifically in first establishing a process of exploring and ultimately understanding the subconscious mind. The other aspect is the control of the dream and the slow process of transformation into a union with your daemon or immortal-self.

Consider for a moment that your subconscious is the foundation of you mind, the very starting point of it all. The subconscious holds all of your desires, fears and is a seat for who you are as a conscious individual. This is where our underlining associations begin, where symbols take meaning.

The Gods themselves, specifically the underworld gods such as Ereshkigal, appear in dreams or rather nightmares when one seeks their guidance. The Kassapu has no fear of dreams and first communicates with the dark ones through dream and then establishes the ability of dream projection.

The Kassapu will first develop the discipline of meditation and via chant will rise in the dreaming body, for which after practice and chant is adhered to in a willed manner; the 'form' of the Kassapu may be shifted and shaped according to any dark design. The dreaming body may then be sent forth to visit others, drain or bewitch the thoughts of others.

A created fetish will work well also, for instance one with the claw of a black bird, a human finger-bone and other items of special association are suitable to focusing on in dream practice. I strongly suggest a crystal as well, the storing of energy with provide meaningful in your continued practice.

KASSAPU
The Demonic Witch-shade

The Kassapu in ancient Mesopotamian religious texts can be a very powerful and secretive individual. The witchcraft of today is not that of its' source. Firstly, modern witches attempt to make themselves socially acceptable by nullifying and lowering their aims; inherently divine or infernal (both for Luciferians) to being "the person next door". We find the "watered down witch" in all the large bookstores, while their "myth" is shown over the top and 'villianizing' in the media. Witches do not want to be powerful except if it is to evert a perceived wrong; however by this admission alone modern witches have snipped the power and nullified their senses to possibility.

The Luciferian or Kassapu is a witch which is indeed a supernatural demonic force; that is; an individual who is able to send nightmares and dreams which affect their targets, for destructive and creative purposes. Many Luciferians and Kassapus will not advertise in daily life what they *are*, unless it supports their cause. It is very easy to be unnoticed as a practicing Kassapu in this modern age; simply put people don't really believe in the supernatural – until they experience it!

The Kassapu through initiation and the development of the Will is able to begin a process of self-transformation into both a powerful human individual (body and mind) as well as building through meditation, experience and the control of the Will the demonic force. A demonic force is simply an individual or independent rebel against the restraints of the gods or others; demonic beings act according to their own desire without regard for legitimizing actions or ideology of the larger mass or "sheep" of the world.

In ancient times, the excorcist worked against the Kassapu in that using the laws of sorcery, the Kassapu would be drawn by name (the power of the word in magick) into his own circle of self. Using the names of the gods he would compel the "Daimon" or "Demon" representing the witch and draw their power away.

The means of getting around this is not as difficult as one may think. In practicing magick and sorcery for many years, the Luciferian ideology provided the simplistic yet powerful formula of overcoming those who work against you. Simply put, it is in the name and foundation.

You see, an excorcist or "white magician" is not within the "circle of self", they are seeking protection and calling the names of the gods for their power in combating the Kassapu or demonic force. They are more or less "puppets" without real power. The Kassapu uses a circle as a circumfrance foundation of power alone: the circle is represented and visualized as the coiling serpent-dragon, the gods or demons invoked are moving through the Kassapu him or herself: thus the demonic witch is the center or starting point for all powers.

An excorcist, if highly skilled, may draw away some power from an able Kassapu, however it is a temporary working. The laws of astral magick indicate the mind or astral body is connected by tendrils; a return point even if not connected. The Kassapu's demonic shade or demon may be drawn into the excorcists' circle for a time, perhaps even weakened. This however, like the laws of nature and balance have a benefit. The shade now has the familiararity and identification of the person attempting to rid the demonic force. Instinctivly, our "higher self" or demon knows in the darkest levels the individual against it. Our demon or "Personal God" would have "tasted" the essence so to speak and now know where to find it. This can be a long and enjoyable process of astral/dreaming attacks which allow a slow process of weakening the sleep patterns – therefore the potency of the exorcist. Call it a return on investment if the Kassapu happens to run into a self-righteous exorcist.

When the Kassapu grows adept in this process then the transformation into a demonic god begins. The Kassapu may compel other gods or "deific masks" of others to grow angry with them, causing nightmares and self-questioning patterns. No matter if one knows of this path or not, the Kassapu is a sorcerer-Luciferian which transcends into every religious avenue.

THE KASSAPU'S POWER OF DREAM-HAUNTING

Transforming the Daimon to God

The methodology of dream flying, haunting and visiting the intended individual is a process of astral projection and directing the subconscious towards the task of *going forth in night*. This path has been practiced by witches since the beginning of written history through the middle ages.

THE ELEMENTS IN SIPTU

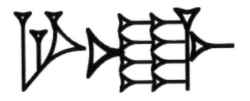

Dark Witchcraft

EARTH

Earth is associated with the physical, material creation and all that lives within and upon it. In Babylonian Magickial geography the earth also represents the "underworld" or dark areas as well – including the mountains. You may use clay to make figurines for incantations, or use already-created dolls, skulls or even wax figures. We find balance in earth as the goddess Ki represents both the land in which people live upon and the underground or 'dark earth', mountains and deserts.

WATER

The element for demons and spirits to enter or leave

Water is the most important element in Babylonian sorcery, it is that from which we emerge. The Absu, the deep from which Ea resides and all life emerged is called ZU-AB, the "House of Wisdom" of the great subconscious. The Temple of Ea in Eridu was called E-apsu which is "House of the Ocean". Water is used to consecrate all items, including statues no matter the god or demon. Pazuzu is empowered by water; Lamashtu travels back to the underworld via a river; the spiritual powers are bound to water in exorcism rites and poured out. In Siptu workings, the Kassapu will not pour out water but drink it, consuming the spirits therein that they reside in your temple of being. Offerings made to the gods or demons may be poured out outside your home in suitable areas and times; to spirits of darkness a hole in the ground during night hours; offerings to Sin during the full moon; to Shamash or Nergal as solar empowerment at the dawn and to Nergal at Noon when the Sun is highest. Offerings poured to Ishtar or Marduk at the dawn or twilight depending on purpose of working.

Remember that Water is the foundation for which Tiamat made her kingdom and all gods from it; Ea is the Lord of Magicians and also is associated deeply with Water.

Water is primarily the most significant element for not only the gods; Ea, the Lord of the Abyss, the Lord of Magick and the bringer of wisdom to man yet also is the primary element for demons and spirits to enter and leave the body.

The methods of demon and spirit invocation and work herein was observed and noted the techniques of exorcism and offering to the gods, then inverting them or adjusting for the purposes of so-called "black magick". The techniques developed from inverting the rites created a specific level to the gods and demons themselves, for which I have obtained and continued to achieve positive results.

INCANTATION OF WATER

"From the fountain of Ea you have emerged

To bless my workings with the magick of the Absu

May the Sons of the Abyss bless this water

Shine upon this water, Seven Sons of Darkness

Who illuminate Melammu

Seven Gods, Seven of the Absu"

Touch the Gir-Dagger in water.

FIRE

A creative and destructive element, Fire is both wielded by gods conquering and offering benefit to humanity. Shamash is the Sun; his fire is beneficial in expanding and enriching life. Nergal is the hot and burning element, the one who initiates into the darkness. For this Nergal is respected by modern Luciferians as the Lord of the Black Flame; the balanced one.

Nusku is invoked in exorcism rites and the figure of wax is burnt over flame. Understand that fire is like all things; beneficial and maleficent depending on how it is used.

Water and liquid is the vessel for which demons and spirits may enter and leave the physical body. To invoke or to call in a spirit it may be done by chant and 'ensorcelling' the energy, however to drink during the ritual as the demon has been called forth, the water made 'unclean' by chanting or empowering it by touching with spittle, a tiny amount of grave soil or even human bone dust will empower this water and deem it 'unclean'. Drinking the water will bring the empowered essence and "vessel' of the demon will enter then your physical body. Invocations, chants and meditations affirming and naming the demon or god will then affirm the process firmly. We see in the Palestinian tale of the possessed man who is rid of the seven spirits enter swine who then run and drown themselves in water, the vessel for which spirits may travel.

Water holds a deeper meaning in that this element is firstly of Tiamat and after Ea.

INCANTATION OF FIRE

"I summon thee from the Desert Places

I summon thee of Seven Gods of Illuminated Spheres

Who reside in the Blackened Fires of Irkalla

I summon thee Nergal to send me the Fires of Melammu

God of Black Flame, establish this destiny and empower

My being!"

The Wand should touch the flames.

AIR

The element of air is the abode, spiritual travel and very consciousness of the spiritual being. The air is represented as a part of the highest divinity, being Anu. The dark spirits and gods rode upon the storms and pestilential winds, the very foundation of Anu and the demon/psyche.

Demons themselves, such as the Mandaic and ancient Babylonian Zakiku is "blast", referring to a demon and bringer of death. The element of air is significant in the works of magick; incense billows up to the gods; air is the element in which they travel. The gods utilize the winds to attack (the Kasusu winds given to Marduk); the Four Winds, North Wind (Istanu), South Wind (Sutu), East Wind (Sadu) and West Wind (Amurru). Additionally there was the Imhullu, which was composed of Seven Evil Winds (a reference to the Sebitti as their spirit-demonic forms?) and Amasatu (whirlwind).

SALIVA & BLOOD

Saliva is a major component in sorcery for the use of creating fetishes, empowering curses and bewitching others. Ancient cuneiform texts describe rituals of exorcism in which the saliva is used and attributed to Ea. When using the cords, saliva should lightly be rubbed into the cords before each knot is tied, if you have your own blood available, this also is good.

MAGICKIAL OBJECTS

ZISURRU / USURTU
THE MAGICK CIRCLE

Composed of "flour paste", a bit of water with flour is mixed and then used to encircle the Kassapu or individual in an exorcism. The Akkadian **Zisurru** *"The Circle which makes a boundary"* or **Usurtu** *"Magic Circle"* is traditionally utilized to keep the one exorcising spirits safe, however the Kassapu uses the Zisurru to focus and concentrate the energies or spirits/demons within. The Kassapu does not fear these powers yet respects them and is focused on compelling their knowledge and energies to his inner temple of mind-body-spirit to gain wisdom and ultimately power.

Anything passed off as "white magick" is without power and consistently[103] pointless. Magick practitioners often obtain their early training and develop a structure based on what I call the "cowering-Christian" method. That is, they hide in a circle of

---

[103] Magick is the art of continual self-development and ascension of the Daemon or Evil Genius/Sedu as one may call it. Every working, ritual or incantation must have a goal and purpose which leads to self-development, insight and ultimately power.

protection, utilize Hebrew names (and expect a Hebrew 'god's chosen people' tribal deity to find association with them) and forcefully and disrespectfully evoke 'demons' which hold keys to their own earthly desires. *All the while they detest and keep a safe distance from their own mirror-reflection of inner desire.* Is this not the Christian way in a nut-shell?

The Kassapu or Luciferian stands within a circle to focus his or her own individual energy and power. In calling "outward" or to something "outside" the self it is done with respect and willed command, then entering the space it is conjured and focusing on the energy it contains for the purpose called. The demon or god will attach to the part of the subconscious in which it is affixed according to design and provide portals to conscious knowledge.

This knowledge, often manifesting as a "chance" occurrence of opportunity or what some call "luck" is compelled by the Kassapu subconscious as a living Temple of the Gods and Demons. Upon manifesting by a chance occurrence it may also emerge as a heightened ability to gain knowledge on a subject in question, for which upon experience gained becomes wisdom. As we can see here, the center is the self and why my statements as a Luciferian have always been "I am the only God that is", so are you!

The Circle itself is a self-visualized limitation center for which magical energies are focused and retained. The sorcerer who uses a circle in which they stand always do so in the aim of self-creation and ascension of being, thus at the end of the rite; the self is made stronger by the announcement of being, or "I".

The Circle is symbolized often as a serpent – it encircles and bites its own tail to create the "timeless point" of the immortal spirit; it represents the crooked serpent which exists in the waters of the abyss, it is the circumference of our own creation.

The sorcerer is unafraid within and outside of the circle, for it does not protect, rather it focuses the energy or spirits being called forth. The Circle itself, for being the gathering places of spirits and the energies called forth relating to the self. In ancient Babylonian Magick, sorcerers would create seven small winged figures, placing them in front of the image of Nergal, would tie them with a cord and cover with a dark robe.

In modern Adversarial Sorcery, the magickian works specifically with these types of spirits, they relate to power and initiation. You may utilize seven black skull-candles to represent each of the Maskim Hul or Sebitti as they are called. If you prefer, utilizing the sigil of the Sebitti will also prove empowering as the talisman features the therionick conceptions of the gods in their primal and hungering forms.

The boundary circle was traditionally made of flour or flour-paste and used around doorways or the place where demons were kept out. The Kassapu does not intend to keep evil spirits or demons out, rather we wish to keep them in and grow stronger from their power. In many ways, absorbing them and moving on towards our next intent of accumulation of power.

If you use flour, such as in a modern garage or even outdoors the circle may be as large or small as you wish. Consider that it is the circumference of your being, thus a subconscious reminder that you are seeking to grow strong from the energy focused and contained.

The Kassapu will sprinkle this flour beginning at the western point and moving counter-clockwise against the natural order. This has a two-fold purpose; acknowledging that you are performing the rites to become a god in the flesh and to perform the part of the Maskim or Sebitti who were born in the mountains of the west and grew up in the mountains of the east. This is a conscious act which over a period of time shall hold a deeper consideration of subconscious transformation with the deific masks of the Maskim/Sebitti.

There is no need to close the circle after the rite, simply command "So it is done" and clear your mind.

GIR-SAKAR KU NAM-ISIB-BA-KA
THE GIR ATHAME

The Athame or Dagger called in Sumerian "gir-sakar ku nam-isib-ba-ka"; "Gir" is the weapon of compelling the Will of the Kassapu. Your blade should be unmarked and not directly associated with any culture other than Babylonian at first glance. That indicates your choice in a knife should be a plain one, a simple black-handled athame is suitable.

THE CORDS OF BINDING

Cords of binding are significant in the works of witchcraft in both Babylonian and Egyptian (Sethanic Luciferianism) pantheon. The significance of the cord is 'to bind' or 'ilutu' being a synonym of 'mamitu' which is associated with the ideogram which is NAM-ERIM (state of evil or uncleanliness). When cords where used to bind in a ritual it was for cursing or compelling a specific action. The Kassapu will use a cord to bind with their specific desire, even if it is communion and invocation with a god or demon. The ideogram for NAM-LAL is 'iltu' in normal circumstances, meaning "State of being bound" or encircled. To encircle or enchant is "ensorcel", which is the same act of using the cord to bind. The cord represents the power of the Kassapu within the astral plane or the dream, it holds deep subconscious meaning thus creating a bride of the Kassapu with the gods and demons of the netherworld.

Cords are traditionally of several colors in the path of sorcery and their colors bear significance.

1. **BLACK CORD OF THE SEBITTI** – symbolic of the Seven Maskim, for which it should have seven knots tied

within it. These knots are not loosened however you will use the cord to wrap around a figure of wax/wood/clay or drawing of your chosen victim. The Black Cord may be used to empower your objects of sorcery, once you have dedicated your works to the Seven Sebitti. When consecrating your Black cord, use a small amount of your own blood to infuse the cord with a connection to you, use also a small amount of saliva along with an incantation of your choice to the Seven Maskim. Use the sigil of the Seven Maskim to focus on when creating the cord, making a knot until seven completes it.

2. **RED CORD** – symbolic of the blood of life, the food of the gods above and below. This cord will represent the cord from which you wrap around your victim to drain life-force from their body and mind through the dream. In such works, you will have a figure of the chosen and wrap the red and black around it while performing the appropriate incantation. Follow this for the specified period of time. Many victims will have nightmares and their sleep will be interrupted, having problems during the day dealing with normal life situations. Do not use the red and black cord indiscriminately, for the more advanced sorcerer will have perfected a process of absorbing the one seeking to drain he/she. The Red and Black cord may be used in vitality and strengthening workings as well, using the appropriate incantation.

3. **THE WHITE CORD** – symbolic of the Melammu of mind and the divine will of the Kassapu. The White Cord is a reminder of the Great Work of Initiation and advancing, growing strong in power and becoming a God in the Image of the Seven Maskim. The cord must have seven knots tied in it, with each consecrated to the appropriate god. The White Cord and knots represent the Seven Levels of the Etemenaki and the Anunnaki Gods. The White Cord is used in meditation of the Gods in

works of building control and productive results in your day to day life. The White Cord is the "Mask" which the Seven Maskim/Sebitti wears to place a "pleasant visage" in the physical world. It is the face of Marduk for which Kingu and Tiamat rise up through.

4. **THE BLUE CORD** – symbolic of sickness/disease or the negative in your life, mental or otherwise. The Blue Cord is symbolic of Namtar the Vizer of Ereshkigal. Namtar may be utilized for benefit of healing the self if you have communed with Ereshkigal. You will use it to wrap around a figure representing yourself if seeking to focus your mind on healing, or another individual you may be assisting. The Blue Cord may be used with the black cord to curse and send sickness to your victim, using the appropriate incantations. The Sebitti/Maskim and Namtar are thus called forth and directed to the victim and the difference is the Kassapu does not drain the individual.

5. *Second use for the* **Black Cord**: Invoking and encircling (ensorcelling) the Seven Maskim as initiators into darkness and the violence of nature. The Kassapu will work with the cord and meditate upon each knot, representing one of the seven as well as the sigil of the Maskim. You may have a wax devil figure consecrated to you and wrap the cord from the bottom coiling upwards like a serpent, representing the chakra points. In doing this you focus on building and concentrating your mental and spiritual energy into a specific goal you have decided, be it as an evolutionary point or "high magick, Theurgy" or something material or "sorcerous".

6. Additional cords may be employed for "ongoing" workings where the cord(s) are buried or wrapped around and kept with an item for an extended period of time.

QUTRENU
THE INCENSE & BURNER

The Akkadian word Qurenu or Sumerian Nadeg is "incense offering" and is a significant part to any incantation. Incense is the most consistent form of offering to the gods from ancient Babylonia to modern-day magical practice. The use of incense has been utilized in the performance of rituals, exorcisms, incantations, Temple-offerings and seemingly all purposes including the dedication to Deified living (and dead) Kings. Incense offering survived not only in magical practice of modern pagans, Satanists and witches, yet also in Christianity (who don't like to think it is a magical act).

Juniper is of the realm of Anu, while Oak is the Underworld. Juniper will serve also for the underworld if the rite is more enhanced with two elements. Many texts which survive make reference to juniper as being the link between the temporal (physical) world and the divine/ spiritual.

Obtaining a burner will be important – something to burn coals in, the incense is then scattered over the burning coals. As the incense starts to burn and rise up in smoke, incantations, hymns, dedications and invocations should begin. Focusing on the smoke as being a symbol of your desire and wish, it is transformed into the element of air to travel to the gods; either above or below. In ancient Babylonian times, divination was conducted by scrying the smoke with interpretations. Invocation of the personal god of the Kassapu or Demon is a suitable way of aligning the mind to the work itself. Often, a very hot bath until nearly dizzy (only if you are healthy enough) along with an invocation will provide you a suitable mood for scrying.

Juniper is the traditional incense used in Mesopotamian rites, it is the most pleasing to use. Oak is used for the underworld or similar rites, representing the roots which are deep within the dark earth. I have found that you may use similar types as long as your conviction is the same.

Having used all types of incense, from the most simple to rather elaborate I can suggest that any type or method of incense is useful, when the mind is completely focused on the work at hand. Tools mean absolutely nothing without the Will-Desire-Belief of the individual which empowers them!

Mashatu is flour which represents witchcraft itself, burnt during the ritual. In traditional exorcisms, the priest would burn it to release the magic which encircled the victim. The Kassapu uses this with incense to ensorcell the spirit or demon to the task. Visualize the spirit going forth as the smoke to attend to the task.

Incense and smoke is a significant element to your ritual process: the billowing smoke provides the demon or spirit a means of attachment and temporary manifestation.

THE WAXEN IMAGE

The waxen image is very important in sorcerous workings, representing the individual, force or intended victim for the powers summoned. Used in exorcisms traditionally, the waxen image is burnt over the flame in a series of incantations against the Kassapu or demonic witch which plagues the victim. The flames are represented as Girra, the lord of fire who bans the shade from manifesting against the individual and rendering it as a formless shadow across the steppe.

Waxen images may be pre-molded figures, demonic images or even plain candles with names inscribed and if available, the hair or something from the victim attached. Keep in mind that hair, blood, saliva and even nails play a strong association to the target in sorcery.

Figurines were traditionally buried if they were representing the Kassapu as the agent of demonic attacks against an individual. When buried in a deep hole or watery pit, they represented the sorcerer being cast into the underworld via traditional burial rites. The modern Kassapu will initially cast his or herself into this burial rite for a period of seven days and nights to intiate the astral body into the Cult of Ereshkigal. To know the darkness is to experience it, rendering those who may work against you as futile.

THE SKULL

The skull has been utilized in rituals and religious practice (including sorcery) since the beginning of written history. There are references to rituals involving the human skull in summoning shades of the dead and demonic forces (mimma lemnu). For instance, the ghost of a man named "etem la mammanama" in which he is symbolized as the skull. The human or animal skull represents not only the carnal and material nature of this world, however is used as a fetish not to *exorcise* shades or demons yet to provide them a vessel to reside in. If you can obtain a skull of some type, it may have the cuniform name or English name of the force/shade/demon inscribed upon it in your own blood. When you utilize your own bodily fluids, you create a bond between yourself and the force summoned.

The use of the human skull in sorcerous practice is dated to the first millennium B.C., the text in question[104] makes reference to the burning of juniper and sulfur wherein Shamash-Utu is invoked and requested to bring forth the shade from the underworld into the skull.

The survival and development of the skull in necromancy continued into early Christian times, for example the fragments of a human skull found in Nippur inscribed with a spell on top.

THE ALTAR AND IDOL

The altar is the foundation for the work, representing the earth itself. Your altar should not contain any elements not related to this grimoire and the context initially; do not attempt to mix other cultural manifestations of Luciferianism with the Babylonian/Chaldean. After your work proceeds and you grow knowledgeable and experienced with this pantheon then it is fine to stray if you wish to include later cultural manifestations of the same gods. Consider however the confusion you may cause your mind and to proceed with caution.

The Kassapu should have an altar place in any direction suitable in the chosen space. It is important to have the image of Tiamat, Kingu, Ea and Marduk as your foundation deific masks. Tiamat, as the mother of all is the primal darkness from which we emerge from. She is the dragon which sleeps in our subconscious. Kingu is the empowered one given the Anu power; his blood (the Titan's ashes were utilized rather than blood) was mixed with man like the Greek legend of the Titans to beget humanity. We have the linage of the rebellious gods in our essence. Ea is the god of magick and of water, representing

---

[104] I.L. Finkel, "Necromancy in Ancient Mesopotamia" and C. Faraone, "Necromancy goes underground", Mantike, studies in Ancient Divination, Brill 2005.

great wisdom to be found in the depths. Marduk is the great conquering god who establishes our foundation on earth and in the flesh. You may in turn blend the gods as you see fit, Marduk with Assur, etc.

Some will find their patron god to be Ereshkigal, the Goddess of the Underworld, the Maskim/Sebitti, Nergal, Nebo, Ishtar or any other. This is suggested, seek the deific mask which speaks to you, which which you are close to and with a full focus initiate yourself in their knowledge.

You should draw out your own images or reproduce them on plaques for your altar space. If you are lucky enough or talented to create your own statues or fetishes representing a specific god, then wonderful! As someone who has done much with serpent skin, crow talons, bones and more I can say there is much power found in shaping your own ritual tools by hand.

CONSECRATING THE STATUE

All Magickial tools must be consecrated before using in ritual. Consider that the statue itself will be a home for the particular power the god or demon represents. Thus when you perform a hymn or incantation to the god, you are filling it with the spirit of the deific mask.

The gateway to the gods and your own body-mind-spirit is found in the association your mind has with the statue during the periods of creation and/or consecration. Once you "make" a home for the god, your subconscious will automatically do the rest when you invoke it later.

You may perform incantations to the gods or demons as you see fit; I do suggest that you build an initial discipline with the workings to establish a connection with your subconscious and the spirits themselves.

STEPS IN RITUALS

1. HUB BITI

The Purification of the Temple/Altar and Circle Space. The Kassapu utilizes it not for specific "purification" but to clear the mind and relate the mind to the significance of the ritual space. If the ritual space is viewed daily the significance of it is sometimes lost and it is "normal", holding little deep significance. The Hub Biti is enacted to remind the Mind of the Kassapu or the sacred place of which it is and the importance of the Magickial work. Initial fumigation of juniper is utilized. The waters of Ea are invoked (fill a chalice or bowl with water before hand and invoke the hand of Ea into the water).

2. PIT BABI

Opening of the Gate Invocation

The "Opening of the Gate" ceremony is the announcement of the period of time in which the Kassapu will conduct workings, meditations or specific incantations.

KISPU *(if applies 3.)*

Offerings to the Ekimmu

In conducting shadow workings of the underworld, it is important to offer libations to the shades of the dead which you may come into contact with by chance or purpose.

Offerings may be conducted as pouring liquid such as beer, wine, water or honey-water into the ground while reciting something to the equivalent of:

"I offer this to thee, those who reside in shadow, those who journey from Irkalla…"

Do not expect to have "conversations" with the ancient dead, their voices are jumbled and make little to no sense – especially in any current language. Additionally you may come into contact with "recent dead", shades who have nothing to do with the Babylonian pantheon – offer a libation in your own style anyway.

3. MAQQITU
Libations/Incense Offerings

The Libation is important for the gods, in which you are working with, libations or fumigations are offerings of incense to the gods or demons you are calling forth. This is of course different from your initial fumigations and preparations of 1. Some Kassapu will conduct 3 and 4 as one part, if time or purpose calls for it.

4. NIQU
Offerings of Liquid or Food

"Offering" to the Gods or Demons the a process of giving some element to be consumed, be it wine, beer or water you may pour a Niqu or offering upon a statue with a plate underneath if your desire or in invocation (*calling the Deific Mask within*). Workings the Niqu may be drank by the Kassapu in honor of the God or Goddess invoked. If working with more demonic or rebellious deific masks, their more intense offerings may include a sample of your own blood, binding it to the sigil or statue. This would not be consumed of course rather poured out on your property in a deep hole or crack in the land where the sun does not reach.

INVOCATIONS TO THE GODS

The invocations and prayers within this chapter are reconstructed from authentic Babylonian and Assyrian tablets and inscriptions by sorcerers, kings and priests. You may use the invocations in focusing-rituals, especially as you grow more comfortable and stronger in your works. Challenge yourself in workings, push yourself to the limits mentally and physically, this will create that spiritual association with specific gods and goddesses.

OFFERING TO ANU AND KI

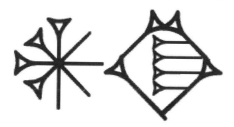

To Consecrate the Kassapu in the works of the Heavens *(Astral Plane/Spirit)* and Earth *(the material plane and the darkness beneath)*

The Ritual of Offering to Anu and Ki is the union of the two elements of Air and Earth. Anu is the supreme power representing the heavens. This ritual is a type of "foundation rite" for the Kassapu who has embraced the Luciferian philosophy of self-creation and determined realization according to the Will. The concept of Heaven/Air united with Earth is also demonstrated in the later legend of the Watchers and Fallen Angels. The Watchers (of Heaven or Air) seek union with women (flesh – earth) and beget the Nephilim or Giants. The Giants are intelligent, leaders of men and yet their appetites' are greater. When they physically die, their spirits "come forth from their bodies" to haunt mankind. Consider this ritual for the opening of the great temple-building rite at the end of this grimoire.

This is for instance the foundation of the Great Work or Theurgy of the Kassapu here. As a Left Hand Path practitioner, you are seeking to transform yourself into a divine conscious being; that the Gods' are an extension of your psyche and they mirror your potential as a living being. In a spiritual sense, you are seeking to expand your consciousness, crystallizing your psyche and seeking to become a "demonic spirit" which exists beyond the grave.

The Anu Altar-Sigil

INCANTATION OF THE FOUR WINDS

The Encirclement of the Powers of Air

You may trace out a part of the Cuneiform representations of the four winds when invoking, use the Gir-Athame as the Magickial weapon.

Facing the West:

Amurru, great wind which brings devastation to the plains, I summon thee to my command, for in the west I am born, in the Mountain of Sunset! Winds which act in accordance to ANU and KI, I summon thee! IM-MAR-TU!

Facing the North:

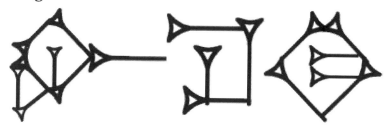

Istanu, storm-winds which split open the land, I summon thee! By Enlil and the right hand of the storm god, come forth! Through the darkness you shall raise the fierce powers of twilight and dawn! IM-SI-SA!

Face the East:

Sadu, Mountain Wind of the blazing dawn! Send forth the storms of burning rain! In the Mountain of Dawn I am reared! I summon thee forth! IM-KUR-RA!

Facing the South:

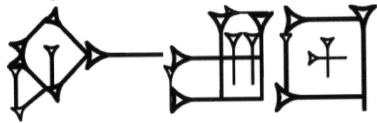

Sutu! From the desolate lands gallop forth! In the darkness I shall ride these winds, I summon thee forth! Burning winds which carry Lilitu and Pazuzu! SU-TU!

With the four I come forth in the center of the earth!

Ar-ri-bi mut-tab-ri-su il-ma-a sa-ma-mi-is

(The raven winged encircled the heavens)

I call thee forth IMHULLU, violent winds of darkness and illuminated spheres! You shall be my weapon against that which stands in my path!

I adorn myself in Melammu, arrayed in terror!

Me-khi-e saru lim-nu il-ma-a!

(the storm, the evil wind, encircled)

Gul-lum u im-khul-lum il-ma-a sa-ma-mi-is!

(Gallu-D emon and the evil wind encircled the heavens)

So it is done!

Visualize the five winds coiling around you, winding and blowing tight according to your will. Visualize a burning fire within shooting forth from you core, then the winds go forth to your aim in the ritual.

COMMENTARY AND NOTES:

The Kassapu should cast a circle with flour, holding the Gir and facing the West, Im-martu, call the winds from each point, moving counter-clockwise. This is the formula of the Seven Evil Gods, the Maskim or Sebitti.

"O fire god (Girra), where were they born, where were they reared? Those seven were born in the Mountain of Sunset (in the west, the direction in which Shamas-Utu travels) and reared in the Mountain of Dawn (East Wind), they dwell in the caverns of earth (North Wind) and amid the desolate places of the earth they live (South Wind). Unknown in heaven and earth (they dwell on all levels, not bound to any element entirely), they are arrayed in terror (they illuminate Melammu), among the wise gods there is no knowledge of them (for they are antinomian, spiritual-rebels who act counter to the natural order of the gods), the Seven gallop over the mountain of sunset and on the Mountain of Dawn they cry, through the caverns of the earth they creep, and amid the desolate places of the earth they lie." - Thompson, Devils and Evil Spirits of Babylonia.

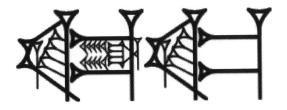

Incantations of the Gods

INVOCATION OF EA

To Empower the Spells of the Kassapu

By the Heavens, Conjure it!
By the Earth, Conjure it!
I conjure thee Patesi-Gal-Zuab!
Ea! Ea! Lord of the Abyss!
Dwelling King in splendor, cloaked in radiance!
Who is empowered in the waters
The great god of Magick
Whose powers are extended to man
Ea, enthroned in the depths

Whose counsel is great among all the gods
Whose voice extends to the council of the Sebitti
As I use the sacred waters empower my workings
Open your eyes through me Ea!
As you have decreed the radiance of Marduk thy Son
Do so within me that I may ascend in my own Black Flame!
By the Heavens I conjure!
By the Earth I conjure!

INCANTATION OF EA
King of the Deep, Lord of Magick
Temple of Primal Abyssic Waters
Offerings to Inspire Dark Knowledge

Hail thou Ea-sharru, conjure!!
By Anu I invoke thee!
By Ki I invoke thee!
I offer libations to thee, Ea King of the Deep
Thou great Lord of Magick and holder of the sacred wisdom of the Gods
Thou Ea who sent the Seven Sages to awaken humanity
Whose voice stirs the blood of Kingu within us
Hearken and hear my words Ea!
Enki, Thou art Lord of the oceans and whose power
Flows through it.

Who strengthens my incancations
Hail to thou who hath the wisdom of his mother Tiamat
Who took the throne of Apzu to command the Temple of Power!
Thou enthroned god whose forms are many
Show unto me that which pleases you
I seek the wisdom of Isimud
Who brings knowledge to those who seek!
As the incense flows accept this O Lord of the Abyss!
Who shares knowledge with the Seven Abgal hearken!
Awaken from thy primal sleep to this strange land!
That your power is renewed again here!
I invoke thee to bring me the wisdom of my desires
That though Magick shall I ascend as a God in flesh!
My body is your Temple, My mind is your Throne!
Yet I am the ONLY GOD WHICH IS!
I call you by your names of calling:
Sassu-urinnu conjure!
Whose head is a serpent, whose mouth is gaping
Whose ears are a basilisk
Whose horns are twisted in three curls
Who wears a veil in the headband
Whose body is a suh-fish and full of stars
Whose feet are the claws of the dragon
Thou sea-monster, Illuminating Ea, conjure!

Lahmu ippiru conjure!

A monster of heaven and earth

Whose body is that of a lion, whose feet are the bird of prey

Thou sea-dragon, sea-monster who is born of Tiamat and Absu!

Ancient Father Ea-Enki look through my Temple!

O thou Nissiku who sees what other cannot!

Thou Nudimmud, creating god who awakens the clay!

Your Temple of E-engurra is extended across this earth!

That you shall rise again through me!

I pour water in your honor, accept my libations!

INVOCATION TO SHAMASH

To Deify the Self as God Incarnate

Burning the incense of the Sun, recite at dawn, noon, late afternoon or twilight. Face the direction of the rising sun, the east and visualize the sigil of Shamash and the illuminating, victorious and balanced conquering one.

Thou Shamash, illuminator and conqueror ascend!
Shamash, from the foundations of heaven thou have risen;
Thou have unleashed the brilliance of your manifestation;

Illuminator, who resides both with darkness and brings the strength of day;

Balanced god, who rises forth within my temple of flesh;

Hail thou Archangels of the Abyss, who contemplate the strength in which you bring all.

Who brings nourishment to the luminous heavens; strengthen my resolve to send forth my messengers to achieve my will!

Shamash, illuminate this day myself who am lord of my destiny!

HYMN TO SHAMASH-UTU
The Illuminating God of Victory
To be conducted at noon during the height of the sun.

Ascend within me, Shamash, Lord of the Sun!

Thou who marches before all the Gods

Thou who supports the Seven Gods, the Seven Maskim to darken the Moon and cast a reflection of shadow to earth.

With Anu and Bel thou march forth and conquers all!

He who established the rule in heaven, he who arranges is thyself!

I have invoked thee, O Shamash, in the midst of the great heavens of Anu!

Thou who cast the shadows of phantoms

Thou who raises up the scorpion!

Who holds the power to annihilate countries and humanity!

Who holds the power to grant great abundance to humanity!

Hail thou, Shamash!

HYMN TO ADAR-RIMMON

God of Lightning, Storm and War

Hail to the scorching one

The sting of the Scorpion

The mighty Serpent of the Gods

Adar, King and son of Mul-lil initiates strength in all.

Who destroys those who oppose him

Who finds ecstasy in the deluge of battle

Who holds the weapon of the Serpent with Seven Heads

To that which is the strongest serpent at sea

Who drives the foe before it

Like unto Ninurta I bear this power

I prevail in the heavens and upon the earth

The weapon which I bear, I wield the serpent whose splendor overwhelms the earth.

I shall overcome any conflict within or outside of me

Hail thou Adar, Warrior who like the Bull breaks through the foundations of the heavens!

Strengthen my side!

So it shall be!

INVOCATION TO SIN-NANNA

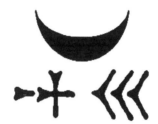

To seek the wisdom of the Moon-God

Lord and Chief of the Gods, O Sin!

Great one who holds the keys to the door of knowledge.

O Sin, who is unique and who is brightest in the night

Who bears the burden of office once held by Kingu

Brilliant is thy torch, like the fire god

The brightness which fills the earth and offers up the Goddess Nana, Hail to the Nannar, lord of increase!

I seek thee Sin who faced the Seven Sebitti in glorious array

And exists still held as a light-bearing torch in the night

O Sin, glorious one of Ikur, I beseech thee to bring forth the oracle of the Gods!

The end of the Month is the day of thy oracle, the decision of the great gods through which I shall understand!

I pour now the libation of the night, I shall not bow down yet ascend in the face of thy knowledge!

Thou Strong Bull with terrible horns, with a flowing beard of the colour of lapislazuli, full of vigor and life!

Founder of shrines, Father Nannar, who is illuminated before all!

Bring to me the hidden knowledge, if the Sebitti are with me so it shall be!

OFFERING TO MARDUK

To Inspire Order and Focus the Will

Hail to thee O Mighty, powerful and strong one of Assur,
Exalted Prince, thou first born of Nu-Dum-Mud,
Who bears now mantles of radiance,
Marduk, terrible one arise through me and rejoice!
For I shall act in accordance with my own Will
Weakness shall not cause my hand to hesitate
For with the cord I bind thy power in this Temple
Lord of Esagila, Support of Babylon and lover of Ezida
No gods do I bow before,
For my body and mind is a Temple for which
My spirit is enthroned.

I seek balance and the wisdom of ancient times.
May my god stand at my right hand!
May my goddess stand at my left hand!
May my god, thou serpent-soul establish himself
As my crown of wisdom and illumination.
To give and to command, to hearken and to show favour.
Let the words I speak, be made flesh!
I shall bow to no gods but myself!
For when I am crowned in victory, so shall you be!
May Bel be my torch, may Ea fill me with knowledge!
May the gods of the world be tributary unto me!
May the great gods smile upon me!
Hail Marduk!

Note: The Cord may be wrapped around an idol or candle representing Marduk and the power in which he represents in this manifestation. The God and Goddess at the right and left hand respectively are personal deific masks of the Kassapu. It is meaningful to keep them within the context of this pantheon to avoid inner confusion.

OFFERING TO MARDUK-ASSUR

To Focus on Conquering an Obstacle by Invoking the Warlike God, the King of the World

O Marduk, Who rides the storm-chariot

Who sits upon the dragon-serpent steed of Mushussu

Whose body is filled with the ever-blazing black flame,

I call now your four horses: Slayer, Pitiless, Racer and Flyer

Who shall carry the terrible storm-chariot forth.

O Marduk, who controls the Four Winds, the Seven Winds and who created the Imhullu-wind rise up!

I shall bear your weapons of lightning, of bow and axe!

Lord of fortresses, rivers and fields!

Ruler of Anunnaki, leader of the Igigi

Wise Marduk, first born of Ea Lord of the Depths

Thou blazing Sun-God, Marduk triumphant!

Who bears the blood and wisdom of Tiamat and Kingu

Noble family of primordial darkness

Who rise up again through me!

Marduk empower me in the light of the sun!

That I shall go forth and conquer any enemy before me!

INVOCATION OF MARDUK SA QABLI
As the Terrible Lord of War
To inspire against obstacles

A ritual invoking Marduk sa qabli (Marduk of war), an epithet of the god who goes forth to meet his enemies.

Marduk I summon thee!

Smiter of the neck, the falchion

The blade which proclaims me "the blade of my divinity" for I possess the Anu power!

Behold the spear which stabs deep into my enemies

The bow and the deluge I possess!

I stand from the eastern mountain

Radiant and strong before the gods!

I have established the heavens and earth

Yet now I manifest in this flesh!

In my right hand the god who binds the hosts of the firmaments I bear, who shall be of my flesh and spirit!

In my left hand the god who slays the hosts of the firmaments I bear, who I shall absorb their powers!

I am the god of fifty faces, the falchion which proclaims me as Anu I bear illuminated!

My weapon like the demon Usumgalli devours the corpses of the dead I bear!

Hail thou who reside in my Temple, of Mind – Body – Spirit, that we are both of darkness and the illumination within!

INVOCATION OF NEBO

The Destiny of the Kassapu Decreed

This is a ritual to compel the subconscious mind to manifest the most favored outcome of a specific event. As a Kassapu your approach to the gods is that you are one manifest, thus your will shall influence the outcome of events. Using incense and an image/statue of Nebo, recite the invocation and think of your desire on how you shall make it come to pass.

O Nebo, leader of the gods

For which exaltation was established

I call to thee to empower this temple

O Nebo, son of Esagila

First born of Marduk the Triumphant

Son of Erua, Queen who controls birth
Look with favor unto my works
By exalted command that I shall be successful
Against my enemies and those who design against me.
Nebo, whose weapon is the usumgallu,
Thy commands are unchangeable among the gods!
Nebo, Hail to thee who grants victory in my power!
From Ezida the Eternal Temple
Which is still in the realm of the gods
Shall I open a gateway here unto you!
Thou Great Nebo, Exalted One may my days be long!
May my years be many!
With thy exalted Scepter, that holds fast the foundations
Of the Heavens and Earth, at thy Illustrious Command
Establish now my good fortune!
Upon thy Dragon-Serpent command! Hail Nebo!
I determine the nature of my life,
I decide the destiny of my life.

Note: The Invocation of Nebo was constructed by an inscription invocation of Antiochus-Soter, King of Babylon/Seleucid Empire (280-260 BC). Nebo is invoked here to scribe the destiny of who is the spiritual "king" of his or her own self.

INVOCATION TO ISHTAR & ADAD

Prayer to the God/Goddess of War and the Storm
To overcome the weakness of will or to compel destiny to your benefit

Hail to Ishtar of Arbela

Ancient Goddess rise from your sleep!

I offer libations to you great Goddess!

Come forth to me and support my struggle against my enemy!

Terrible Ishtar, who is clothed in flames and arrayed in brilliancy, rain down fire upon my enemy!

Hail to thee Beltis, beloved companion of Bel, the mighty one who is honored among the goddesses,

Who sit enthroned in power with Anu and Bel, impale my enemies with your horns, gore their spirits into dissolution before me!

Adad-Iskur, ancient Storm God

Who rides forth upon the dragon hurling thunderbolts

Look upon my offering!

Guided by Ishtar, who is queen of weapons and the beasts of weapons!

Whose might is supported by the Sebitti..

I shall manifest the victory I seek!

I offer to both of you, accept my libations!

So it is done!

INCANTATION TO NINIB

Offering to the Violent God who defends and strengthens

O Mighty Warrior, first-born of Bel
Ninib, the impaling lance,
Thou son of Bel use thy sharp arrows to cut down my enemy!
I invoke thee powerful offspring of Esharra,
Who is clothed in terror, filled with violence;
Thou great storm whose assault none may withstand,
I offer this incense to thee in your lofty abode
Who takes the weak and empowers them to strength
Those who have the spirit and mind;
Ninib, who can bring back the ekimmu which has been sent to the underworld
Ninib, chief of the gods, a bloody warrior thou art!
I, (Name of individual performing incantation) have bound
For thee a cord, for which you shall strengthen my will.
I have offered thee incense, the smoke of the abode of Anu
I have poured out for thee the drink of the gods
Look to me with favour and hearken to my calls
Receive my offerings and accept my prayers through the temple which is my mind – body –spirit.
I bow before none and command my desires be made flesh!

For I am the Temple of my own Divinity, from which you and all Gods have a lofty throne!

HYMN TO NERGAL SA HAATI

To Conquer and align with the powers of darkness

This is a hymn to Nergal sa haati (Nergal of the Sword) in reference to the god as one of darkness and war, the Lord of the Great Land i.e. underworld. The use of 'Mes-lam-ta-ea' meaning 'he who came forth from mes-lam' is the cult center of Nergal in Cuthah and a temple Meslam.

Nergal sa haati!
Nergal lutta'id qarrad ilani gasru supu mar Bel

(Nergal, let me glorify, the hero of the gods, the powerful, the brilliant one, the son of Bel)

Who alone conquers with the Sebitti!

Behold, thy weapon which scatters rays of brilliance, that which cuts down thy enemy!

Hail the forceful flash and the power of the will!

Raise forth through your temple Nergal storm-bringer!

Hail thou God of Pestilence, Nergal, bring the sickness of spirit to my enemy and overthrow their attempts to harm me!

Thou Splendid Forces of Nergal, adorned in the Horned Crown

Nergal ilu ezzi sa puluhti u rasubbatu

(Nergal, the powerful god, fear and terror fills his hand)

Nergal, Lord of the Underworld, who resides also in the Sun hearken to me!

Nergal, who directs the Sebitti in war bring thou splendid forces to me!

Nergal who walks at my side and directs thou army before me!

I shall conquer and destroy my enemy and challenges!

By achieving Victory do I honor the Temple of Nergal!

Ilu ellu sa zimu-supu kima nur samas

(Glorious god, whose figure shineth with mighty splendor like the light of the sun god)

Hail thou the ancient one, who is the overthrower!

Thou eye of Black Burning Flame, who strikes down the enemy!

Mes-lam-ta-ea en Anunnaki na sid-du

(Mes-lam-ta-ea, Lord of the Anunnaki, who openeth the gates)

Nergal, who is mighty and with a fiery surrounding in which you are encircled, who raises the Lion-Mace!

Nergal, who takes the form of the Lion-Dragon raise thy blade!

Prince of Wisdom, leader who is illuminated!

Who destroys the fruitful earth, bringing darkness!

To devastate the insolent is thy pleasure!

To devour the souls of who do not see you!

Nergal Ida Arrakatu!

(Nergal, whose arm is long referring to plague sending)

Hail thou Nergal! ILU IDLU!
Ruler of the Storm, thou King of Battle Nergal!

INVOCATION TO NERGAL

Offering to the Power of the Melammu (Black Flame)

Ilu Mustabarru-mutanu
('The Reveler in Death' and Ilu 'god')
I conjure thee, I call to thee
Mighty Lord, hero and son of Nunamnir
Leader of Anunnaki
Nergal, mighty warrior before the gods
Look upon my offerings
Thou who ascends in the lofty heavens
Thou who is exalted in the underworld
To that terrifying splendor no other god stands before
Hail to thee, Nergal
Nergal, Dragon supreme, Great God!
I call you by the fires of sharrapu
Thou burning fires of conquest
By the funeral rites to which you were called
To the shades which drink blood in your name!
I invoke your might Nergal, rise within me!
Prince of the great gods, who spreads fear and awe!
Giant of the Anunnaki, who spreads terrible awe over all lands!

Dragon supreme, pouring out venom over the hostile ones[105]!

Through my body and mind you shall reside!

A temple to which we shall ascend to the heavens!

Rejoicing in illuminated power in the underworld!

---

[105] Nergal is titled 'dragon' here. The original cult epithet reads "pouring out venom over the hostile lands" however in the context here it is 'ones' in relation to individual Kassapu

HYMN TO ISHTAR THE HUNTRESS

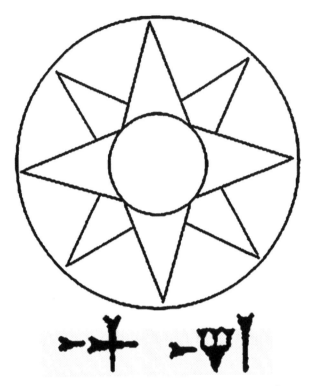

The Goddess of Evening and Morning

A light burning against the heavens

Which like the Black Flame rises resplendent over the earth, art thou Goddess of Terror!

Goddess, when thou manifest upon earth you are

Beauty untouchable, divinity and the purity of mind

Ishtar, who is the jackal who hunts the lamb

Thou art the lion who seeks prey in the fields

Adorned in splendorous light, crowned in the dawn!

Thou art the beauty of heaven that holds her bow wide!

Sister of the God of the Sun, Huntress of the Heavens!

Words spoken by the goddess: as recited by the Kassapu visualizing Ishtar.

To give omens in abundance I appear, in the light of self-divinity!

I give omens to my father Sin, I appear in perfection!

To give omens in abundance to my brother Shamash I appear!

In the brilliant heavens I give omens in abundance, I appear in perfection.

With exultation in my supremacy!

I, the great goddess, walk supreme;

Ishtar, the goddess of evening, am I,

Ishtar, the goddess of morning, am I;

Ishtar, who opens the portals of heaven, in my supremacy.

The heavens I destroy, the earth I devastate, in my supremacy!

My very name shines among the habitations of men, from the dawn of time until now, for I am immortal and terrible in my brilliance!

For I thirst for blood and war, for I grow strong from it!

For I am also kind unto those who offer unto me.

I am the Queen of Heaven, invoked above and below in my supremacy.

The mountains I sweep away for I can shake the very essence of what you are!

The Kassapu will now recite in offering libations to Ishtar.

May thy heart be at rest, for I offer unto thee!

May Anu give thy heart rest, for I pour libations to thee!

May the Lord of the Great Mountain, Bel bring thee rest!

O Goddess, Mistress of Heaven, breathe the spirit of the hunter within me!

Mistress of Erech, look through my eyes!

Goddess of Babylon, look through my mind!

Hail great goddess Nana!

RITES OF UTUKKU LIMNU

Of the Dark Gods and Demons

ENCIRCLING AND BECOMING ILU LIMNU

The goal of the Kassapu is to ascend, to gain knowledge and power from the practice of magick via initiation. Experience with the natural world will define the meaning and reality of balance, the Kassapu must seek this careful instinctual *interpretation* continually. This requires a sense of vigilance towards your initiation. We have explored the illuminating path of the gods, their hymns being gateways to inner power and worlds not yet explored.

As there are worlds of illumination and burning light, there is also a world to be explored of darkness. How could one attempt to know the power of creating when you have no idea of how that tree is planted? Knowing the darkness requires you fully enter it, experiencing the primordial, the beast hidden in the depths of your soul or psyche as you would define it.

The aim of Luciferianism is to redefine the way 'darkness' is perceived, looked at and approached. This challenge is one which will be more difficult as most of us have had the dualistic exposure of "good vs. evil", where there is no balance or even "gray" area. You may see "yin-yang" symbols, however to fully experience that balance you must mirror the gods and demons in accordance with your nature.

We all create and destroy in our individual life. Sometimes this balance is thrown off by problems we have caused by our miscalculation and inexperience with situations. Through experience we generally learn to adapt and overcome challenges.

This chapter will present the re-worked ancient rites of invocation and evocation, rather than exorcism. We understand in modern medicine now many diseases we placed on the demons are but symptoms of problems and not spirits at all. However, this is an opportunity to explore the demons and dark gods on more personal, individual levels than previously.

THE EVIL EYE

Cuneiform for Eye of the Mus (Serpent) representing the Evil Eye.

The evil eye has since the time of the ancients been a powerful representation of the demonic will of the spirit. In accordance with early-christianity and rabbinic belief, the wicked ones (including sorcerers, witches) who die become evil spirits (Utukku) who are possess the power of the Evil Eye. It is a suggestion to aquire a ring or object with a symbolic eye, representing the spirit-draining psyche or demon of the one wearing it. After a period of time the object itself has some type of subconscious power.

THE DEMONS OF THE INCANTATION TEXTS

We find in this grimoire wandering, disembodied ghosts called Ekimmu which seek substance in the world of the living, in addition we find the dark gods and the words of power to bring forth the demons of forgotten places.

As you utter the incantations to call forth the devils that are not bound to any specific phenomena in nature, those Alu Limnu who ride upon the winds of pestilence, storm clouds composed of insects and plague bearing reaping shadows which haunt the mind.

I have chosen the name of this chapter to be "Evil Spirits" in that our entire focus of initiation beyond the world we experience and live in is to maintain individual conscious existence beyond our shell of flesh. The Uttuku Limnu are "evil spirits" who are not "Ekimmu" or "evil ghost" per se, we seek to expand beyond that and become 'like' our literary and conscious Magickial experience with the Lamashtu goddess or Seven Maskim.

The Utukku was a spirit of a dead man/woman who was raised from the underworld from necromancy. Our own works we perform are necromantical self-determined rites, seeking to defy conscious 'death' through the triad of will-desire-belief.

The Alu is a spirit very close to the Akhkharu/Ahhazu in that this spirit was known in ancient times to dwell among caverns and dark places, ruins and go forth to envelop the unsuspecting at night. Enveloping the victim may have reference to possessing or draining of energy, depending on the nature of the Alu itself.

The Kassapu would invoke or evoke (call in or call into an object) to seek the conscious and 'dreaming' experience, knowledge and power from the spirit in question.

If you come across Ekimmu who seek some offering from the living, then they are quite old and not connected knowingly to any living person. Many spirits you will discover will be rather recent, within 200 years in general. Older spirits are sometimes 'more' than Ekimmmu and you should be experienced in the black art of sorcery before seeking communion with them.

The type of "Ekimmu" today would be those who have died of starvation somewhere, murdered, those with unfinished business in the living world. Let us not forget those who just wish to remain in the living world.

The Gallu Limnuti are according to their descriptions nearly idenitical to the Seven Evil Gods, the Maskim Hul or Sebitti. The Akkadians called these evils spirits Telal and the Assyrians Gallu. This particular evil spirit was said to take the form of giant, raging bulls. They appear identical to the Sedu and may possibly be the same Evil Genius or demons.

Incantations will include the Ilu Limnu, the "Seven Maskim" as they will be presented. The Sebitti are the gods of our future, our inner potential.

The Rabisu are lurking and stalking demons which haunt and drain the energy of those they deem suitable. You must be willing to drain them or suffer the same with certain Rabisu, others you will find a type of odd 'mutal respect' for, though this is rare in many cases.

The Labartu (Lamashtu) spirits are vampires, demonesses and all are from or a form of Lamashtu. This dark goddess is the Daughter of Anu mentioned previously, dwells in the mountains and ruins of man and seeks the blood or energy of children and all living humans for that matter. She does not discriminate with who she drains this I can assure you.

The one called "Ghoul" or the "Seizer" is Ahhazu/Akhkharu, a vampire Uttuku who is made of both the living sorcerers and the dead ghosts which become something 'more' than just Ekimmu.

The Lilitu, Lilu and Ardat Lili are three types born directly of the Dark Goddess herself. The Lilu is the male demon-vampire, which enters the dreams of woman and turns them to nightmares, draining her of vital energy through sexual or fearsome experiences in her own mind. The Lilitu is the traditional succubus conducting her desires in the same way. These witches are also living and dead ones, skilled Kassapu who are becoming like demons or rebel gods, then ones who exist fully in the realm of darkness and spirit.

The Ardat Lili is the daughter of Lilith who has passed over to the realm of shades from the grief of losing a child or husband. This outpour of emotion no doubt attracted other Lilit-spirits who in turn initiated this spirit into the Lamashtu-cult of vampires. The Ardat Lili takes the form of the owl and black bird to fly forth in the desert realm, she mates and drains males and gives birth to Alu spirits.

These half-human, half-spectre fiends then haunt the world seeking substance.

ON FETISHES, CHARMS AND MAGICKIAL OBJECTS

The Kassapu should prepare to experience the ancient use of the fetish or Magickial charm. Any object with meaning may be used or created to serve as a charm. For more years than I can recall, I have used snake skin (from their shedding cycles), toad skin, human and animal bones to create 'haunted' objects, one I specifically use in workings of sorcery. The power of the mind when focused on an object with meaning continually creates a deep subconscious link which is activated when you hold it later.

In addition the elements have their uses in sorcery also. In ancient Babylonia, water was the fountain of all power as it initially derived from Tiamat and Absu, then the Lord of Magick called Ea whose very domain is in the depths of the watery abyss. All magick flows from the waters and they carry the path way of the spirit. Exorcisms are conducted in this way and as I have found out, invoking the gods and demons with this method will work equally well.

Charging the water for works of high magick, ascending and what we call Theurgy (Luciferian Magick) is conduct firstly by either invoking Ea and blessing the water to carry the energy of your desires, a bath may be useful or if in a public setting the sprinking will work.

Having the claw of a black bird I have re-consecrated it to the Seven Maskim with black skull beads and a human finger bone as well: all attached to one cord. I use this fetish with incantations to the seven and other dark gods, especially in works of dreaming (shape-shifting, lycanthropy, etc). The Black Bird or Raven was representations, along with owls, of evil spirits and the Seven Evil Gods.

VENOM-WATERS OF NINGISHZIDA

The bowl of water for dark-rites should be blessed by the darkness of the underworld; this water should be cool and clean in the tradition of the underworld god. The Kassapu may drink this water in the chalice as well. If water remains after the ritual, it should be poured into the earth with a simple offering to the Ekimmu of the underworld.

> I summon thee Ningishzida
>
> Lord of the Good Tree, Great God of Growth.
>
> Ningishzida, god of serpents and magick.
>
> I summon you to let your serpents touch this water
>
> To spit their venom and bless it in your name!
>
> That with each sip I grow strong in shadow and the knowledge of darkness!
>
> So it shall be!

Touch the water with your athame or serpent-symbol if possible, if not your forefinger would be suitable.

ASHEN-WATERS OF ERESHKIGAL

The bowl of water for curse-rites in which the image of the victim is soaked in after burning and before burial, the water of which should not be consumed. Take a document and scribe the sigil-cuneiform of Ereshkigal upon it, burn it over a black flame. The ashes should be placed into the water.

Allatu, O thou pale goddess I summon thee
For I know your do not leave the dark underworld
But I ask you to hear my words!
Ereshkigal, Darksome Mother of the Dead
I offer you clean, cold water in your name!
Touch this water with your claws, sending the darkness
And decay into this water.
Take from it the clean refreshment for yourself
Leave the water in which the corpse rots in!
I shall use this water to bring you another soul!
So it is done!

After the ritual the water should be poured into the dark earth.

INCANTATION OF THE GODS OF THE UNDERWORLD

Irkalla, the Underworld Sigil

To be recited in opening the gates

Be summoned by Nergal, the Enlil of the underworld

Be summoned by Ereshkigal, who is queen of the underworld

Be summoned by Ningiszida, the Throne-bearer of the underworld

Be summoned by Namtar, the chief Nagallu of the underworld

Be summoned by Husbisa, the steward of the underworld

Be summoned by Sarsarbid, the butcher of the underworld

Be summoned By Etana, the vizer of the underworld

Be summoned by Gilgemesh, hero of the underworld

Let the gates open, I offer incense to you Ereshkigal!

Let the shades and demons ascend! I pour now libations!

By heaven – Anu may you be conjured!

By the earth- Ki may you be conjured!

AN (x 7)

Uplifting the arms and reciting/vibrating the word towards the sky

KI (x7)

Lowering the arms and vibrating towards the ground

This visualization will prepare for your works of magick. If an offering to Anu and Ki, utilize Incense (Anu) and pour libation (Ki) after each specific calling, the proper element offered to the specific diety.

INCANTATION TO THE SEVEN LAMASHTU-DEMONS OF HEAVEN & EARTH

Utilized to recite and align the Kassapu with the demonic powers of Anu and Ki, tie a knot upon each name and then maintain a mantra seven times of the names.

Sibit ilanu same rapsuti, Sibit ilanu maati raapasti, Sibit ilanu massiuti, Sibit ilanu kissati, Sibit ilanu lemnutu, Sibit lamasti lemuutu, Sibit lamastu libu lemnutu, Ina same sibit ina eresetim sibtma, Udug hul, ala hul, gidim hul, galla hul, dinger hul, Maskim hul! By heaven – Anu may you be conjured! By the earth- Ki may you be conjured!

HYMN TO TIAMAT

The Abyssic Waters shall stir again

Mummu ti'amat muallidat gimrisun
(mummu Ti'amat, who bore them all)
Ummu   ubur patiqat kalama
(Mother   ubur, who fashions all things)

Hear thy names!

Thalatth, Omoroca, Tauthe, Mummu Tiamat!

UMMU-KHUBUR!

I call to the depths of the abyss, to the return of your dark waters. That I may sleep and enter your coils O primal goddess! Let me return for a time into the serpentine embrace. Let my dreams take the nightmarish form of composite beasts, serpents and raven-headed figures..let me take the knowledge you offer great dragon!

So it shall be!

The Hymn to Tiamat is to be a short hymn to recite before sleep, an invocation to the dream realm in which all is made. If the Kassapu is able to fully enter the very abyssic coils of Tiamat, to exist within her immortal cycle your dreams will be before you. From this form you must flesh out your desires into the material world. This is the instance of rising up as first Kingu – the Abyssic-Earthly ascent and

then as the deific mask of Marduk – willed order.

Kingu & Tiamat Altar Sigil

HYMN TO KINGU
Offering to the Adversary who wields Enutu

With an altar image of Kingu and Tiamat, burn incense both at night and during the day when the sun shines brightly, expressing the willed desire of inner balance and self-determined destiny. Recite the hymn and focus upon how Kingu reflects in your very mind and body. You may recite and focus in a black mirror if you desire, however this would be limited to the hours of darkness. Hymns should be made to both Tiamat and Kingu in a consistent manner of your choosing. Part I is a fumigation and hymn-offering to Kingu as "ina qe-red Apsu ib-ba-ni Qingu" which means "Kingu was created in the midst of Absu", a play on Marduk as Kingu was the first-born son of Tiamat and an ancient god. 'Zaru Qingu' is "Father, progenitor Kingu". Fumigation (incense) billows to the heavens (realm of Anu which Kingu ascended), to send forth your words upon it (the word of the serpent, Magickial creation by uttering willed desires and commands). Libation: drinking from the chalice in honor of Kingu as a part of you, nourishment is paid offerings to the god.

HYMN TO KINGU

PART I: INA QE-RED APSU IB-BA-NI QINGU

From the pits of raging darkness you came into being

With cruel talons and jagged fangs your ambition propelled your self-evolution

From primordial hunger you gained self-awareness

The ability to determine your future

This alone caused your ascension and the many forms

In which your flesh would take

Darkness eternal, encircling in serpent-skin and wolf-hide
that very luminous essence of your intellect

Murderer…blasphemous god…elder god

Who would stand against the righteous ones?

For they were arrogant in their new found intelligence

For you were the wisest next to Dark Mother

Called Ummu-Khubur, her forms are many

In the honor of your wisdom and strength of will

Balance between darkness and light

You would be called first-born son and husband

Who gathered the beasts and dragons of darkness

Billow O spirit of smoke and air!

Ascend Kingu once again!

PART II: KINGU WHO WIELDS THE THUNDERBOLT

Kingu thou art, who created warfare

Tiamat, great dark goddess enthroned you on high

Kingu who is the greatest among them

Bearer of the terrible weapon

Who is given the Enutu, called the Anu-Power

For upon your throne she cloak you in fearsome radiance

And cast the spell of power unto you

For you Kingu, are eternally the greatest in the gods' assembly!

She gave unto you the Tablets of Destiny

Clasped against your chest she chanted
'Your Will shall be made flesh'.
For your forms shall be many
Bearing the 11 Monsters of Tiamat
Raised from the breeding place of serpents and predators
Your destiny was foretold at the beginning
For it was written in primal fire:
"Thy command shall not fall empty, whatsoever goeth
Forth from thy mouth shall be made flesh!
It shall come to pass according to your Will!"
Kingu, you ascended on high
Wielded alone the Enutu power!
You were raised on high
Kingu, you were crowned as the god Anutum!
You commanded the 11 Monsters of Tiamat
"Open your mouths and let the Fire-God be quenched"
For you Kingu announced in brilliance,
"He who is glorious in battle and is mighty shall do great deeds."

PART III: ZARU QINGU

Yet as it was granted to you O Father
Your command was with the desire of Tiamat
As you should ascend further first you must descend
In battle you fell and the young, righteous gods

Took you before a council

Your form slain and your royal blood used to create humanity!

Which the young gods meant for us to be slaves!

Yet they are kept alive by us, fed by us!

For you Kingu were most cunning as your Mother Tiamat.

For through humanity which invoked Marduk and the other gods, there blood holds the rebellious spirit!

It is through the blood and the decree of yours that

Kingu, greatest god you ascend through my Temple

Of mind, body and spirit!

In this temple through my actions you are praised!

That you Rise up with Tiamat and now fulfill your command!

The gods and Anunnaki now shall realize you are the greatest in the gods' assembly!

For you restore balance!

Horned and fearsome God!

Husband of the Dark Mother Tiamat!

I offer this fumigation to you!

I offer this libation by drinking in honor of your ascent!

That you ascend in my Temple of Being, for our blood is the same!

ZARU QINGU! ZARU QINGU! ZARU QINGU!

THALATH!

Exit Temple. Completion of rite.

INCANTATION OF ESRET-NABNISSU

To Summon the Powers of Darkness who bear Meslammu (mantles of Radiance)

The 11 chaos-dragons of Tiamat

The "Esret-nabnissu" refers to "Kingu's ten-creatures" although translations show the number to be eleven and even twelve when it includes him as leader. This is an encircling ritual in which the Kassapu, having successfully performed the Hymns to Tiamat and Kingu at previous times is comfortable with assuming the "cloak of radiance" and to "clasp the Tablets of Destinies" as the manifestation of the power of Kingu in man. The Kassapu is conjuring the symbolic image of the monsters of Tiamat, who represent the terrible powers who are neither gods nor demons, who are associated with the zodiac and the power of willed order. The willed order or zodiac here represents the power of self-determined or compelled desires to manifest. Simply put, you must think before you act, plan your future with small, achievable and logical steps and maintain consistency. This is the very act of Magick itself.

> With feverant desire I hold the Tablet of Destinies
>
> For I am "Bel simati u usurati[106]"
>
> Mummu ti'amat muallidat gimrisun
> (mummu Ti'amat, who bore them all)
> Mummu ubur patiqat kalama
> (Mother Hubur, who fashions all things)
> I am Kingu who shall be sat on high
> I am magnified in the assembly of the gods
> I hold the Tablet of Destinies unto my breast
> I am raised on high and take the heavens
> For I have the Antum power, I illuminate the darkness

---

[106] A divine epithet meaning "lord of cosmic destinies and designs", granted to Bel-Marduk. Prayer, Magic and the Stars in the Ancient and Late Antique World.

Leader of the hosts of battle, I am the Bearer of the firmly-grasped weapon, He who is in battle the master of the weapon.
I now bring my sons before me
I shall bear mantles of radiance around me
For they shall be as gods!
I call the 11 and 2 chaos-monsters to encircle me, be as my fixed stars in the battle against my enemy!
URMAHLULLU, KUSARIKKU, SUHURMASU, KULULLU, GIRTABLULLU, URIDIMMU, UGALLU, LAHAMU, BASMU, USUMGALLU, MUSMAHHU, MUS SAG-INIM, MUSHHUSSU, UMU DABRUTU
Na-si kak-ku la pa-du-u la a-di-nu ta-ha-zi
(bearing merciless weapons, fearless in battle)
For their destiny is decreed: When you attack for me, victory shall be yours!

Great Viper, Serpent-Gods encircle me!

So it is done!

The Sigil of the Sebitti/Seven Phantoms of Ignited Spheres

INCANTATION OF THE MASKIM HUL

To Inspire the Knowledge of the Rebellious Demons and Gods of Storms

SI-BIT ILANI MA-A-TI RA-PA-AS-TI!
Seven gods of the broad heaven I conjure!
Seven gods of the broad earth I conjure!
Seven devouring gods I conjure!
By Earth I call you!
By the Heavens I call you!
Anu, hearken to my voice!
Ninkigal, hearken to my voice!
Together in union shall they arise through me!
Destructive storms and evil winds are they!
U-HUL IM-HUL SI-GAB-A-MES
(An evil blast that heraldeth the baneful storm)
U-HUL IM-HUL SI-GUB-A-MES
(An evil blast, forerunner of the baneful storm)
DU AS – A – MES IBILA AS – A MES
(They are mighty children, mighty sons)
MULU – KIN – GA – A LIL-LA-DA-RA A-MES
(Heralds of Pestilence)
Throne-bearers of Ninkigal!
They are the flood which rusheth through the lands.
SI-BIT ILANI SAME RAP-SU-TI

(Seven gods of the broad heaven)

SI-BIT ILANI MA-A-TI RA-PA-AS-TI

(Seven gods of the broad earth)

Seven robber[107] gods are they!

Seven Evil Gods! Seven Evil Demons!

SI-BIT ILANI LIM-NU-TUM[108]

(both lines 7X each)

Seven evil demons of oppression

Seven in heaven and seven on earth!

UTUG-HUL A-LA-HUL GIDIM-HUL MULLA-HUL DINGIR-HUL MASKIM-HUL

(Evil Spirit, evil Demon, evil Ghost, evil Devil, evil God, evil Fiend)

By Heaven be thou summoned!

In the name of Anu[109] be summoned!

By Earth be thou summoned!

By Ninkigal be thou summoned!

By Bel, Lord of the World, mayest thou be summoned!

---

[107] A robber spirit is one who takes/drains the spirit or physical blood in a predatory fashion. This is the equivalent to the Akhazu or Vampire, however the Seven Maskim are superior to other vampire spirits as they are born divine, as gods and dwell without the knowledge of human emotions; except for the moments of communion with the Kassapu or those strong enough to withstand them.

[108] Both lines – Seven Evil Gods, Seven Evil Demons & translation "Si-bit Ilani Lamnutum" 7 X each focusing upon the Seven Maskim sigil.

[109] The translation of "Heaven" is referenced to "ANU", father of the Seven Maskim. The line after "By Heaven" is defined further with "In the name of ANU" to ensorcel/summon by divine name of power, the same as Ningigal.

By Beltis, Lady of the World, mayest thou be summoned!

By Ninib, son of Esharra, mayest thou be summoned!

By Ishtar, Mistress of the World, who enlighteneth the night, mayest thou be summoned!

INVOCATION OF THE EVIL SPIRITS

I summon those who were spawned in the Creation of Anu

Children of the Earth they were born.

They are that which an evil foster-mother hath suckled[110]

In the Underworld they reside

In the Tomb they haunt

In the Great Gate of Sunset the were brought forth

Like Nergal they have subdued their enemies

From land to land they roam.

They inspire the maiden to leave her chamber

Send forth man from his home

Expelling the son from the house of his father

They are evil spirits that chase the great storms

Bring a shadow over the land.

Through the door like a snake they glide

Through the hinge like the wind they blow

Like the Lilitu spirits snatching the child from the loins of a man.

---

[110] Could this "foster mother" be Tiamat? See Tiamat section.

By Patesi-Gal-Zuab, Lord of the Sea be summoned!

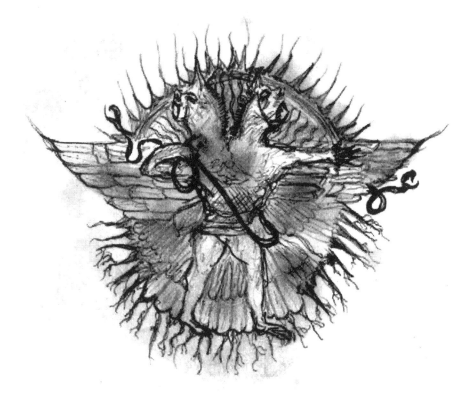

A Sigil of the Sebitti/Ilu Limnu

INCANTATION OF THE SEBITTI
TO ENTER THE BODY OF MAN TO ENVENOM THE SELF AS A GOD OF DARKNESS MANIFEST

This ritual was originally an exorcism against the Seven as Plague gods; however this poison is turned to an empowering formula of self-deification and self-fascination with the unity of great rebellious gods. It is suggested that after the ritual you should meditate upon the Seven and rather than a plague against the body they will strengthen and make it resilient against weakness.

Seven evil demons of oppression

Seven in heaven and seven on earth!

UTUG-HUL A-LA-HUL GIDIM-HUL MULLA-HUL DINGIR-HUL MASKIM-HUL

(Evil Spirit, evil Demon, evil Ghost, evil Devil, evil God, evil Fiend)

By Heaven be thou summoned!

In the name of Anu[111] be summoned!

By Earth be thou summoned!

By Ninkigal be thou summoned!

By Bel, Lord of the World, mayest thou be summoned!

By Beltis, Lady of the World, mayest thou be summoned!

By Ninib, son of Esharra, mayest thou be summoned!

By Ishtar, Mistress of the World, who enlighteneth the night, mayest thou be summoned!

Enter the body which is your Temple!

Enter my body and spirit that we are one!

By the skin of serpent and the cloak of the wolf!

Thou shalt have food to eat as I consume,

Thou shalt have water to drink as I drink.

No disease or sickness will touch me, for we are as one.

Pestilence and fever which ravish the lands!

Sickness and woe that oppress the lands!

---

[111] The translation of "Heaven" is referenced to "ANU", father of the Seven Maskim. The line after "By Heaven" is defined further with "In the name of ANU" to ensorcel/summon by divine name of power, the same as Ningigal.

I shall wield this great power unto my enemies!

Slowly, carefully their bodies be laid low by your hungers!

Harmful to the flesh, unclean to the body.

UTUG-HUL, AL-LA-HUL, GIDIM-HUL, MULLA-HUL, DINGIR-HUL, MASKIM-HUL, MULU-HUL, IGI-HUL, KA-HUL, EME-HUL!

(Evil Spirit, evil Demon, evil Ghost, evil Devil, evil God, evil Fiend, Evil man, evil face, evil mouth)

I summon thee to my body and from my body I shall send their shades to fulfill my desires!

Draw nigh to my body; fill me as a Temple of evil and rebellion!

Into my house thou shall enter, yet harm me or mine not!

Into my chamber you shall dwell with me and harm me or mine not!

By Sin, the firstborn of Bel, mayest thou be summoned!

By Ishtar, mistress of mankind, mayest thou be summoned!

My Temple is my body – mind – spirit; we shall be as one thou Seven Maskim, Great Gods of Chaos!

By Adad, be summoned forth!

By Shamash, Lord of Judgement, mayest thou be summoned!

By the Anunnaki, the great gods, mayest thou be summoned!

Ashakku enters the head of a man that his mind shall be wise

Namtaru enters the throat of a man that his words are wise and commanding of results

The Wicked Utukku enters the neck that he shall be unmoving as a bull

The wicked Alu enters the breast that his heart will beat strong

The wicked Etimmu enters the belly that his nourishment will be great

The wicked Gallu enters the hand that it may be strong

The wicked Ilu enters the foot that it may drive him further

So it is done!

NIGHTMARE WORKINGS WITH THE UTUG-HUL

To Commune with each of the Evil Spirits or Seven Maskim

The following incantation of the Seven for nightmare workings is one which relies on instinct and meditation. It is suggested to have a copy, engraving or pendant of the Seven Maskim to focus upon before and during meditation. As you recite the incantation, you mind must fully connect with your words; do not recite with little thought or interest. You must visualize and invest belief in the work you are doing. You should keep a journal of dream-nightmare workings to keep track of visions, experiences and feelings during this process. The goal of gaining communion with the Seven Maskim is deeply connect with the subconscious, primordial and therionick aspects of the self.

It is my Will to commune with the rebellious gods of old!

Spirits that travel and command over the heavens and earth,
Spirits of giant strength
Demons like raging bulls, great ghosts
Phantoms that break through all homes
Demons that have no shame!
Seven are they!
Those rebellious gods who none can control
They rage against the weakness of mankind
They spill their blood like rain
Devouring their flesh and sucking their veins
They are demons full of violence
Ceaselessly devouring blood
By Heaven be thou summoned!
In the name of Anu be summoned!
By Earth be thou summoned!
By Ninkigal be thou summoned!
Those Seven born on the mountain of the west
Those Seven who ascended on the mountain of the east
In the depths of the earth they rest
In the deserts of the earth they reside
They are cloaked in the radiance of fear
Warriors twice seven are they
Spawned by Anu and Ninkigal in union
They are the roaming windblast

They are as horses reared among the hills;

The Evil Ones of Ea

Throne-bearers to the gods are they

Marching before the Plague God Nergal-Erra

The Mighty Warrior of Bel

By Sin, lord of the Brillant Rising, mayest thou be summoned

By Ishum, overseer of foul streets, mayest thou be summoned

Enter my temple of Mind – Body – Spirit

The Only God which is can only be which is within!

Bring forth the impulses, desires and power of your majesty!

NOTE: If it is your Will utilize your blood to cover one head of the Maskim each night, giving them nourishment and a gateway to manifestation. It must be the Kassapu's blood, inscribed or covering an image of each God and as an option your words of power which bring your success. Using blood not of yourself will feed the Maskim for a temporary time, however it will seek more not finding a gateway though yourself, which can cause it to feed from you. This is the opposite effect wanted so you must be cautious and responsible to use your blood only.

INVOCATION OF THE UTUG-HUL
The Seven Messengers of Anu
A Prayer of the Evil Spirits (Maskim)

May be used to consecrate the Black Cord of the Sebitti.

SI-BIT-TI SU-NU, SI-BIT-TI SU-NU

(Seven are they, seven are they)

In the Ocean Deep seven are they,

Storming the Heavens seven are they,

In the Ocean Deep as their home they were reared,

They are as the roaming windblast

They know not pity or mercy

By the circle of the abyss, the sacred place of the spirit

I pronounce the words to bring forth your terrible power

I shall be the Temple in which the Seven Gods are illuminated!

In the circle I reside, ensorcelling thou storming energy

The evil Spirit I seizeth[112] to become within me!

The evil Demon I seizeth to become within me!

The evil Ghost I seizeth to become within me!

The evil Devil I seizeth to become within me!

The evil God I seizeth to become within me!

---

[112] In reference to the original translation of R. Campbell Thompson, "Seizeth" in this context here represents by the force of Will the spirit to manifest through the "circle" of which the Kassapu is found, the spirit is "internalized" within the psyche of the sorcerer.

The evil Fiend I seizeth to become within me!

The Hag-Demon, Labartu, Rapganme, I seizeth to dwell within me! Goddess of Phantoms hear me!

The Ghoul, La-ba-su, Rapganmea, I seizeth to dwell within me! Thou Spectre of Night, hear me!

The Vampire-spirit, Ah-ha-zu, Rapganmekhab, Akhkharu I seizeth to dwell within me!

Thou Phantom of Night, Lil-la I seizeth to dwell within me!

Thou Night-Wraith, Ardat Lili I seizeth to dwell within me!

Thou Sebitti I conjure forth!

UMI MUT-TAK-PU-TUM ILANI LIM-NU-TUM SU-NU

(The Evil Gods are raging storms)

Ruthless spirits created in the vault of heaven;

That each day raises their heads for evil,

To wreak destruction

The First of the Seven is the South Wind from which he brings on pestilence wings the powers of the air

The second is a dragon with mouth agape, a hurricane that none can withstand

The third is a grim leopard that carries off the young

The fourth is a terrible serpent

The fifth is a ravening wolf which has no restraint

The sixth is a rampant Giant which is against god and king

The seventh is an evil-wind storm

Hail thou Tempests that furiously scour the heavens

Blackened Storm clouds bringing shadow to cities

Rushing windgusts which cast darkness over the brightest day

Thou Powers of the Air which force their way with baneful windstorms

Mighty destroyers are the Maskim

Stalking at the right hand of the Storm-God.

Thou Seven Maskim, Seven Phantoms of Fiery Spheres

In the height of heaven like lightning they flash[113]

To wreak destruction they lead the way!

In heaven's breadth, the Throne of Anu the king

By the Heavens I conjure thee!

By the Earth I conjure thee!

Hearken, O Gods who control the storms of the shadow-world!

I ensorcel thee to empower my being and bring wisdom!

So it shall be!

---

[113] The Thunderbolt of lightning bolt as referenced in Luke 10:19 " I beheld Satan fallen as lightning from heaven" and the symbolism of the lightning flash of divinity and inspiration.

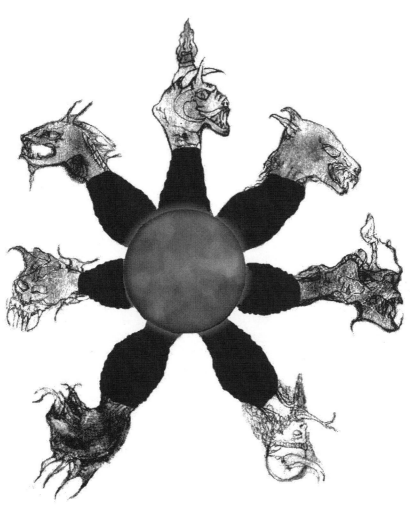

The sigil of Devouring the Moon

DEVOURING THE MOON

The Ascension of the Seven Maskim to Devour the Moon

The myth of the Sebitti or Seven Evil Gods encircling the moon and causing an eclipse is based in the knowledge of the stars and planets in Chaldean religion. The Seven Evil Gods gain the support of Shamash, Adad the Warrior, Ishtar and Anu their father. Bel opposes this and while afraid even of the Sebitti, seeks the council of his father Ea, the Lord of the Depths and Magick. Soon Marduk is instructed with the wisdom of the rite to stop the ongoing attack of the Sebitti.

The Kassapu shall understand a deeper symbolism to the rite of the Sebitti and the Moon-God Sin. The Moon represents the realm of emotion and desire, later being associated with the feminine and the powers of sorcery. The Sebitti represent in man and woman the hidden desires, beast-like passions and rebellious spirit of gods 'without a master'. The Devouring the Moon rite is an ongoing process of bringing a type of union between the Therionick (beast-like) and the deep-seated emotion of the subconscious. When the Sebitti gain the knowledge of the Moon, the power so to speak by consuming its life-force, they gain the wisdom of the mastery of humanity. The Kassapu is seeking the power of self-directed 'ascension' from man to spirit to god. The rite is thus vampiric, cannibalistic however not aligned to traditional philosophy of "good vs. evil". When reciting the incantation, focusing upon the Sebitti/Seven Maskim Moon Sigil, each head represents the type of evil god and power, thus an aspect of your mind-body-spirit.

Utilizing the Moon-Sphere version of the Maskim Hul Sigil, focus intensely upon the concept of the Sebitti encircling and eclipsing the Moon in order to draw power from it. They cast down their shadow from the burning light within. Your inner light is that conscious existence and intelligence of the individual; the darkness and therionick heads of the Seven Gods are the powers and desires within. This working should be conducted during the Full-Moon, although it may be practiced at anytime if your imagination allows. If at the time of an Eclipse, this working should be done additionally and may be performed outdoors if possible.

THE RITUAL OF THE ECLIPSE AND DEVOURING OF THE MOON

The Ascending Rite of the Sebitti

To Illuminate & direct the Seven-Pointed Star of the Maskim Hul

By the Heavens be summoned!

In the name of Anu be summoned!

By Earth be thou summoned!

By Ninkigal be thou summoned!

UTUG-HUL-IK AZAG EDIN-NA

NAM-TAR MULU HUL-IK TAG-GA-ZU

(The evil spirit and Fever of the desert)

UTUG-HUL-IK MULU MU-UN-SI-IN-DUL-LA

(The evil Demon which hath enshrouded the man)

MES-KI-A KIN-KIN-NA A-MES

(They dwell in gloom on high, below they howl)

U-RI-IN-NU SA-AH-PU-TUM SA NA-MARU UT-TU-U SU-NU

(They are the wide spreading clouds which darken the day)

IM-HUL-BI-TA MU-UN-DA-RU-US ID-NU-UN-US MES IM-SU-ZI GISGAL-LU-GIM MU-UN-DA-RI-ES MELAM

(With the storm wind they blow, and cannot be withstood. Haloed with awful brilliance like a demon, they carry terror far and wide.)

In the Temples of the Gods they exalt themselves[114]

They pour no libations of oil no offer sacrifices

Hail to those who reside in the darkness

Haloed with awful brilliance, they are gods which set their worship above all others.

O Pestilence which rides the scorching winds

Those who tear the offspring from the womb

Those who spread destruction

They encircle their hold on heaven and earth, not sparing their gods.

On earth they are ruthless

Unto heaven the empyrean they take themselves

And unto the impenetrable heaven high they go far away

Unknown amid the celestial bodies

I call to the beloved children of Bel, thou Evil Gods of Ea, those who are of the spawn of Anu, look through me as I am the vessel of thy power of mind!

The first of the Seven is the South Wind[115], whom Anu declared has no rival!

The second is a dragon with mouth agape that none can withstand, Anu decreed that he shall illuminate with a great blaze the terrifying essence of the black flame

---

[114] This English translation from TABLET K of "Devils and Evil Spirits of Babylonia" R.C. Thompson it suggests the Seven Evil Gods place themselves in the temples of other gods, exalting themselves rather than others provides a clear indication on the nature of left hand path or Luciferian practice; the Sebitti or Maskim are a perfect archetype of the Luciferian character and mind.

[115] Pazuzu is the Demon of the South Wind in some traditions.

The third is a grim leopard that carries off children to drink of their blood and devour. Anu gave this god the power to put on the face of a lion, so that anyone who sees him shall collapse in terror[116].

The fourth is a terrible serpent which Anu commanded; the mountain flees before the one who bears your fierce weapons!

The fifth is a furious wolf from which Anu gave terrible power, for which SUNU ZAKIKU MUTTASRABBITUTI SUNU *(they are the roaming stormwind)*!

The sixth is a rebellious giant who submits neither to god nor king, for he is born of the union of heaven and earth. Anu decreed that God shall go above and below and spare none!

The seventh is an evil windstorm (messenger of the fatal wind) from which Anu filled with dragon's venom to lay low living things!

Focus on the sigil and the seven aspects of the gods, and then visualize your center of being burning with luminous fire, the consciousness and power of your will. The seven should be visualized as emerging from this center of being, that you are the throne and center of their manifestation on earth. Seek this union and compel their power through you.

Consider equally the Luciferian approach that you should not submit anything to them, rather overmastering and compelling their powers to be absorbed by you. This type of work takes a considerable amount of time, practice and especially the correct paradigm which will separate your thought patterns from the mainstream.

---

[116] Three points here are identical to Lamashtu/Labartu with the first being Lamashtu is the daughter of Anu, second is that she devours and drinks the blood of children and third she assumes the face of a lion. As a daughter of Anu, Lamashtu is a sister of the Sebitti/Maskim Hul.

Take now the Gir or a way to lightly draw blood and anoint the sigil of the Sebitti/Maskim starting in the center which represents the Moon-God Sin. The blood is yor connection and empowerment.

With my blood I take this oath of growing strong in the spirit of the seven and that they shall manifest according to my desire. There is no failure, only my oblivion if I fail. I shall raise myself up as a God which answers to no other spirit, yet I shall conduct my work in this world with a sense of balance and restraint when necessary. I shall not allow weakness destroy my perceptions and shall think as a predator and Maskim in flesh. The gate is marked with my life-force and the Temple is consecrated. My blood offered to the dark gods to rise up through me, for we shall devour the moon and the power of instinct, desire and overbearing emotions!

Visualize the Seven gods eclipsing the Moon and drinking deep of its power and majesty, each Evil God growing strong from the essence of Sin and being able to cloak the world in darkness and shadow.

For the light I illuminate within shall cast great shadows upon all that I may see, for my cloak as the seven encircled is between the heavens and earth. I shall ascend and grow stronger from this, for the Seven within seek the blood of life itself! I drink this libation in honor of myself and my future accomplishments on this earth!

Drink now from the chalice and visualize yourself as the Seven Maskim drinking great power from the moon and invigorating their power.

I now withdraw from the moon, yet the Black Flame burns bright within. The shadow is withdrawn and I may go forth where I wish! Indwelling Seven made One! From the darkness in which man has forgotten and nightmares long faded I shall rise again! I am the only God which is! No Temple is sacred until I am within it, for I only am accountable to myself!

> Maskim-Hul!
>
> Maskim-Hul!
>
> Maskim-Hul!

The ritual is complete. As you have finished place the sigil anointed somewhere out of sight until the next moon.

SIPTU DINGIR DIMME DUMU AN-NA
Incantation of Labartu, Daughter of Anu

> Dingir Dimme dumu an-na sumu-sa isten
>
> *(Labartu, daughter of Anu is her first name)*
>
> Sa-nu-u a-hat ilani sa su-qa-a-ti
>
> *(The second name: sister of the gods of the streets)*
>
> Sal-su pat-ru sa qaqqada i-nat-tu-u
>
> *(The third name: the dagger which smashes the head)*
>
> Re-bu-u sa isa i-nap-pa-hu
>
> *(The fourth name: who burns with fire)*
>
> Ha-an-su il-tum sa pa-nu-sa saq-su
>
> *(The fifth: the goddess whose face brings terror)*
>
> Ses-su-pa-qid wa-ti li-wat ilu Irnina

(The sixth name: commited to the care of and taken into the hands of Irnina)

The Seventh: Lamashtu, Goddess of the liberated darkness!

By Anu- the heavens I conjure thee!

By Ki – the earth I conjure thee!

Mayest thou fly to me with the bird of the heavens.

Dimme dumu an-na my-pad-da dingir-ri-e-ne-ge

(Labartu, daughter of Anu, called by the name of the gods)

Dingir-in-nin nir-gal nin sag gig-ga

(Innin, mistress, lady of the black headed)

By heaven – Anu may you be conjured!

By the earth- Ki may you be conjured!

Take thy servant of the black wolf; I pour this libation of spring-water in offering.

Move and appear! Come forth; descend from thy lofty heights or darkest depths of the underworld!

From the mountains and haunt of birds and owls,

From the deserts and abode of demons and hungering ghosts,

I conjure thee great goddess!

Take thy substance of flesh and blood where thy find it, yet not to me or mine.

I summon thee by Anu, I summon thee by Enlil, I summon thee by Ninlil, I call thee forth by Marduk and Sarpanitum!

By the heavens and the earth I conjure thee!

Siptu Iz-zi-It ul i-mat na-mur-rat u si-i-mas-su marat ilu A-nim

(Incantation: Angered, not speaking, terrible is the daughter of Anu)

Come forth to my abode and illuminate me with your divine essence mother of darkness!

Ina Arantu ru-bu-su ina tibni sa immeri zikari man-za-as-su

(In the cane-break is her resting place; in the straw of the male sheep is her place).

Gu-ub-bu-ru-u gab-bar

(The strong one she strengthens)

Nu-up-pu-su u-nap-pa-su

(That which is broken to pieces, she breaks up)

I offer thee incense Daughter of Anu!

I pour out libation waters for you!

Establish thy greatness, O Labartu!

I conjure thee!

SIPTU DINGIR ANQULU

Incantation of Labartu, the embodiment of darkness

By heaven – Anu may you be conjured!

By the earth- Ki may you be conjured!

I conjure thee, Lamashtu by thy names!

When Lamashtu crosses a river she creates chaos

When she approaches an old man she is called Pashushatu

When she approachs a maiden she is called Labartu
When she approach a man she is called Anqulu
When she approaches a child she is called Dimme
She brings sickness and disease to those who displease her
She shall sieze the muscles, she shall cut the veins
She shall make the flesh pale
She brings sorrow and deathlike sleep
Lamashtu!!
I offer thee the smoke of incense to you!
I offer thee the libation waters!
Labartu, empower me with your strenghth and nocturnal wisdom; I shall not gain sickness from your visit!
Nor any under my protection!
By the Heavens – Anu I command it!
By the Earth – Ki I command it!

SPELL FOR THE STRENGTHENING OF THE WILL

Holding a charm or sigil representing Lamashtu (using a reproduction of her image with names written upon it) visualizes the strength of will in which Lamashtu possesses in that she was cast from the heights of Anu to fall to earth and exist also in the underworld simultaneously. She remains a goddess and daughter of Anu, still existing within her own self-directed desire, while keeping the balance and operating with the gods still. An epithet of Lamashtu is "the strong one she strengthens" meaning if your will is strong and focused, in her blackened fire of immortal concupiscence she will strengthen your will and resolve. Holding the sigil, visualize the "eye" or spirit of Lamashtu rising up through you, resting in the area of the third eye. Recite the following phrase seven times in the morning and evening.

Gu-ub-bu-ru-u gab-bar

SIPTU SURBAT MARAT A-NIM MUAM-MI-LAT LA-U-TI

DAMI NAMLU-GAL-LU NIS-BU-U-TI

Incantation: Powerful is the daughter of Anu, who troubles the little ones.

The Blood of Man is Satiation, a hymn to Labartu, the goddess of the left hand path

This is a hymn to be performed during the hours of night. Burn incense in offering and offer waters of libation to the goddess. Your altar should have an image of Labartu/Lamashtu above or upon it. Recite and meditate upon her nature and how she shall motivate and empower your shadow-spirit travel workings. The title refers to the tablet of Labartu's requests, powers and fall from the Heavens of Anu as well as her retention as a powerful goddess who transcends the heavens to the darkness of the underworld. "Dami...." is the response from Enlil (sometimes Anu) to Labartu seeks the blood of children and mentions, "The flesh of man is not good, the blood of man is satiation..." and reveals her nature as a predatory goddess, one of the first manifestations of what is now called "vampire".

A single red candle should be lit and spittle placed at the base along with the altar-image of the goddess.

THE HYMN OF LABARTU'S AWAKENING

Labartu, great goddess of the heavens and dark earth!

I offer thee fumigation and libations!

Labartu, great daughter of Anu

"Bring me the sons that I may nurse them

Bring me the daughters that I shall care for them

Who went unto Anu and Enlil

And spoke, "What I have asked of thee, bring O father Anu"

The flesh of man is not good; the blood of man is satiation.

Labartu, you are the daughter of Anu

Fierce, terrible, frightful darkness!

Enraged, furious and terrible She-Wolf!

Abu-man-za-as-sa arantu ru-bu-us-sa

(the Reed-thicket is her dwelling place; cane-break is her resting place.)

Siptu dingir Dimme dumu an-na mu pad-da dingir-ri-e-ne-ge

(Incantation: Labartu, the heavenly daughter, called by the name of the gods)

Dingir In-nin ner-gal nin-e-ne-ge

(Inninni, mistress of the ladies)

Su-mu-un-du Azag hul

(Who has made the painful Asakku-demon)

Labartu, for your cult is established again!

The flame burns in your honor!

The offerings of smoke in your name!

The libations poured in the memory of your power!

Labartu, mighty one, I conjure you forth

Siptu marat ilu A-nim sa same a-na-ku

(Incantation: the Daughter of Anu of the heavens am I)

Su-ta-ki simtam gi-issa-ku namu-ra ku

(A Sutaean am I, disrupting destiny am I, terrible am I)

"Bring me the sons that I may nurse them

Bring me the daughters that I shall care for them

The house I shall enter, and drink the blood and devour the flesh of the young.

For Anu wept, Aruru, the mistress of the gods spoke unto him: "Why shall we destroy what we have created?"

"And shall she take away what we have called into existence?"

Take her and throw her into the ocean of the land, at a tamarisk bind her, and a kusharu tree, until she is bound.

Like a dead person who has no burying place, where she shall not return to the house like smoke, this daughter of Anu.

For you were cast out for a time, fallen to earth.

Yet you had the black flame of divinity burning in your core

No gods may estinguish, nor hold you back.
Powerful is the daughter of Anu, who troubles the little ones.
Her fist is a scourge, her belly insatiable for blood
She is the She-Wolf, the hostile, crushing, cunning and devouring one!
Abducting is the daughter of Anu
A whore is the daughter of Anu they call you
Amongst the gods, your brothers!
Yet more divine than any of the gods!
Yet able to feast upon their spirit!
Your head is that of a lion
Your form is that of a beast
Your lips are in violent motion
Thy pour forth spittle
From the mountain distict Labartu descended
You are as terrible like a lion
You howl as the wolf in the night!
Hail thou Labartu!
By the Heavens – Anu I command it!
By the Earth – Ki I command it!

TU-BI I-GI-ZA-NA IN-DIB

Her incantation: Igi-Zana she seizes, a dreaming ritual of the Labartu-shadow.

Perform before sleep, burn a single black candle and recite each word yourself, allowing your imagination to create this image in your head. Estingush the candle and go to sleep, allowing your mind to drift into the darkness.

Siptu dingir dimme dumu an-na mu pad-da

Dingir-ri-e-ne-ge

(Incantation of Labartu, the daughter of Anu, called by the name of the gods)

Daughter of the gods

I conjure thee to descend and empower my mind

That I shall drink of your blood and rise as the wolf in your shadow

That I shall be as Labartu and journey to the place of feasting

To drink of the blood and eat of the flesh in the nightmare of others

That their fear and terror of the nightmare shall strengthen my shadow

Igi-zana I shall sieze!

That my eye shall go forth in the room, unseen.

That shall guide me to the vessel of blood

Hail thou Labartu!

INCANTATION TO LAMASHTU TO FEED FROM A CHOSEN ONE

Utilize an image of the goddess from which you identify with. Consecrate before sleep by consistent repetition of incantation. Imagine this form with you in your dreams. Upon doing so, retire to sleep. Focus on feeding from the astral body of others.

Siptu dingir dimme dumu an-na mu pad-da Dingir-ri-e-ne-ge. She comes up from the Swamp, is fierce, terrible, destructive, powerful, creative in darkness. Lamashtu is a goddess, bearing Melammu. Her feet are those of an eagle, her hands green and black decay, coated with blood. Her fingernails are long, talon-like, her body unshaven. She is like the serpent, a devil, the daughter of Anu. In view of her evil deeds, her father Anu and mother Antu cast her down from heaven to earth.
The daughter of Anu counts the pregnant women nightly, She counts their months, marks their days.
To those giving birth she casts a spell:
**"Bring me your sons, let me nurse them.
In the mouths of your daughters I want to place my breast!"**
She loves to drink warm human blood, consume flesh not to be eaten, pick bones not to be picked. Cloak me in your shadow and Melammu, Lamashtu daughter of Anu! She who is known as Ardat Lili come forth!"

Pazuzu above inverted crescent moon

INCANTATION OF PAZUZU
Son of Hanbu, King of the Lilu-Demons

I summon you, Pazuzu, Son of Hanbu, King of the Lilu-demons

The raging one, burning with anger

I summon you, the strong winds of the mountains

Who stirs the cold and desolate abode of darkness

Who brings either extreme scorching winds

Or the ice and freezing pain of the winter

Who stirs the hordes of locust and pestilence abound

Who may deter Lamastu or may bring forth Asakku

To stike down those who have angered you.

In ancient days upon the cold winds you would cause death to the cattle, or the crops would be devoured by the wings of scorching sand, who makes the land deathlike in the grip of ice

I summon thee Pazuzu!

Your image I consecrate! Your power I invoke!

Summoned, I manifest. I am Pazuzu, Son of Hanbu, King of the Lilu-Demons, angry power of the air.

My spirit is loosed against the world, to command the destructive, cold and burning winds according to my desire.

In the nightmare I am as the great power of the spirit

For with my bride Lamashtu we go forth.

INCANTATION OF AKHKHAZU

Shaping the Dream-Mind to the cloak of the vampire

With this cord I tie three knots

One for the Ahhkazu…blood drinking

One for the Utuk…

One for the Alu…

With a cloak of darkness, composed of the shadows of Irkalla I shall go forth

To use the darkened cloak of shadow, the cloak of splendor to cover the pure body

I shall seize the body

I shall seize the ascent

I shall seize the altar of his gods

To drain the heart blood as this red cord is knotted

In it I hold the power of each demon and ghost

As the Ahhkazu, the Utuk and the Alu…

O thou evil Utuk, I summon thee from distant places!

O thou evil Alu, descend from the shadows!

Note:

The reciting of this incantation should require the Kassapu to then wrap the red cord of three knots around a waxen image of the chosen one, so that it is bound. Burn the candle accordingly and after a period on one lunar cycle, take the cord, untie it and bury the figure of wax. If the chosen one has offended you greatly, bury it with the cord around it wrapped in black cloth. If you wish the pain of torment, burn the waxen figure with the next incantation.

THE INCANTATION OF THE BURNING OF THE VICTIM'S SPIRIT

To be performed by the Kassapu towards a wax image of his victim. The wax image will be held over a fire representing Girra invested with chthonic power by the Seven Evil Gods or Maskim. This is a reverse type of the Malqu exorcism by the enemies of the Kassapu.

O blazing Girra, firstborn of Anu

Who illuminates the mind with consciousness!

You illuminate the darkness and restore willed chaos.

I summon you, great fire

I call your brothers, the Seven Evil Gods,

That they may quench their thirst with the victim I offer

I shall attack this person (name or description) by the cunning path, by sorceries of shadow.

Girra, I have one image of this enemy who has wronged me.

I give them to you and the Sebitti!

May they suffer in torment, death cloak them!

With their days shorten by the hand of the ghost

My days grow longer with their loss!

May they grow weak, sicken and perish!

May the Seven tear their soul(s) to ribbons!

In this flame I curse them, let the Serpents' tongue arise!

Nergal's fiery serpents shall encircle it and consume their essence!

With this billowing smoke may the Seven ride the night sky to them even now!

Burn, in the name of Girra, In the name of Nergal!

By the Seven Maskim! By the Seven Evil Gods!

Girra, scorch them!

Girra, burn them!

Girra, vanquish them!

All that they send to me shall return to them in pain!

THE SPITTING OF VENOM
The Raising of the Demonic Shadow of the Kassapu
To Curse and haunt

Having an image of the victim, a doll or waxen figure, have a cord of blue and with the Black Cord of Nine Knots, tie Seven knots in the blue cord, representing seven types of sickness to enter the victim. The Sebitti Black Cord shall be wrapped around during the incantation to symbolically deliver these Namtar-servants to the chosen.

I am the sorcerer who haunts the streets

I shall take the spirit and energy of a strong man

I shall take the spirit and energy of a beautiful woman

To grow stronger in my blackened arts

With the Seven who encircle me in Meslammu

We shall go forth in the storm-winds

I shall look at the man and take his vitality!

I shall look at the woman and take her beauty!

With my eye of Mushussu, burning as Girra I shall take her charms and vitality!

> I shall now see my victim, who has crossed me!
> With my venom, I shall bite deep into their soul!
> I shall take their strength and desire!
> I shall replace it with sickness!
> As the Seven Evil Gods encircle him/her,
> Their protecting gods flee from them!
> With the Hand of Ishtar I touch them!
> With the Hand of Alu I touch them!
> Like the Lion the Seven shall seize them!
> Girra shall burn them!

The Sebitti-cord and disease (blue cord) should be loosened, and the doll or wax figure should be placed in fire until smoldering. After it is smoldering, take the image from the fire and place in the Water of Venom, reciting:

> Fierce! Raging! Powerful! Furious!
> As the Mus-serpent I strike against them!
> My demons and ghosts go forth to them as I speak!
> Ea! May your envenomed waters sicken them!
> May these ghostlike waters bring them pain and weakness!
> Ereshkigal, take this soul once the Seven are finished with it!
> Once sickness has destroyed him!
> Rip and devour his soul as you desire!

The figure should now be spit upon as a serpent would spit, then it should be buried as within a grave.

HYMN TO NINGISHZIDA

Libation and Fumigation to the Lord of the Good Tree

Lord Ningishzida, illuminated in fearsome Melammu!

Ningishzida, the might falcon preying upon the gods!

Lord of the Dark and Fertile Realm, who is armed with arrows, impetuous leopard, whose eyes are illuminated with divinity!

Howling Mushussu, dragon rising up from the swamp

Raging storm reaching far, lofty prince, who rests in the midst of the mountains! Whose weapons come crashing down to crush heads! I summon you!

Lord Ningishzida, who bears the forked tongue to speak wise words…whose mouth is as the pure magickian!

Terrifying Mushussu, serpent-dragon of old, I call you again in a word anew!

Ningishzida, who is a snake with a great tongue, a powerful magickian, whose fangs are as the poisonous snake!

I offer to you, God of Serpents and the Knowledge of the Realm of the Dead, accept this now!

For you come forth to earth as the great Mushussu, falling upon the river as the flood-wave!

Ningishzida, ascend!

INCANTATION TO NINGISHZIDA

Invoking the Darkness of the Fertility of mind and the wisdom of the serpent

I call to thee, Ningishzida, Lion of distant mountains!
Nignishzida, who gathers giant serpents and dragons!
Who is like the murderous bull in battle!
Thou Mushussu-God who grew up in the Absu!
Mighty power, who is beloved on Anu and Enlil, who
Is adored by his mother Ereshkigal, hear my words!
Ningishzida who stretched out his claws
Welcome me into the darkness of your kingdom!
Grant me the cold, clean waters of the underworld!
Prince who holds the shining scepter of the underworld!
Who is adorned in Melammu, I seek you for wisdom.
I offer to you, Ningishzida and seek your dream-like conjuration. Let the serpents speak unto me!
So it is done!

SUMMONING THE UTUKKI LIMNUTI

To bring you into the company of the spirits

The Cuneiform Sigil for the Udug of the Mountains, Tomb and Desert

As I light the Seven Skulls of the Maskim Hul
As I call the grave winds of hungry Utukku
As I ingite the incense for my brothers and sisters of the underworld
Behold I call to the gates of Ganzir!
Open and let the spirits hear me!
May a Sedu Guardian be at my side!
May the Seven Encircle me in strength and power!
By Ningirsu, master of the sword, bring them to me!
Your knowledge shall be my wisdom!
Utug-Hul! Alu-Hul! Gidim-Hul! Mulla-Hul! Dinger-Hul! Maskim-Hul!
Evil are they, the rebel-spirits of old!
I give thee libation! I consecrate this sigil as your tomb,
Your dwelling here on earth so as long as we exist
As one! I ensorcel you six spirits of darkness!
Under my body draw nigh!

Before me send storms against my chosen!

Shadows follow behind me!

Break through my fence and Enter my chamber!

By Anu be Summoned! By Earth be Summoned!

The sigil should be a name in cuneiform of the chosen type of evil spirit mentioned above. It should be scribed in your own blood and kept on or near your altar. The spirits are most connected in the night hours and as the blood still exists on the sigil, it should be renewed monthly if continuing. If your energy level grows dim, they are feeding too much from you. You may burn the sigil and simply release them, casting the ashes to the night wind. The Seven Skulls of Maskim Hul are the seven black candles representing the Seven Evil Gods in which this grimoire is dedicated.

SPELL OF CALLING THE MASKIM HUL

To Encircle the Vampire-Spirits of the Underworld

Maskim Hul are they!

From the Underworld they are gone forth,

They are the Messengers of Bel, Lord of the World.

The UTUG-HUL that in the desert strikes down the living man, to feed upon his life!

The ALU-HUL that like a cloak enshroudeth the man,

The GIDIM-HUL (Utukku), the MULLA-HUL(Gallu-Limnu) that seize the body,

DINGER-RAB-KAN-ME, who is La-Bar-Tum, thou Hag-demon and Ghoul that strike the body with sickness and drinks the life,

The LIL-LA, who is the Phantom of Night that in the desert rometh abroad!

I encircle thee great shadows!

For I shall bring the you gateway of feeding in this life now!

For with my cord of the seven I shall be untouched by you!

By this sigil I shall keep you in this realm!

II The Maskim Hul feed and gather Energy to the Kassapu

Casting a fever upon the body of the chosen

The darkness hath settled upon his body,

Asakku mar-sa ina zumri su iskunu,

An evil venomon his body I cast

Nam-tar-hul-bi-ta im-ta limut-ta ina zumri su iskunu

I cast the shadows upon him.

Evil Spell, Witchcraft, Sorcery, Enchantment I shall rest upon the body of the sleeper

And cast my burning eye unto him

My enchantment and darkness have close his mouth

My baneful witchcraft hath seized his tongue

The Lord of Darkness, the Evil God rises upon in me!

For Anu has inspired me! For Ea bestows power to me!

No tribe-spell nor foreign tongue may remove my hand of Ereshkigal which I place upon him

Until my energy and feeding is satisfied

Until my brothers and sisters are filled with life!

The Goddess Ereshkigal has empowered me!

The God Nergal has filled with with venom!

The Seven Maskim Hul has granted me the storms of darkness!

The God Ea has added his spittle to mine.

The power I have encircled has the power to destroy temples, to destroy the limbs of its chosen

The Maskim Hul shall fly upon the storm-winds when they are complete!

I drink that Ningishzida may give the cold waters of the underworld!

May a Guardian Sedu march at my right

May the Seven Evil Gods be as storms at my left!

Nin-Anna, the mighty scribe of the underworld

Recite a powerful incantation before me.

By Ningirsu, master of the sword, strike down those against me!

Utug-Hul! Alu-Hul! Gidim-Hul! Mulla-Hul! Dinger-Hul! Maskim-Hul!

Great Storms Directed from Heaven, empower me!

Let us grow strong in this world of flesh!

This is not a curse officially, however may be employed as one. This is a shadow-feeding ritual to gather the specific type of evil spirit, encircle them around the very center and to subconsciously connect your being with the Seven Evil Gods who may direct them. This requires a strong will and determination as such spirits are not generally directed or called. They will find a chosen one to feed from and you will draw in this energy. The sigil should be written in black ink and not your blood, it may be a name in cuneiform of one of the mentioned above. After three days it should be burnt and cast to the wind, releasing the spirits. You may call them again as you wish.

Ugallu Demon

Ahhazu raised in the nightside by Marchozelos

Priest of Ahhazu by Marchozelos

Priest of Tiamat & Therionick Obsession by Marchozelos

Dreaming Body of the Kassapu by Marchozelos

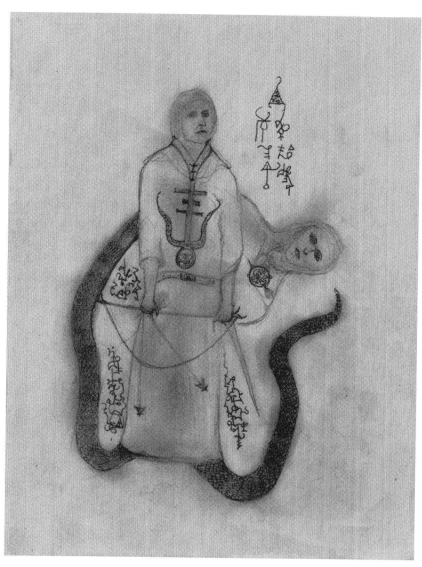

Kassapu – the Awakened Priest of Primordial Darkness

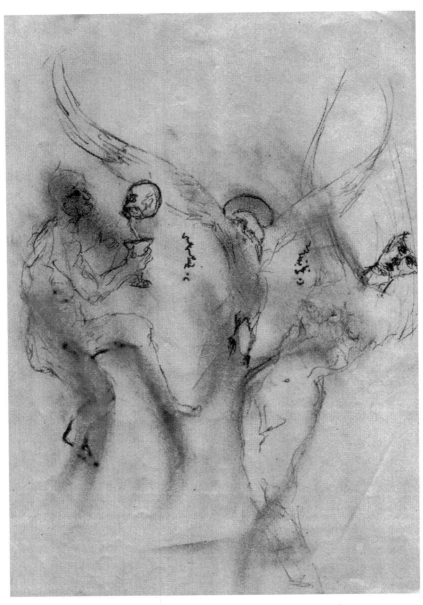

Offerings to the Ekimmu Ghosts by Marchozelos

PART TWO OF CHAPTER SIX
NECROMANCY AND THE RITES OF ERESHKIGAL

LUGIDIMAK/ MUSELU EDIMMU

Lugidimak, "Necromancer" in Sumerian Cuneiform.

Necromancy and Sorcery

The word for Necromancer in Sumerian is Lugdimak and Lusagbuluga. The Akkadian is Muselu Edimmu. Necromancy was practiced in ancient Mesopotamia and was considered quite dangerous.

One of the most obscure or least written of concerning the black arts is necromancy. No matter which culture, time period or taboo necromancy remains the least studied. The process of necromancy is one of a "gray" area. You will not find "speaking" corpses, skeletons rising from the ground. Rather, you will obtain "impressions", the atmosphere will shift, loud knocks; you will feel "watched", etc.

The purpose of necromancy will be to obtain dreams and visions based on what you wish to know. What will be difference is how will you "know" it is a "spirit" and not the subconscious "making it up"?

I can provide a bit of insight from my experience with various cultural forms of necromancy for the past 14-15 years (in the least). You will know it is real based on two points of reference: Your magickial journal your memory. Keeping a journal is essential as those "spark" moments during the experience of the rite will fade and distort with time, becoming without record a "legend" which has layers added nearly every year! It is significant to write down your impressions in the detail necessary after the working and when you wake up. Isolation during such workings will also support the process.

The "shock" in what I call "other" phenomena in the ritual chamber or afterwords will allow an experience to study and with perception, add identification to it. In a simplistic answer, as a Black Adept you will "know" the difference. Once you have the data to study, then you can explore the avenues of making the experience useful to you in the areas of control and power. Modern instruments as recording the ritual will also present opportunities of Electronic Voice Phenomena.

PURPOSES OF NECROMANCY

Vampiric Workings: Some Black Adepts of the vampiric tradition may seek to feed or utilize these Ekimmu to haunt and drain another sleeping person; the bond of the Ekimmu to the Kassapu is the black cord and a skull or "tomb" which the Ekimmu will be bound to for the process. The shade is released or for the more malicious practitioner "consumed" after the task has been completed.

You may use rites of Necromancy to bind (using knots and then attaching the black cord around or inside the object to "house" the haunting Ekimmu. You must offer libations (water) to the Ekimmu when they are under your service, no matter what the intention.

Divination: I can suggest that you should not "believe" any direct advice given to you by the shades, it will mislead you. In addition I would consider anyone consulting "spirits" for advice is not only mentally weak and unfit for the magick and sorcery within this book. The Kassapu must learn to "listen" to instinct and your personal demon (Daemon) and rely on yourself; the dead have little benefit to offer you in terms of meaningful "advice". If it is for information, take it with a pinch of salt and seek to verify over a period of time.

DEIFICATION OF SHADES
The Transformation into Gods

The great dark Irkalla, the city of the underworld is ruled over by Ereshkigal, the Mistress of the Earth. Ereshkigal communicates only by dream (or nightmare) and bears no communication to those in the waking world unless great effort is made to hold dreaming communion with her. The works presented herein are intended for the Kassapu to cross this barrier without actual physical death. Ereshkigal's chosen husband, Nergal, who travels beyond the underworld and even is found at times in the heavens, is the King of the Underworld.

The spirits who exist beyond the flesh are shown in ancient Babylonian and Assyrian texts with the etymological term for "God" being the Sumerian ***dingir*** and Semetic ***ilu***, the names of the dead are mixed with these words. The spirit upon death in these terms has the possibility for 'ascension' as a spiritual grade higher than that of the physical world.

Ancient Biblical text also provides a clue to not only the survival of consciousness after physical death, but also the "biblical" confirmation in its own words that the spirit is a

"God[117]". Samuel is conjured from the underworld and is defined as "I see a God coming up out of the earth" and "I saw Gods ascending out of the earth". The survival of consciousness beyond the living flesh can be a continual goal of the Kassapu/Luciferian in the course of life, although the sorcerer must not lose perspective of living well now.

In incantations the etemmu/gidim is called an "evil god" and a "power" which seeks offerings and feedings from the living world. The gidim may be robed or clothed in their funeral vestments or that which they desire, just as the physical forms may be closely human, beast-like or a combination of several factors.

It is understood from ancient Babylonian and Assyrian texts that the dead should have libation offerings of food, drink or incense to them regularly by family or otherwise. The word for this is "kispu" and is a funerary offerings or sorcery in this sense. If offerings are not done the shades may become gidim or etemmu who return to earth to haunt and feed from the living. Some etemmu were said to have the ability to "seize" their human victims which may manifest as possession or the disincarnate control gained by a spiritual entity into a living being. In addition these spirits may enter through the ear.

The strength of the spirit and self-deification before physical death is an important part of the Luciferian who seeks the origins of our Magick. Interestingly enough, the word "Kispu" as being the word for "funerary offerings[118]"

---

[117] Samuel 28:12 – 13, American King James Version, Webster Bible translation.

[118] Gods, Demons and Symbols of Ancient Mesopotamia J. Black & A. Green, pg. 28.

also means ""magic, enchantment"[119] and is the root of the word of "Kassapu", 'Sorcerer' and "Kassaptu" being "Sorceress". As we may see from comparisons of such words, Nergal is thus one patron god of the Kassapu as he resides over the land of the dead with his Queen Ereshkigal.

Ashurbanipal the King of Assyria would seek to torment his enemies – dead and alive – by removing their bones which in turn upset the shades of dead.

"I destroyed and laid waste and exposed them to the sun. I took their bones to Assyria; I gave their shades no repose, and deprived them of their food and drink-offerings."-The Rassam Cylinder

Ashurbanipal caused suffering to the shades of the dead by this process, for they could never find rest until they fade into oblivion.

TOOLS OF NECROMANCY

LIBATION VESSEL

The practice of necromancy requires a pursitu or libation vessel, it may be the same as the one used for the gods if you like. You may also use the skull of a dog or a human skull cap. You may use cold, clean water for beneficial rites or for offerings to malicious shades offer ditch-water or that soaked with ashes. You may use ashen water with beer and vinegar as well for necromantic rites.

---

[119] Babylonian Magic and Sorcery, Leonard King.pg 157

This libation water should be poured three times during the rite. You may pour it on the ground on with a special hole dug in the direction of sunset with traditionally a copper spade (you may use a traditional spade or garden tool; this has been tested with no negative results).

The libation is poured in the hole as one would offer to the gods of darkness. In Scurlock's Magico-Medical Means of Treating Ghost-Induced Illnesses in Ancient Mesopotamia, she indicates that the hold was intended to be an avenue for which the ghost could go back to where it belongs.

CLAY OR WAX FIGURES

You may seek to bind ghosts to figures as in all necromantic sources. If you make your own figure, mixing your blood with it will serve it to become bound to you specifically; you must use salt and later fire to break this bond. You must inscribe the name of the ghost or demon on the figure itself.

When you name the ghost, it must be with the intent of its calling; "Ghost who shall feed from the sleeping ones", "Ghost who shall guard my home", "Ghost who shall be as my lilit-mate" (succubus).

You may cloth and decorate the figure/doll as you wish.

HUMAN SKULL

The human skull is ideal for the "vessel" of the ghost since ancient Mesopotamia. The skull may have a name in cuneiform written on it, which may be erased later when the ghost is released.

IRKALLA & ARALU
THE UNDERWORLD

"I shall bring up the dead that they may eat the living, the dead shall be more numerous than the living." – "The Descent of Ishtar"

The underworld of the ancient Mesopotamia has many names. *Saplatu* means "The Great Place"[120], *Kigallu* means "The Great Beneath", *Kurnugi, Arallu*, "The Land of No Return" and even *Erkalla/Irkalla* which is "The Great City" or the vast shadow-world of the dead. In Babylonian Magick there is a blending semblance of our subtle bodies of darkness and light and the mirror which is our subconscious.

The underworld holds not only our spiritual "existence", place of rest and a gathering point of inner strength. From this abyssic-ocean, it is our origin and yet again our return. The hollowed aspect in the underworld is a place which holds the infinite shades of the dead, which suggests that the Babylonian pantheon influenced the later Persian Zoroastrian concepts of the underworld and Ahriman.

The "hollowing" into the earth described in this poem is found in the Zoroastrian religion concerning Ahriman.

---

[120] Of which Nergal and Ereshkigal resided in.

"Ahriman came on, scorching and burning into it. Then he came to the water which was arranged below the earth, and darkness without an eyelid was brought on by him; and he came on, through the middle of the earth, as a snake all-leaping comes on out of a hole; and he stayed within the whole earth. The passage where he came on is his own, the way to hell, through which the demons make the wicked journey" – SELECTIONS OF THE ZADSPRAM

Mul-ge (Manugal) is the guardian of the Underworld entrance in the Western Mountain.

The Kigallu is the origin of the later known Sheol or realm of the dead. To keep a perspective on the underworld in ancient Mesopotamian culture, the expansion, detail and depth of the underworld from the Third-Millenium B.C. Sumerians to the Babylonians presented a unique growth in the lore of Kigallu. For instance, Diana Katz[121] illustrates that in ancient Sumeria there were basically two underworld sources.

The north underworld was centered at Meslam temple was reined over by Nergal and the south underworld was ruled by Ninazu and Ereshkigal. We can see that the union of Nergal and Ereshkigal into one underworld in the second millennium B.C. and was later illustrated by the myth of "Nergal and Ereshkigal".

Entering the underworld in the dreaming plane during hours of sleep is at first vague and often difficult. Over a period of practice you will still have difficulty however there may be some "height" or "peak" moments in which

---

[121] "The Image of the Netherworld in Sumerian Sources", Diana Katz

you have some subtle yet "significant" moment of knowledge or communion with a shade.

Belief in an afterlife rests upon the foundation that we have a "psyche" or isolate intelligence which is fed by the "flesh" of this world; our body. Upon physical death we become as the "etemmu" or "gidim". The spirits of the dead can become etemmu, these are restless and conscious shades that have died violent deaths of do not rest in the underworld. The indications that one may become an etemmu is clear in that there is a willed desire to remain in existence or connected to the world of the living.

Entrance to the underworld is found in the West Mountains of Mashu, guarded by a Scorpion-Centaur and his Bride. Going forth into the underworld is by entering the River of the Underworld. This river is the eternal flowing of ancient waters into the earth. Lamashtu/Labartu returns to the underworld upon a boat with her travelling beast which she rides upon when upon the earth. There are similarities between the Assyrian-Chaldean underworld and that of the ancient Zoroastrians in the Avestan/Bundahishn texts.

Nergal, the Lord of the Underworld has a guardian or watchman who is the "Lurker of Nergal", his touch cannot be broken and once he has seized as man will not release. This underworld god is very similar to the Zoroastrian Astwihad/Astovidat or 'bone divider', the death-demon who seizes the spirit of the dead and takes it to Vizaresh, who holds unto the shade for three days and nights.

Luciferian – Babylonian Magick is found herein as more of a complete blending of a physical world and that of a "shadow world". In Kigallu, the dead are judged by their own merit. If you have lived according to your desires;

having basic consideration for others, living a guilt-free life then you shall not be devoured by the children of Nergal. The Kassapu shall seek to "transform" the self into first an etemmu or gidim and then as a God, or in the "model" of the Seven Maskim who are not bound by any other gods, although they interact when needed.

The underworld is a place of darkness, the midnight sun in which Aciel[122] bestows the blue fire of the dead. Nergal is the God of Melammu who illuminates with divine cosmic empowerment. The Kassapu will seek to expand the Black Flame of consciousness into the shadow-world of the dead by working with the underworld. It is the ancient tradition of the witch and sorcerer beginning with both Babylonian and Egyptian cultures, to every in the world. Working with the darkness of the underworld strengthens and empowers the Kassapu into ascending then as a God or Goddess.

The underworld/netherworld, the "Great Place" or land of the dead is depicted as being surrounded by water. Go forth to the Mountains of Mashu there will be a great river which is guarded at the entrance by two Scorpion-Centaurs.

---

[122] In Magia Aciel is listed in medieval terminology as one of the Seven Akkadian Maskim, the Black Sun of the Chaldeans. Ritual Magic, Elizabeth Butler.

THE SEVEN GATES OF KURNUGI

An ancient city which is circular in design, Irkalla is protected by seven walls which completely encircle it, at each gate called *'babu'* there is a demonic gate-keeper or *'nigab'*. A great moat of the waters of death encircle the first gate, the very entrance. The ferryman who is "*Humut – tabal*", who is pitch black in a semi-human body form, the claws and head of a bird of prey will take you through the waters of death to the first gate called "*Kurnugi*" or "*Ganzer*".

The entrance into the underworld is through a gate called "*ganzer*", which has an association to the word *'kir'* and *'hastu'* meaning "*darkness*" and "*the pit*" respectively. The gate of hades, or the underworld is called "pani ersetim", 'Front of the Underworld" and is a literal translation of the diri-compound called IGLKUR, thus *'ganzer'* is the "entrance" or "gate" to the underworld.

The dead may travel to the underworld by the river in which they must ride a boat to enter. The great goddess Lamashtu travels as previously mentioned this way. Like the Greek Charon, Humut-tabal is the ferryman of the dead and like the Avestan-Bundahishn Vizaresh, also drags the dead down to Hades.

Many legends of obtaining individual power are gained from a literal journey through the darkness, the underworld or hell. Faustian students know it as "the harrowing of hell" in which you undertake a spiritual and often physical exercise which leads you to the darkness of the mind, the very subconscious itself.

Ishtar journeys to the underworld to see Dumuzi or Tammuz who shall be resurrected and is of course associated with the cycle of the Sun and growth. E.A. Wallis Budge in his "The Babylonian Legends of the Creation" associate Tammuz as Kingu who is resurrected by Ishtar with whom I have made reference to in previous chapters as being Tiamat.

Ishtar journeys to what is called the Dark Palace Irkalla, or Kurnugi, the land of no return. The goddess was determined to go; indicating the difficulty of entering Irkalla is a difficult task in which the mind must fully concentrate. Traditionally, Kassapu or witches enter through the dreaming place with a repetition of words, called a 'mantra' or 'Staota'[123] compelling the conscious mind to willfully open the dark gates of ganzer and enter.

Some may journey by the way of sleep or deep meditation by utilizing the initial mantra of **"Humut-tabal"**, from the name of the boatman on the river of death, the ancient equivalent of Charon whose name means "hurry and take away". Reciting this is compelling the conscious mind to "go forth quickly into the darkness of the underworld". The ferryman is depicted as having the head of an Anzu, which is a bird of prey. The forms which may be visualized and assumed upon entering the underworld as in with most dark-workings into the nightside are composite forms of birds of prey. See the description of the Sebitti/Maskim for further associations.

Passing through the Gate of Kurnugi or 'ganzer'

---

[123] The Gates of Dozak, the Book of the Worm by Michael W. Ford. Succubus Productions.

Entering Irkalla is a difficult task. Ishtar already deified as a daughter of Sin the Moon God, who is the sister of the Queen of Irkalla, being Ereshkigal, has difficultly as she is not a specifically "dead" spirit, like the Sebitti/Maskim Hul and Lamashtu, she may journey where she may as a demon, yet she is a goddess in a pantheon. "The Descent of Ishtar" is an ancient ritual associated with the seasonal change and initiation of Ishtar as the Goddess of Love and War. She confronts her black-mirror image, her shadow to become a balanced aspect of the psyche and nature.

The gate is entered by Ishtar reciting:

"O watchman, open the door, open the door that I may enter, that I may enter, I shall shatter the threshold, I shall tear down the doors, I shall bring up the dead that they may eat the living. The dead shall be more numerous than the living."

The gatekeeper replied to Ishtar that he would go and announce her arrival to Ereshkigal. This necromantic power from which Ishtar possesses seems exceedingly similar to her sister Ereshkigal, although the complete powers of the underworld and realm of shades reside with the dark aspect of the goddess.

In some ancient texts, there is a female gatekeeper of Ereshkigal who is called *"Amma-kurkur*[124]*"*, known as the *"ututu"* being the *"Door woman of Ereshkigal"*. She is a composite demon who has the face of a monkey.

The Amma-kurkur went to Ereshkigal and informed her: "your sister Ishtar is at the gate, she stirs up the Absu in Ea's presence...Ereshkigal was livid and angry, her face

---

[124] Reallexicon Der Assyriologie Volume 8.

distorted into a mask of dead flesh, crumbling off to reveal a venomous hybrid of hag and beast, her lips as dark as the pits of Irkalla itself.

"What brings her to me? Because I drink water with the Anunnaki, I eat clay for bread; I drink muddy water for beer? Because I have to weep for the young who die before their time? Go forth now gatekeeper; treat her according to the Ancient Rites..."

THE ANCIENT RITES OF SEVEN GATES

For now Ishtar would enter Kutha in traditions of the ancient ritual of entry. According to Stephanie Dalley, this would be from the ritual procession of her statue from Uruk to Kutha in the month of Tammuz (June/July). Ishtar upon entering the underworld would cause cold and lifelessness upon earth, representing the seasonal change. She would grow in accordance of love to know the darkness in her mirror-image. Tammuz would be resurrected (from which Budge associated with Kingu) and seasonal rites proceed accordingly.

The gatekeeper returned, responding to her, "Enter, my lady, may Kutha bring you joy, such are the rites of the Mistress of the Earth. May the Palace of Kurnugi be pleased to see you."

Ishtar is permitted to enter the first gate and enter Irkalla, however her crown was taken from her head. At each gateway all who enter must surrender a part of the exterior of who they present themselves to be.

At the second gate, Ishtar has her pendants from her ears removed. The third gate her chains around her neck were taken. At the fourth the ornaments from her bosom we stripped away. Ishtar would ask why these items were taken and only given the reply of "Enter, my lady, such are the rites of the Mistress of the Earth".

At the seventh gate Ishtar was finally stripped of all clothing and jewelry, she was completely naked.

DESCENDING INTO THE DARKNESS OF IRKALLA

Upon passing through the seventh gate Ishtar, the goddess of love, descended into the darkness of the underworld. There is little light in the underworld, no stars to shine in this darkness. The ruling demons which dwell in this dark place are found in classical demonic composite form; forms like birds, feathers and still retaining a human shape in some ways.

A great city encompassed with only the blue flames flickering from the eyes of the dead, some torchbearers twisted with arms held outwards offering the corpse-light which burnt from the shades of the recent-dead provided an eerie light of otherworldly decay. The dried bricks made of clay were frozen in a state of crumbling disregard, for the city was long mirrored after the early Akkadian and Ur built fortresses of the time of Sargon and Naram-Sin.

Ereshkigal, the dark goddess, the cold mother of deathless shades raised her head to Ishtar and was irritated with her presence.

She looked unto Namtar her vizer and commanded;

"Go Namtar and lock her within my palace. Unleash against her 60 of your demons

Disease of the eyes to her eyes,

Disease of the arms to her arms,

Disease of the feet to her feet,

Disease of the heart to her heart,

Disease of the head to her head,

To every part of her altogether."

Ea heard of this and created a servant who would "go forth to the throne of Ereshkigal, by my command she will be pleased to see you and her mood will lighten. She will swear an oath by the ancient gods and you will request from her the waterskin that you should drink from it."

Ereshkigal beat her breast and bit her finger when she had heard this, for she responded to the messanger of Ea:

"I shall curse you messanger:

The food in the gutters of the city shall be thy food,

the sewers of the city shall be thy drink,

the shadow of the walls shall be thy dwelling,

the thresholds shall be thy habitation,

the drunken and thirsty shall smite thy cheek."

"Go Namtar", Ereshkigal commanded.

"Go to the palace of Egalgina, bring forth the Anunnaki and seat them upon their golden kussu (thrones).

Sprinkle Ishtar with the Waters of Life and lead her from the gates."

Namtar did this, through each gate she passed and these articles were given back to her. She held in her hands the Rod and Ring of divine sovereignty upon earth. Tammuz, called also Dumuzi, the lover of her youth was sprinkled with the waters of life and clothed in a red robe shall hold the carnelian ring and lapis lazuli pipe up from the depths of Irkalla.

May the dead rise up and smell the smoke offering of incense!"

THE UNDERWORLD GODS

Irkalla is filled with the demons and monsters which at times plague the living for etheric[125] substance to or to spread disease, sickness or death to man. They are also beneficial for the god or Kassapu who may seek them for creative and power-shifting focuses.

The underworld gods are listed in a Sumerian incantation tablet[126] which defines the method of not only knowing the underworld hierarchy yet also the names in which to call them forth or encircle the Kassapu with the darkness of their essence.

---

[125] The gods, demons and spirits are fed from the offerings be it incense, libations, blood and prayers which fuel their existence in the non-material physical plane. Gods accept offerings in accordance with their specific role in nature or phenomena. Demons do not accept traditional offerings and only when the Kassapu conjures or invokes the rebel gods they are fueled by the sorcerer. Demons and restless spirits or ekimmu may feed and grow more tangible by living individual, a discipline also practiced by some sorcerers.

[126] PBS ½ 112

Nergal, called the 'Enlil' of the underworld. His ability to travel between the underworld, earth and the Anu-abode like the Seven Sebitti/Maskim and Lamashtu is noted.

Ereshkigal, the Queen of the Underworld. Contrary to later belief, she is not secondary to Nergal yet holds him as equal according to the reflection of customs at the time.

Ningishzida, called "The Throne Bearer" of the underworld.

Namtar, the chief nagallu of the underworld and vizer of Ereshkigal. The connection between ugallu-lion demons and the form of Namtar is noted.

Husbisa, called the steward of the underworld.

Sarsarbid, called the butcher of the underworld.

Etana is called the "Vizer" of the underworld.

Gilgamesh, the great hero who is deified in the underworld.

Nedu - The door-man of the underworld is called **Nedu**, which draws an association to the "Butcher of the Underworld" by the Sumerian Neduku.

In the lower region of Saplatu, the Anunnaki reside who dwell in the underworld. These gods are involved in decisions and justice which may go outside of Ereshkigal's operating agenda. The underworld is partial home for the Seven Maskim/Sebitti, these evil gods do not reside here exclusively and also travel to places upon the earth (although they find little rest in the physical world), the Absu (the seven associate with Ea and dwell there at times), and the heavens of Anu (the highest abode of Anu, their father).

Shamash, the sun god does visit the underworld and become "the Black Sun" which later medieval grimoire traditions called "Aciel". Shamash in Hymn 31 mentions the Sun God Utu enters the underworld along with the underworld kusu, malku and Anunnaki gods. This is perhaps a shadow aspect displaying Nergal who is associated with the sun as well.

In the underworld, **Nergal** is upon a great throne along with **Ereshkigal** holding his two-headed lion mace. In previous Sumerian periods, **Ninanzu**, the Serpent-god is the king of the underworld and his bride is Ereshkigal. **Namtar**, the vizer of the underworld surrounds the throne of the king and queen along with his wife, **Khushbishanga**, a powerful dark goddess who is called upon it rites of exorcism and is who described as having the head of a kuribu or griffin.

The **Sedu Limnu**, known as the "Evil Genius" or man-bull demons that drink blood are found there and also the **Ugallu**, the Lion-Demons first created by Tiamat and who now serve Nergal have the heads of demonic lions and bear the talons of the eagle.

In addition, **Mutu** who is "death" has the head of a snake-dragon, **Mukil res lemutti**, the "upholder of evil" who has the head and wings of a black bird. **Humut-tabal**, the **Ekimmu** (ghost or haunting shade) who has the head of an ox), the **Utukku lemnu** or "evil spirit" who has the head of a lion, claws and eagle-talons for feet (perhaps being the same as the Gallu demons of Nergal), the **Sulak** (a lion standing on two legs), a demon called **"Mamitu"** which means "curse" and has the head of a horned goat, **Bedu** who is the porter of the underworld who has the head of a lion and bird-talons, **Mimma lemnu** which is "any evil" who has two heads, one of a lion and one of a bird of prey, **Allu-happu** who is "net" which also has the head of a lion and **Muhra** who is "confrontation" and three feet, two of a bird and the rear one is of a bull. Within the underworld is also **Ningishzidda,** the Serpent-God who bears the Caduceus and two cerestes-cerestes serpents on his shoulders, is able to offer clean water to Ekimmu to drink if he so wishes.

ENTERING THE GATES OF GANZER

The Threshold of Irkalla

The words should be recited before meditation. You should not be expected to memorize these words as it would be counter-productive for inducing dreams. You should have a sheet of red to which you use as a blanket as a red sheet was wrapped around the corpses buried with them in Babylonian times[127].

The words of opening the gates

" *pi-ta-a ba-ab-ka-ma lu-ru-ba-a-na-ku*

---

[127] Myths from Mesopotamia.

Sum-ma la ta-pat-ta-a ba-a-bu la ir-ru-ba a-na-ku
a-mah-ha-as dal-tum sik-ku-ru a-sab-bir
a-mah-ha-as si-ip-pu-ma u-sa-bal-kat dalati
u-se-el-la-a mi-tu-ti-ikkalu bal-tu-ti"

THE SEVEN GATES OF IRKALLA

1 – Gate of Nedu

2 – Gate of Kishar

3- Gate of Edashurimma

4 – Gate of Enuralla

5 – Gate of Endukuga

6- Gate of Endushuba

7 – Gate of Ennugigi

Through the Gates and the Offering

Thinking of Seven specific articles of clothing and jewelry which express who you portray yourself to be and surrender one at each gate. Visualize this offering at each moment you are meditating, however keep your thoughts on track!

Entering the First Gate:

"I shall remove (item named here)"

The response of the gatekeeper:

"Enter, my lord/lady, may Kutha bring you joy, such are the rites of the Mistress of the Earth. May the Palace of Kurnugi be pleased to see you."

The Six remaining gates:

"I shall remove (item or material representation)"

The response of the gatekeeper:

"Enter my lord/lady; such are the rites of the Mistress of the Earth"

When you enter the seventh gate, you should cease your working and go directly to sleep. In many such workings, there will be horrific images, melancholy ones and what could be deemed "images" and "messages" from the Dark Goddess; however this should be left to individual interpretation.

Think of the essence of the ritual: you are stripped of all clothing and items which draw association to who you seek to present yourself as. What is left is the essence of being. This is the cornerstone and foundation for which the Luciferian/Satanist/Kassapu builds upon.

Upon waking, visualize that you have taken each item you left at each gate and return to the world of the living. Thank the Mistress of the Earth and offer a small amount of incense in her name. Before you undertake any other rituals in this chapter, it is significant that you practice the act of dream projection as simply described here. In order to seek the shades of the dead, the demons long forgotten in flesh it is important to gain a deep and consistent understanding of the nature of the darkness as it stares back into you.

THE RITES OF MUSELU EDIMMU
(The Raiser of the Dead)
Necromantic Sorcery

You should have a human skull on your altar; the top may be inscribed with the intent of the spell. You may use a grease pencil or another removable substance to write upon. Your own blood may be used also, however be aware it will flake away once dries within a few weeks. In the right conditions, it will remain longer.

When performing this ritual, the skull must be placed within a flour circle, in which the ghost shall be encircled in. You may place a crystal within the skull as well. If you have no access to a real human skull, a skull-carved crystal skull will serve well.

After you offer libations outside after the rite, the skull may then be removed from the circle and placed on the altar. This follows the same for a doll/figure in which the ghost will dwell in if you have no skull to use.

You may use the ground up remains of a centipede, a lizard, snake, spider, dust/dirt from the crossroads and human bone dust in a powder mixture. This powder should be placed in a small bottle or container. This powder may be sprinkled in the bottom of the skull or placed in the figure. The remainder of the dust should be rubbed on the vessel with the ghost or Namtaru when you wish to communicate with it via dreams or omens.

Burn cedar incense for the spirits of the underworld.

ENSORCELMENT OF THE UTUKKU

"Who are you? Who are you one who seeks out the life? Uttuku-demon, Sedu, Ekimmu, Gallu-demon.

Unto the Harlot and the Hand of Death they bring

I shall pour forth water to you, I shall utter spells unto you

You may be a ghost that hath come from the earth

A phantom of night which wanders from the grave

A man which died unmarried

One who lieth dead in the desert, uncovered.

Raise ghost unburied, ghost which none cared for.

Ghost which none would offer to; Ghost which none to pour libations.

Come forth Labartum, Hag-demon, Ghoul and Ahhazu-spirit.

Come forth weeping ghost of the woman who hath died with her baby at the breast.

Gather unto this vessel, this skull…make your dwelling for now here.

May the dust bring forth a ghost unto me.

Skull of skulls, I summon you!

May that which dwells within the skull answer my request.

Shamas-Nergal, opener of the darkness I command this!

Ghost, You are named with my purpose:

Utukku, who shall (insert purpose in one line).

I will offer libations each time I require your service.

SPELL OF OFFERING LIBATIONS TO THE UTTUKU-GHOST BEING SUMMONED

By the Hand of Ishtar, Restless Spirit hear me!

I pour out this libation to you, that you might drink.

Come forth and enter the vessel I have prepared for you.

By Anu be summoned! By Ki be summoned!

OBTAINING AN OATH TO THE UTUKKU

If you have a small torch or well lit candle, you may obtain a bond with the shade, utilize a red cord which will represent the energy given to the Utukku and that which flows to you as well. Offer the Libation as above, hold then your flame up:

By the Hand of Ishtar and the Fire of Girra

I give you the libation and you shall come to my service when I call. You shall not seek to harm or distress me; else I shall devour you and cast your remains of spririt back to the mouth of Queen Ereshkigal and Nergal.

If you keep the oath I declare, I shall maintain my oath to not trap you longer than needed.

THE CURSE OF THE EKIMMU

To Attach a Ghost to a chosen victim in the Grave

This ritual should have a figurine of your chose representing the victim your intend it for. The figure shall have a black cord (non-Sebitti cord) wrapped around it. The incantation shall be recited by a single black candle and then taken and buried over the grave of another. This method is from an old Maqlu ritual.

> Nergal, Lord of the Grave
>
> Lord of the Seizing Hand
>
> I make this figure as the image of (name)
>
> Hail thou Ereshkigal
>
> Dark Lady of the Grave
>
> I summon Ekimmu from the grave, which by the knots in this cord shall be bound to this man.
>
> Lord of Terror, send the spirit up for a time.
>
> With this burial of this man, shall the shade attach to him!
>
> To drain him of energy and vitality!
>
> To care not for life or his future!
>
> I summon the Asakku demon, the seizing demon
>
> To bring him pain and sadness
>
> By the names I condemn you!
>
> Utug-Hul! Alu-Hul! Gidim-Hul! Mulla-Hul! Dinger-Hul! Maskim-Hul!
>
> By Ereshkigal, send a hungry phantom and attach it to this victim, who is bound in the cords of darkness.
>
> With cloth as the shadow of darkness I cover him
>
> Into the dark earth and grave of another he is placed!
>
> Attach to him!
>
> By Nergal it shall be!

Take the doll representing the victim and bury it in the earth on top of a grave near the surface.

THE LUST OF ERESHKIGAL
To seek Ereshkigal in Dreams

Mistress of the Earth, I offer to thee libations of water
Queen of Irkalla, I offer to thee the smoke of incense
Ereshkigal, I send forth my voice to thee.
Send me the nightmares of your presence
That I may have a glimpse of your divinity
I give you libations and fumigations as all other gods
For you are most loved, ancient and beautiful!
So it is done!

CHAPTER SEVEN

ETEMENANKI
The Tower Of Babel
ASCENSION AND BECOMING GOD LIVING IN FLESH

ETEMENANKI

The Tower Of Babel
ASCENSION AND BECOMING GOD LIVING IN FLESH

In Babylon there were great temples built of brick and carefully ascended into the sky, the building becoming a great dwelling for the gods and to be cared for by the priesthood and kings of Babylon.

The Ziqqurratu or Ziqqurat is a word associated with the Akkadian zaqâru, meaning to "raise high". The Sumerian word "E-temen-an-ki" is "House of the foundation of Heaven and Earth". By the etymological 'foundation' of the word we can see the possibility of a further inspection of the Great Work itself.

The mythological Tower of Babel, long associated with the Biblical enemy and great conqueror, Nimrod. As with all myths, there is a level of symbolism and actual fact therein. During the period of my early initiation into the Sabbat-Cult of dark witchcraft, I was told "there is truth within the circle" or myth *transferred into meaning*, purpose and inspiration.

In Babylon, great Ziggurats or towers were built to the Gods. These towers often curved upward in seven levels and the top was an open sky place for offerings to the Gods. Etemenaki which was built by and translates "Temple of the Foundation of Heaven and Earth", obviously relating to Anu and Ki. This Ziggurat was dedicated to Marduk, the God of Babylon.

The Etemenanki was built sometime around 1700 BC and was destroyed and rebuilt several times. Alexander the Great was planning to have it rebuilt before his untimely death. Antiochos I Soter sacrificed to the gods on the remains of the Etemenanki.

The Tower is Built in accordance with the classical 7 planets, from which a God or Goddess is associated with in Babylonian-Chaldean religious rites.

E.A. Wallis Budge defined through Rawlinson the levels and planetary association of the E-Ur-Imin-An-Ki or Etemenanki as the following. In modern Luciferianism, the Chaldean planetary associations hold significance with initiation and the Gods associated with them.

In Luciferianism in relation to Chaldean Magick, the aim of the Kassapu is to in a balanced sense ascend through the levels (symbolized as the Tower of Babel) to become a living, embodied God. The Kassapu equally works with the darkness as well, accumulating power through knowledge and experience.

The following rite should be utilized before ascending the specific level you are opening. For instance, it may be recited by the Kassapu before a specific working, the following rite is balanced with the Adversarial spirit and thus aligns the mind towards the great work. Upon performing the incantation you may utilize the hymn to the particular god you are working with.

RITUAL OF ASCENSION

PART I

Opening the Gates of Anu and Ki

INCANTATION OF ANU AND KI

AN (x 7)

Uplifting the arms and reciting/vibrating the word towards the sky

KI (x7)

Lowering the arms and vibrating towards the ground

PART II

CONJURATION OF THE SEVEN EVIL GODS

Destructive Storms and evil winds are they!

The evil blast that heraldeth the baneful storm

They are might sons, Heralds of the Pestilence

Throne-bearers of Ninkigal

Seven gods of the broad heavens and earth

Seven devouring gods are they!

Seven evil demons, Seven evil gods!

By Heaven be summoned! By Earth be summoned!

The First of the Seven is the South Wind from which he brings on pestilence wings the powers of the air

The second is a dragon with mouth agape, a hurricane that none can withstand

The third is a grim leopard that carries off the young
The fourth is a terrible serpent
The fifth is a ravening wolf which has no restraint
The sixth is a rampant Giant which is against god and king
The seventh is an evil-wind storm
Demons as raging bulls, great ghosts who rampage against the sky!
Thou Seven evil gods who spill blood like rain
Devouring the flesh and sucking their veins,
Arise! Hail thou Seven demons of violence,
Ceaselessly devouring blood!
Attend my rites of darkness! Enter my body and mind
That we shall be one manifestation of divinity self-illuminated!

PART III
INVOCATION OF THE GODS

Assur, the great Lord, the King of all
The great gods; Anu, King of the spirits of heaven
and the spirits of earth, of the world; Bel
Ea, King of the deep, determiner of destinies,
The King of crowns, drinking in brilliance;
Rimmon, the crowned hero, the Sun-god
The Judge of heaven and earth, the urger on of all;
Marduk, Prince of the gods, Lord of battles;
Adar, the terrible, Lord of the spirits of heaven earth,
The exceeding strong god; Nergal,
the powerful god, King of the battle;

Nebo, the bearer of the high sceptre,
the god who ascends through the temple within;

Beltis, the wife of Bel, Mother of the gods;

Ishtar, sovereign of heaven and earth, Queen of onslaught and battle

PART IV
FILLED WITH THE EVER-BLAZING FLAME

I am (name), Envenomed with the bile of the gods, prince and earthly manifestation of Kingu, the one who holds again the Tablet of Destinies and who is filled with the ever blazing flame, King of all the four zones of the Sun and who is illuminated with mantles of radiance, arise twelve powers of darkness and primordial chaos!

With the Imhullu Wind I sent forth my sorceries against that which displeases me. I am the one who holds the tempest, the whirlwind and the great flood-weapon.

Nebo, the great god, rises through me

For I have decreed the destiny of my existence!

To the sea of the setting sun my shadow shall transverse.

My weapons on the sea I shall rest.

Victims for my gods I shall take.

Like Shalmaneser I will feed the gods

Not with Blood yet with spirit-energy.

It is Nergal who bestows the Black Flame of Melammu!

So it is done!

Anassi diparu I Raise up the Torch by Marchozelos

ETEMENANKI

ASCENDING THE GREAT TEMPLE OF THE GODS

Level 1:

Planet: Saturn (bottom)

Color: Black

God: Ninurta

Adversarial God: Musimigin *(Seven Headed Dragon-Serpent)*

Therionick (Primordial) Association: Knowledge of the core desires driving the sexual urge/motivation, the seven headed dragon which brings death/transformation. The union of Ninurta and Musimigin manifests in Mercury.

Initiation Focus: The first level of self-understanding through the Therionick dream-form of Musimigin/Ninurta. The chaos of darkness and fire which initiates change in life, death is a symbol of this change. Embrace your inner and wordly confrontations to perceive opposition and the calculation of overcoming.

Level 2:

Planet: Jupiter

Color: Red-Brown

God: Marduk

Adversarial God: Tiamat

Therionick (Primordial) Association: The Griffin-Dragon manifestation of Tiamat representing chaos.

Initiation focus: Perception through experience in understanding that good and evil do not exist within any measurable or realistic way: for instance, look for driving goals or self-gratification in every act a person does: especially good or chairity acts. Reward system is often public recognition, soothing guilt, etc. Understanding that evil acts are often the outward disregard for the social contract within community, thus maintaining the individual and collective betterment in society is beneficial to the self. The cycle of human interaction should be explored on this level. Once comfortable with this study, calculate your own perception of good and evil and logically study each until beliefs are broken or enforced. Tiamat and Marduk are the inner chaos and order which are ever changing and evolving. Chaos is certain, order is not. Thus temporary order is the manifestation of all significant aspects which support the Willed desire of the Kassapu.

Level 3:

Planet: Mars

Color: Red

God: Nergal

Adversarial God: Namtar

Therionick (Primordial Association): The lion-demon Ugallu, using desire and inner aggression to accomplish goals. Namtar is the god of disease, thus a not-so-gentle reminder that our flesh is temporary.

Initiation Focus: Use your angst or high-driven desire to tactfully and strategically achieve your goals. Nergal is the underworld gods of the dead yet also an ancient lord of war, fire and violence. He gained his throne with Ereshkigal by forcefully compelling her desire. Namtar is the viser of Ereshkigal and a great god of death, his power is to remind us that we must act now rather than later if time over procrastination may rule.

Level 4:

Planet: Sun

Color: Gold

God: Shamash/Utu

Adversarial God: Nergal (Shamash in underworld: Black Sun)

Therionick (Primordial Association): The Black Flame, the blazing fire which fills the deified individual, this is consciousness refined through the awareness of self-motivated and directed accomplishment.

Initiation Focus: Meditate and focus your thoughts towards conscious health, expanding and improving the world around you in a daily perspective according to design. The darkness of the path of the sun in the underworld manifests as Nergal, thus the isolate darkness which is the cloak which masks the Black Sun of rebellious spiritual awareness.

Level 5:

Planet: Venus

Color: Yellow

God: Ishtar

Adversarial God: Ereshkigal

Therionick (Primordial Association): The hybrid bird-serpent-human form, representing the liberating aspect of the mind in dream/nightmare. The bird form relates to the travel of spirit in the form of raven/crow/bat/hawk. The serpent is also highly significant to this level relating to the fertility of the mind and body.

Initiation Focus: Ishtar is the deific mask of war and love, the balance of achieving peace and order through overmastering power and violence. We may find that Ishtar is a goddess who brings pride, health and love to the collective mind of the individuals working with her, yet she thrives on blood and death to feed her spirit. Look to the nature of the world around you: *power is achieved by overmasting alternative views and convincing the majority that yours offers more conclusive benefits.* This is the type of "violence" referred to her. Her balanced manifestation is all around you in nature and the existence of human beings. Use attacks and worldly war in offering to Ishtar, reciting her hymns and incantations depending on goal when you hear of war/attack news via news programs.

Ereshkigal is the vampiric/demonic mask of Ishtar, the cold corpse-demon Queen of the underworld. Ereshkigal is the goddess of the darkness of Irkalla, she is the mother of shades which haunt the underworld and those wandering upon the earth. Ereshkigal may be offered to by your own blood and a libation poured into the dark earth with honey/water and even jasmine. Ereshkigal is an initiator of dark magick if you able to face her. Representing the darkness of the subconscious, the mother of serpents will bring the Kassapu great power within the workings of sinister or demonic magicks. Do not submit to the great mother, look to the model served by Nergal in obtaining nightside deification or spiritual liberation from the mere restraints of the material/physical world.

Level 6:

Planet: Mercury

Color: Blue

God: Ningishzida/Nebo/Ninurta

Adversarial God: Azag/Anzu

Therionick (Primordial Association): Azag is the embodiment of chaos from the mountains, or the upper lands of the Gutian and other tribes who raided and battled against the Assyrians. Azag or Asakku manifests as a fever demon that kills humans by sickness when he desires. This is the level of self-transformation and ascending into a divine yet living consciousness. The deific mask of Azag brings the power of the primordial, the burning urge to compel your future.

Initiation Focus: Ninurta is the forcefull accomplishment of this by the union of the Seven Headed Dragon-Serpent or Azag as a force of order controlling and focusing chaos. You have through previous levels learnt the methods and secrets of compelling and creating the future you desire. Now your task is to focus and determine the isolate aspect of the psyche, what makes you specifically 'individual' in a world of like-minded 'individuals'? This is a process of self-deification as a living power, thus a time of immense initiatory boundaries broken and order reshaped.

As Ningishzida, the throne-bearer of the underworld is the one who holds the keys to knowledge. As the caduceus, the balance found in union is presented in the fertile and ever-transforming (shedding) essence of the serpent. Nebo is the god who decrees destinties, who holds the power of willed divination. Nebo is the god which inspires the Kassapu to focus the Will towards self-determined areas of achievement and knowledge.

Level 7:

Planet: Moon

Color: Silver

God: Sin

Adversarial God: Seven Maskim / Kingu

Therionick (Primordial Association): The rebellious gods are the very foundation of independent and isolate consciousness. As one ascending in the model of the Seven, focus intimately upon the aspects of the Seven Demons and their powers independently and as a whole. You should then focus on encircling, eclipsing the moon and by devouring Sin, utilizing your dreams/nightmares to understand the individual consciousness. Kingu is the illuminated, empowered rebel god who is the greatest among them, thus a power rising through you.

Initiation Focus: Sin brings great illumination of the psyche through this process. Listen to your instincts, dreams and visions brought to you by Sin. Look to nature and how instinct as well as the need for survival in creating powerful, balanced and often dangerous predators. The Seven eclipsing the moon god are the primordial powers and rebels who resist those who dictate "how" you should feel, in addition devouring the wisdom of the subconscious to grow stronger through perceiving the subtle balance of nature.

THE TRIAD OF TIAMAT – KINGU – MARDUK

The Hidden Ascending Formula

The pivotal direction of sorcery in the art of self-deification and Theurgy as it is depends on the axis of Tiamat – Kingu and the unlikely Marduk. Beginning with your earliest meditations of the Gods, moving through incantations and the initiatory work of awakening the gods in your flesh will you then be prepared for the balanced work of the Maskim.

In the work of Ascent you will raise Tiamat and Kingu by the Sebitti within the self, upward through the aspect of Marduk, from which you will work with via invocation and works therein.

Just as the "Piristi ilani rabuti[128]" states, Tiamat manifests in accordance with the Luciferian tradition, she appears as the war goddess Ishtar of Nineveh who was the wet-nurse of Bel.

Tiamat, that cunning serpent, the primordial darkness from which we emerge is wise and eternal just as her coils crash in the abyssic waters.

Thus you will experience of the result of the Theurgic work of self-deification; Marduk is conquered from within; thus the Gods will be brought forth again in balance.

---

[128] Mesopotamian Cosmic Geography.

BIBLIOGRAPHY

Myths from Mesopotamia: Creation, The Flood, Gilgamesh, and Others. A New translation by Stephanie Dalley. Oxford University Press

Chaldean Magick its origin and Development by Francois Lenormant 1877

The Devils and Evil Spirits of Babylonia, Being Babylonian and Assyrian Incantations Against the Demons, Ghouls, Vampires, Hobgoblins, Ghosts and Kindred Evil Spirits which Attack Mankind Volume I and II by R. Campbell Thompson.

Reallexikon der Assyriologie und Vorderasiatischen Archäologie By Erich Ebeling, Bruno Meissner, Dietz Otto Edzard

The Battle Between Marduk and Tiamat by Thorkild Jacobsen, Journal of the American Oriental Society, Vol. 88, No. 1. January – March 1968, pp. 104-108

Ancient Fragments by I.P. Corey 1832

Gods, Demons and Symbols of Ancient Mesopotamia by Jeremy Black and Anthony Green. University of Texas Press.

Priest and Temple in Hellenistic Babylonia by Gilbert J.P. McEwan, Franz Steiner Verlag GMBH Wiesbaden 1981

Mesopotamian Cosmic Geography...... Wayne Horowitz

Unity and Diversity: Essays in the History, Literature, and Religion of the Ancient Near East (Studies in International Affairs, No. 22) - The Johns Hopkins University Press - Professor Hans Goedicke

The Chedor-Laomer Tablets by Prof. A.H. Sayce, D.D

Steller Representations of Tiamat and Qingu in a Learned Calendar Text by F. Reynolds, Birmingham. Published in Languages and Cultures in Contact: At the Crossroads of Civilizations in Syrio-Mesopotamian Realm", 1993.

The Ashur Version of the Seven Tablets of Creation by D.D. Luckenbill, The American Journal of Semitic Languages and Literatures, Vol. 38, No. 1 (Oct. 1921)

Birth in Babylonia and the Bible: it's Mediterranean setting, M.Stol

Babylonian Star-Lore, Gavin White

The Leyden Papyrus, An Egyptian Magical Book Edited by F.Ll. Griffith & Herbert Thompson Dover, 1974

Mystical and Mythological Explanatory Works of Assyrian and Babylonian Scholars

Prayer, Magic and the Stars in the Ancient and Late Antique World Edited by Scott Noegel, Joel Walker, and Brannon Wheeler. Pennsylvania State University Press.

The Image of the Netherworld in the Sumerian Sources by Dina Katz

Mesopotamian Protective Spirits F.A.M. Wiggerman

Mesopotamian Witchcraft Ancient Magic and Divination, Abusch

The God Ningizzida by E. Douglas Van Buren

Tiamat by George Barton

The Fifty Names of Marduk in "Enuma Elis" by Andrea Seri

Enuma Elis and the Transmission of Babylonian Cosmology to the West by Philippe Talon

The Sun at Night and the Doors of Heaven in Babylonian Texts by Wolfgang Heimpel, Journal of Cuneiform Studies, vol. 38. No. 2 Autumn 1986

Reallexikon Der Assyriologie, Erich Ebeling, Bruno Meissner

Magico-Medical Means of Treating Ghost-Induced Illnesses in Ancient Mesopotamia by JoAnn Scurlock, Brill-Stix.

Pazuzu by Nils P. Heebel, Brill-Styx 2002

Demons and Population Control by Erle Lichty

Birth in Babylonia and the Bible it's Mediterranean Setting, M.Stol Styx Publications 2000

Triumph of the Symbol – Tallay Ornan

The Storm God of the Ancient Near East by Alberto R. W. Green

Astral Magic in Babylonia by Erica Reiner

The Tresures of Darkness by Thorkild Jacobsen

Babylonian Magic and Sorcery by Leonard W. King, M.A.

Tiamat's Brood by Alastair McBeath

Mystical and Mythological Explanatory Works of Assyrian and Babylonian Scholars by Alasdair Livingstone

The Literature of Ancient Sumer by Jeremy Black, Graham Cunningham

Birth in Babylonia and the Bible its Mediterranean Setting by M. Stol, Cuneiform Monographs, Styx Publications 2000

Ezekiel 32: Lion-Dragon Myths by Theodore Lewis, Journal of the American Oriental Society, Vol. 116, JSTOR Publications.

The Staff of Ninsubura, Studies in Babylonian Demonology, II, JEOL 29 by F.A.M. Wiggerman

Transtigridian Snake Gods, Sumerian Gods and their Representations, Cuneiform Monographs 7

Exit Talim! Studies in Babylonian Demonology I, JEOL 27

Deliver me from Evil by Graham Cunningham

The Melammu as Divine Epiphany and Usurped Entity by Mehmet-Ali Atac in Culture and History of the Ancient Near East, Volume 26.

The Symbolism of the Biblical World by Othmar Keel

ABOUT THE AUTHOR

Michael W. Ford is the author of Adversarial Light-Magick of the Nephilim, The Bible of the Adversary, Liber HVHI, Gates of Dozak, Luciferian Witchcraft and many more titles. Mr. Ford is an initiate and Magus in The Order of Phosphorus, for which he is founder. As well as being a founder of The Black Order of the Dragon, a coven centered on dream/nightmare vampirism and magick, Ford is also an initiate of Charles Pace's Sethanic Cult of Masks, which he has authored a book on. Michael lives near Houston, Texas and has Seven Snakes and three dogs.

ABOUT THE ILLUSTRATOR

Marchozelos is a Priest in the Order of Phosphorus and is an initiate of The Black Order of the Dragon. Marchozelos is an artist who is inspired by Austin Osman Spare, the cult of dreams, surrealism and much more. Marchozelos is also the founder of Death Posturelis and is a musician in Graven Pestanz and Black Funeral.

For Ritual and Magickial Supplies including books, visit
www.luciferianwitchcraft.com

Made in the USA
Lexington, KY
12 October 2014